Pretty Good Years
A Biography of Tori Amos

Jay S. Jacobs

HAL•LEONARD®

Copyright © 2006 by Jay S. Jacobs

Photo by Michel Linssen / Redferns Music Picture Library
Cover design by Jenna Young
Book interior by Lisa A. Jones

Published by Hal Leonard Corporation
7777 Bluemound Road
P.O. Box 13819
Milwaukee, WI 53213

Trade Book Division Editorial Offices
19 West 21st Street
Suite 201
New York, New York 10010

Library of Congress Cataloging-in-Publication Data

Jacobs, Jay S., 1962-
  Pretty good years : a biography of Tori Amos / by Jay S. Jacobs. —1st ed.
      p. cm.
  Includes discography (p. 147) and bibliographical references (p. 195).
  ISBN 1-4234-0022-4
  1. Amos, Tori. 2. Rock musicians—United States—Biography. I. Title.
ML420.A5874J33 2006
782.42166092--dc22
[B]
                              2006010620

Printed in the United States of America
First Edition

Hal Leonard books are available at your local bookstore, or you may order through Music Dispatch at 1-800-637-2852 or www.musicdispatch.com.

Contents

Acknowledgments

Thank you to everyone who helped me bring this book to life.

To Leslie Diamond, Debbie Jacobs, and Smudgey, you know what you did. Thanks for being there for me.

To George Seth Wagner, thanks for hiding me from the ghosts and the dinosaurs.

To Dave Strohler, thank you for letting me be you for a while.

To Flavia Abbinante and the good people at Arcana Libri, thanks for the idea and for having so much faith in me.

To John Cerullo, Belinda Yong, and all the people at Hal Leonard Corporation, thanks for giving me this opportunity to share my work.

To Robert Lecker and agency, thanks for helping me get all my ducks in a row.

To all the people who talked to me, both on and off the record, your help has been incredible. Also, to Ken Sharp and Brad Balfour and all the others, thanks for sharing your work. To Web sites like TheDent.com, Toriphoria, and HereInMy Head.com—thanks for putting together such a stunning compendium of information just out of true passion for Tori Amos.

To Ron Sklar, Lou Hirshorn, Eileen Fitzpatrick, Mark and Marie Healy, Bob, Roni, Colleen, Natalie and Paul McGowan, Drew Bergman, John Ruback, Damian Childress, Phil Green, Mary Aloe, George Wagner, Lucille Falk, Wayne Diamond, Alan Feroe, Dave Feroe, Kathy Feroe, Sheila Graham, Christina Feroe, Ron Merx, and so many others.... Thank you for reminding me I still had another life out there.

And thanks to Tori Amos, just because.

Introduction

The first time that I interviewed Tori Amos, back in 1992, she was still flush with the new success of her album *Little Earthquakes*. At the time, I opened the article with a simple, and yet at the same time exceedingly complex, question:"So, who is Tori Amos, anyway?"I then rattled off some of the positions and poses that Amos had touched upon in public."Is she the shy daughter of a minister? The musical prodigy who felt like an outcast? A rock 'n' roll bimbo? A weird chick that believes in fairies? A brutally frank singer and songwriter?"

In the years since, she has allowed us to touch upon many other aspects of her personality. She is a person who has been so immersed in religion that it has made her skeptical toward the very beliefs that she had been brought up to hold in the highest regard. She was a musical prodigy, who was so talented that she became the youngest child ever to be admitted into one of the most prestigious musical academies in the world, and yet so rebellious and taken by her own muse that she eventually was thrown out of it. She was a little girl playing piano in gay bars. She has been a crusader for abused women. She was victim of a violent crime who has tried to teach others from her experience. She is a cult phenomenon. She is a woman who is seen as a feminist, and yet who has serious questions about the values and beliefs of feminism. She is a figurehead of the "Lilith" movement (named for the mythical first wife of Adam, who was thrown out of Eden when she refused to acquiesce to his desires), and yet Amos has never really worked with the people closely associated with it. She is a musical star, filling arenas around the world, although her records almost never get airplay on MTV or popular radio. She is also a shrewd, pioneering businesswoman. She is a wife. She is a doting and loving mother. All of these answer the question, and at the same time, none of them do.

So, who is Tori Amos, anyway?

It's still a difficult question. It is a question that even Tori Amos herself probably couldn't answer, nor would she likely have any inclination to. She constantly drops little hints in her music or her stage patter or her interviews. However, the whole point is, Amos is not someone who can just be easily explained away. Even more than most people, she has many layers, complex dichotomies in her life and personality, and looking at the big picture will still only show the surface. Tori Amos is an artist for a complex age, for a complex world. She will share her passions, her ideas, and her art because it is what she is here to do. It is her calling. It is her job. It is her *raison d'être*. But that doesn't mean she will give you everything. She realizes that sometimes, what we imagine is so much more interesting than the truth.

In a 1999 cover story, *Spin* magazine referred to Amos's fans as rock's most passionate cult.[1] Despite the undoubted protests of the remaining Deadheads or Phish Phans out there (very meek objections of course, because most of them are still too stoned to put up much of a fight), the statement has a serious ring of truth. Tori Amos isn't some prepackaged star that goes for the lowest common denominator. She opens herself up to love and criticism, and if she can't catch everyone, the ones who do get her can be obsessive in their ardor. She knows this full well, even to the point that it has kept her career in the "cult" artist racks of the local music shop. She has a large and, as just pointed out, passionate following. But Tori Amos is still looked at by the mainstream music world as something of an oddity. "You can't control your popularity; I know I'm an acquired taste," she told *Rolling Stone* in 1998. "I'm anchovies. And not everyone wants those hairy little things. If I was potato chips, I could go a lot more places, but I'm not."[2]

She can be political, but she does not wear her beliefs on her sleeve. Instead, she may tease the audience with her ideals, like the way she sampled speeches from George W. Bush and his father, George H. W. Bush, in her cover of the Beatles' "Happiness Is a Warm Gun." However, she doesn't tell you what to believe; she just lays out the facts and lets you come away with your own decision. As a rape victim and survivor, Amos has also been an outspoken advocate of victim's rights. She was instrumental in creating the Rape, Abuse & Incest National Network (RAINN) to help women who have been affected by violent crime.

Tori has often been painted as an off-the-wall interview. For the most part, this is not true. Her words are well thought-out and interesting. She has a very active mind. In that first interview that I did with her, she suddenly stopped right in the middle of an answer to say, "I hope you don't use exclamation points in this article, because I really hate them. I'm into periods." It's part of her makeup. She likes to surprise people. Her lyrics often use unexpected non sequiturs. In her songs, she has the Antichrist yelling in her kitchen, or she's dating a guy who dumps her because she eats the same kind of ice cream as Charles Manson. She tells her father that she killed her monkey, or she has a little blubber in her igloo. She has an angry snatch, or she nearly runs over an angel who is toking on a big old cigar. "I make sexual references all the time," she cheerily acknowledged to journalist Ken Sharp in 1992.[3] She uses language to be provocative.

Provoke she has done. That isn't always a bad word, you know. Provoking a response is an honored goal. Because, for positive or negative, Tori Amos is something of a master in getting people to feel something. People react to her. It is difficult to be indifferent or lukewarm toward her. Her music would never work as Muzak or musical wallpaper. It is too involved, too nuanced, and demands too much of the person hearing it. It begs to be paid attention to, to be explored. Listeners tend to either love Tori Amos's music or totally hate it. She gets people to explore their thoughts and beliefs. She may not change every viewpoint. In fact, she probably doesn't want to. It may be enough to just spark the debate. She inflames a reaction. Then we can sit back and see what transpires.

Maybe this is even taking things too far. She is, after all, an entertainer first and foremost. Tori Amos is an artist, a poet, a chanteuse, a wordsmith, a pianist, and an entertainer. Anything else could be a projection of the audience. Therefore, let's take a look at the muse and the music of Tori Amos. Let's explore the background and the events that have molded her body of work into one of the most memorable of modern years. If, in the end, the music is what matters most, then Tori Amos has let herself be open to her audience in a way most popular musicians would not dare. As has been said throughout the centuries by performers, it's all about the show. So let's get on with it....

And I promise I won't overdo it in this book with the exclamation points. I'm into periods, too.

chapter 1
Baltimore

The first dirty trick that life played on Tori Amos came soon before she was even born. Her parents—a Methodist minister named Dr. Edison Amos and his wife, Mary Ellen—had decided to leave their Washington, D.C.–area home to go to visit Mary Ellen's parents in North Carolina when she was hugely pregnant. She became ill, and it quickly became obvious that the mother-to-be was not fit for travel. A doctor ordered her to stay locally to have the baby. So instead of being born at Georgetown Hospital in Washington, D.C., as planned, the baby greeted the world on August 22, 1963, at Old Catawba Hospital in the faraway hamlet of Newton, North Carolina.

This wasn't fate's trick, mind you. In fact, being born in the wrong place may have been an indication of her future, that the little Amos child would grow up to be unpredictable, original, and persistently individualistic. Little things like plans and people's perceptions and expectations would not bind her. She would see the world and have experiences and live life on her own terms. No, there is something symbiotic about the fact that little Tori Amos decided to come onto this earth about three states south of her parents' best-laid plans.

The real problem was that Dr. and Mrs. Amos decided that their cute little girl should be named Myra Ellen Amos.

Myra. It's not a name that even in 1963 really fit too many people well. It certainly did not suit the young Amos girl as she grew. She was a lively girl, with a tremendous imagination, a probing mind, a flashing sense of humor, an almost immediate love of music, and not a small wild streak. She was the third child born into the Amos family—brother Michael and sister Marie (yes, all three have names starting with M's) were significantly older than their newborn sister.

Over the years, Amos has often suggested that this spirit may have been handed down her family tree from her great-great-grandmother. Mary Ellen Amos came from a full-blooded Indian family. The ancestor that Tori Amos has often expressed the most respect for was this great-great-grandmother, a full-blooded Cherokee woman named Margaret Little. For years, her mother told young Myra the stories of how Little was one of the few Cherokees who survived in the Smoky Mountains after the apocalyptical Indian event known as the Trail of Tears. In 1830, because settlers were moving into Georgia, the U.S. government passed the Indian Removal Act over the protest of many citizens and vocal opponents like Tennessee Congressman Davy Crockett. The tribes fought the law, taking it all the way to the Supreme Court. However, by 1838, the government started forcibly moving the Cherokee from their Georgia homes to faraway reservations in Oklahoma. The army forced them to march a thousand miles, with little in the way of food, shelter, or rest. Approximately four thousand Cherokees died on the journey. Many others were demoralized. However, Margaret Little was able to stay in her home area. She survived the hardships and carried on as much as possible in the horrible situation.[1]

Mary Ellen Amos had told her daughter all about Margaret Little's life and struggles. "[My mother] is a very loyal Christian woman, but she has a spirituality that goes beyond that," Tori Amos told the *Sunday Times Magazine* in an interview she did together with her mother. "She has premonitions and dreams, but she keeps her esoteric side to herself. She made me very familiar with the Cherokee blood in us. I remember she used to read me stories. I had a brother and a sister, but they were seven and ten years older, so my mother and I formed a special bond. She says I played music before I could talk, and I would play the piano for her. I was very close to her father, too. He had a real temper, which she says I inherited. He had been raised by his grandmother, a full-blooded Cherokee called Margaret Little, and he would tell stories about her. When soldiers burnt the South to the ground in the Civil War, there was nothing to eat, so she harnessed the plough to her body and planted the seeds. Margaret Little gave me a sense of integrity. I like her tenacity. She was a survivor, and I share that inspiration with my mother."[2]

Little Myra also felt great love for her maternal grandparents, Calvin Clinton Copeland and his wife, Bertie, or Poppa and Nannie, as they were known to the child. Calvin was a factory worker who had retired from the hosiery mill when Myra was still young. Bertie was a homemaker. One of Amos's earliest memories was going out on daily rides with Poppa in his 1952 Buick. Poppa also told the little girl all about their family lore. They explored Indian legends, nature, the meaning of dreams, and alternative medicine. He was also a wonderful singer, and he serenaded his granddaughter from the time she was a baby. Sadly, he died when she was only nine. "I went to my grandfather's house in North Carolina most summers until I was nine and a half, when he died," she recalls. "He and his wife were eastern Cherokee, and I grew up listening to their stories."[3] It was a devastating loss to the young girl. Years later, Tori Amos would write the song "Frog on My Toe" as a direct tribute to Calvin.

Unfortunately, Amos did not feel the same connection with her father's parents, in particular, his mother, Addie Allen Amos. I experienced that firsthand early in Amos's career. I remember the second time that I saw Tori Amos in concert was at the Keswick Theater outside of Philadelphia on October 20, 1992. By strange coincidence, during the concert, I was sitting next to Amos's parents, who had come up from Baltimore to see the show. I had met them earlier that day with Amos. (Okay, it wasn't that big a coincidence. My tickets were provided by her label, Atlantic Records, as were Dr. and Mrs. Amos's seats. So I guess it was inevitable that I'd have been in the same vicinity as them.) Nonetheless, it was fascinating. I watched as Amos told long, detailed stories of how horrible and repressed her grandmother had been. Each time she did, I looked over at Mrs. Amos (who was seated at my side) trying to figure out her reaction to her daughter's stories about the family.

When I mentioned to Tori the next day that I had sat next to her parents at the show, she said demurely, "Oh, that must have been interesting." In a lot of parts the show got very confessional, or very sexual, or talked of private family matters. I mentioned that I kept glancing at her mother as she spoke of her grandmother. "It wasn't my mother's mother," she acknowledged, good-naturedly. I asked her if she ever felt at all self-conscious when performing and knowing that they are out there? "Sometimes…but you cannot revolve your show around thinking about what anybody else is thinking. There are times when I back off a little bit if I feel that I'd rather have a Mexican meal afterwards than go through it for an hour. If that's what the vibe is…coming from, if it's just a touchy night in general. There's a lot of respect that goes around those that are close to me. Which is, what happens up there is real hands off."

Amos's paternal grandmother, Addie Allen Amos, has received the great majority of the touchy treatment in Amos's work and in her life. Even though Addie died when young Myra was only ten years old, her memory cast a long shadow over the singer's life. Amos's memories of this grandmother mostly revolve around guilt, sacrifice, and repression. "If we met at the River Styx, I don't know if I'd give her a ride in my boat," Amos told the *Independent* (London) in 1994.[4]

She put it in even more brutally frank terms a couple of years beforehand. "I hated my grandmother," Amos told *Hot Press* in 1992. "She'd pound into me the idea that only evil women give away their virginity before marriage. If you even thought about doing that, you were 'out of the Kingdom of God,' she'd say…. And so I waited a long time before giving up my virginity, because of this feeling: 'How can I be a nice, respectable girl and want to do this?' And more than anything I wanted respect from men, my father in particular. And even at that age I felt that Jesus was a real, living presence in my life. That can be a bit of a disadvantage. It's weird when you're giving a guy head at fifteen and you're thinking, 'Jesus is looking at me!' "[5]

The odd thing is, in some ways, Addie Amos *was* a woman that took risks and forged paths just like her famous granddaughter would. Addie was born into hardship in a dirt-poor Appalachian Mountain family. However, Addie was an extraordinarily bright woman. She threw off her financial restrictions and went to summer school at, and graduated from, the University of Virginia in the 1920s, at a time when it was exceedingly rare for a woman to receive a degree. She had a sharp mind and an incisive understanding of literature. "[She] could give you interpretations of Byron and Shelley that would make your head spin," Amos acknowledged to *Rolling Stone*.[6] She became an ordained minister, again a rarity for a woman in the culture of the time. Her husband, James, was also a minister. Addie Amos immersed herself into the gospel. She rejected and repudiated all sin and weakness in herself and those around her. Her granddaughter has often said in interviews that if Addie Allen Amos had lived in Salem, Massachusetts, during the infamous witch trials, she would have been there with her torch ready.

By the time young Myra was only five, Addie was writing to her son, explaining to him how the young girl must be indoctrinated into the world of Jesus

Christ and the church. Of course, the fact that the father was an ordained minister and was undoubtedly trying to do just that did not diminish her zeal in pushing this agenda. This was the battle for the child's immortal soul. However, the whole thing was just confusing the little girl. Even at five years old, she had a probing, intelligent nature. She wanted to figure out her beliefs on her own. She did not like being pushed into something…even something that she was repeatedly assured would lead to her eternal salvation. Somehow what she was being told wasn't quite gibing with what she was sensing, even as a little girl. "There were a lot of dos and don'ts," Amos told Ken Sharp. "Love and lust should never meet. And there was me, five years old, and I had all these feelings."[7]

"At five I really believed that Jesus and Mary [Magdalene] were in love, and there was this whole thing going on," Amos told *Time* magazine.[8] So when she would hear of all these things that seemed to be natural to her being called sins, she could not help but rebel from the ideas a bit. The church was teaching her to feel guilty about her emotions and needs, and this somehow felt wrong to her. Still, it took many years before she could completely overcome the ideas and shame that she felt were pounded into her from the very beginning. Eventually, Amos developed a certain amount of grudging respect for her grandmother, calling her a "tough broad"[9] and acknowledging that attribute has probably been passed down to her. "I hated her, sure, but you had to admire her power over people. She definitely had a mission."[10]

Most importantly, through her parents and both sets of her grandparents, she learned to become the complex and questioning woman she has grown into being. For good or bad, they all contributed to who she is. Through the Copelands, she learned a love and respect for the land, culture, and her background. The Amos side helped her develop toughness and a strong intellectual curiosity. "I always thought of them [her two sets of grandparents] as the 'bad' and 'good' sides," Amos told *Spin* magazine. "It's like the concept of the mango—dry and juicy….Some people get baptized with sprinkles, well, I had my head down in the water for twenty-five years. I learned some really tuneless hymns to sing in the shower and then I started listening to Robert Plant and Jimmy Page and you know what? I realized Jesus wasn't downstairs. But I'd like to thank my dry side, because without it I'd have nothing to write about."[11]

These contradictions come rather naturally. Amos is a minister's daughter. Hearing those words can call up an entire set of very concrete images. To the idealist (or the follower of George W. Bush), a minister's daughter is a pure woman who is comfortable with her God. She only believes in sex only for procreational purposes, assuming she decides not to become a nun, a librarian, a cat lady, or a spinster. Reality is usually very different from these limited views. Much of the time a girl who grew up in a deeply religious house will grow up rebellious, ponder her faith, and go through experimental phases. Tori Amos knows this lifestyle well, because she has lived it. She believes being a minister's daughter has completely stimulated her life and music.

"It's one thing to have tastes of it. It's another thing to be surrounded by it," Amos explained. "It's like when you get your head held under the water. When you're just dunked a couple of times, you don't really know what's down there because you don't see it too much. But you know, God, I didn't like getting dunked. What's going on? You might not remember that has traumatized you. People who go to church once a year; they can't get to the root of it. I had my head held down for so long I know exactly what's down there, how many sea horses there are. What's happening? It took me a while. The problem is, I just stayed down there." Amos laughed. "It took me a while to come up for air and say hang on a minute. Wait a minute. There's another reality. I have compassion for it. There are people that I like that are very much believers, and I respect that. What I am really against is somebody dictating to me how I should believe. That's not okay. That's about control. I can't accept something in the guise of 'God said this, God said that.' No, it's not, man said this so that he could control other men and women. Leave God out of it."

If love of religion was not something that came naturally to the young girl, she found a suitable alternative. Something that made complete sense to her from the very beginning. It was a passion, a joy, and a sensation that filled her up with a feeling of self-worth. She was immediately in love with and enmeshed in music. In 1966, the family moved from the Georgetown section of Washington, D.C. to nearby Baltimore, Maryland. The two-and-a-half-year-old girl watched as her older siblings, Michael and Marie, took piano lessons. One of Amos's earliest memories was of playing the piano by ear in her family's house when she was only four years old. Her mother insists that she had the skill at two and a half. "I was playing before I thought about there being any music world out there," Amos says. "All I knew was there was this massive black piano staring at me. I'd crawl up on the little stool and go, 'I love you. Can we be friends?'"

Amos was about five when she let her parents know that music was where her future lay. She was in the family living room, studying the famous celebrity-studded cover of the Beatles' classic album *Sgt. Pepper's Lonely Hearts Club Band.* Nonchalantly she announced that this was what she wanted to do. They were shocked, but even at that young age, her parents could see that little Myra had a natural gift. Wanting to nurture her talent, they enrolled her in Baltimore's distinguished Peabody Conservatory of Music. In fact, as a five-year-old prodigy, she was the youngest child ever accepted into the conservatory. There, the Amoses felt their little girl could learn classical piano. So rather than just going to a normal elementary school, Amos was thrown into the world of serious potential artists.

"You're five, and you think you're going to be around older people," Amos told *Keyboard* magazine. "It's a very exciting prospect. I knew I was different. I knew I did things that other kids didn't do. But, you know, you don't have an ego when you're five. I didn't want them to treat me like I was weird or special. It would be really great if other people did what I did and we could just hang out.

You just want to have friends and play and eat popcorn together. And life is very simple. You get inspired, it's very exciting."[12]

Amos stayed at the conservatory for six years, though she realized much earlier that she did not quite fit in. Classical music was not what moved her. She had no desire to be part of an orchestra or a chamber quartet—she wanted to explore her own world of music. However, she was a little girl, and like any other little girl in the world, she wanted to assimilate, to be accepted. So she tried to toe the conservatory line. Soon she felt that it was taking her backward. Since she was a toddler, Amos had played the piano by ear. Now she was being asked—no, actually it was insisted—to play music only by sight, by reading it. The conservatory took her back to basics. Instead of celebrating her ability to perform songs by ear, they tried to stifle it and force her to play by the rules. Even as a little girl, Tori Amos did not like to be told to play by the rules.

"They started me with 'Hot Cross Buns,'" she recalled. "When you go from Gershwin to 'Hot Cross Buns' it's a bit of a shock. You don't understand that this is for your good.…There's nothing that you could have said to that girl to convince her. [I] had no desire to do that.…You think you're being punished. What I really learned from the Peabody came from my classmates. I got the music through them. I understood that there was a Jim Morrison and I understood that there was a John Lennon. They spoke to me like I was an adult. Here I was with my little curls, my feet that didn't touch the floor, and we're all sitting in theory class. And I'm turning around, going, 'Wow, he's really cute, and he's black, and he has long hair. Can I go home with him?'"[13]

By the time she was nine, the writing was on the wall for Amos at the conservatory. "All the kids [at the Peabody] were over sixteen, one was nine and I was the youngest," Amos recalled to *Deluxe*. "I didn't fit in. My mother was reading me Edgar Allan Poe at night to help me go to sleep, then you go and read *Dick and Jane* and practice Mozart and Bartók in the afternoon. I was always writing music at my desk. It's not that I was that smart, but I was real creative."[14] Amos was not practicing nearly as much as was expected to keep up. Instead she would just hang out at home, listening to the Beatles and the Stones. Amos would lie in her dark room listening to *Led Zeppelin II*, weaving elaborate plans on how Robert Plant would take her virginity. She realized that this music was what she wanted from life, not classical.

"I heard *Led Zeppelin I, II,* and *III* all at the same time, because I jumped into them around '73, when I was about eight," she told *Q* magazine. "When I heard Zeppelin, it was like, okay, *now* I know why I'm not doing well on my classical piano. Because Jimmy Page was the bridge from acoustic to electric music. He showed me what I could do. I always felt like they tapped into this passion that Mary Magdalene understood, and was the only one in the Bible that represented it. Musically, Zeppelin understood that goddess energy."[15]

In 1973 she also went to her first rock concert, seeing Elton John perform. Here was another pianist who was expressing himself, who wasn't being forced to play "Hot Cross Buns" in conservatory. This was what Amos wanted to do. Eventually, she couldn't pretend anymore. "It stopped being fun," she told *The Concert News*. "Something got lost, and it became deadly serious. It wasn't free expression anymore; it was going to be channeled into a career. I just didn't want to do what was expected of me."[16] In her little girl way she raged against the conservatory machine. By the time she had reached eleven, Amos was dismissed from the school.

Over the years Amos has often spoken about how the institute was a poor fit for her. Even though the school did end up throwing her out, the school doesn't seem to hold a grudge. All these years later, the Peabody Institute Preparatory does mention its most famous dropout on its official Web site. It reads, "Illustrious alumni of the Preparatory include composer Philip Glass, singer James Morris, choreographer Martha Clarke, singer Tori Amos, jazz pianist Cyrus Chestnut, composer Camara Kambon, and violinist Hilary Hahn." It also includes a link to Amos's official Web page in the Alumni Personal Homepages.[17]

The experimentation that she experienced hanging with the older kids at Peabody was not confined to music and boys, either. "I just wanted to lay on my bed and squeeze my legs, which is what a young girl should do, though I didn't realize it at the time," she told Tom Hibbert of *Details*. "I laid on my bed and squeezed my legs together and thought, 'Oh, this is a curiosity!' "[18] She also was a bit curious about artificial stimulants, hearing about drugs from older friends. Being the intellectually inquiring girl that she was, Amos felt she had to find out about them, too.

Amos has told a story of the time that she was twelve and was over at a friend's house. She and her friend and the friend's brother were all smoking pot. "I guess that seems young, but this was a different time," she told *Q* magazine. "We're talking 1974–75. Led Zeppelin were kicking! It was a different time!" The kids had a lot of pot, too. Not just one joint. They were wrecked. Dr. Amos came to get her earlier than he was supposed to. And she reeked of smoke. It was in her hair, in her clothes. Dr. Amos was not happy. So, being a twelve-year-old girl, Myra did what anyone her age would do. She lied. And she lied some more. She swore up and down that the other kids had done it, but she just watched. Being a normal parent, he wanted to believe his young daughter couldn't be involved with something like drugs. So he took her at her word. That evening, Dr. Amos and his daughter had dinner with a man from his church and his eighteen-year-old son. The son pulled her aside, looked at her, and said, "You are so stoned." However, as she proudly pointed out all those years later, she got away with it.[19]

So Myra returned her focus to Eastern Junior High School in Silver Spring, a Maryland suburb near Washington, D.C. When she was only eleven, she got into an empty-nest scenario that occurs to many children much younger than their siblings. Within a few months in the summer of 1975, her brother, Michael, got married, and sister, Marie, moved to Virginia to go to college. Tori fought her loneliness by throwing herself into her music. She took voice and music lessons at nearby Montgomery College. At her father's request, she did try out again at thirteen for the Peabody Conservatory as a singer. Her heart wasn't in it, though, and her choice of song, "I've Been Cheated," probably telegraphed that to the judges at her audition. She was not invited to come back. She did continue to take lessons with Peabody professor Patricia Springer. Springer was also organist in the Reverend Amos's church. Tori Amos now cites her as one of the best teachers she ever had.

Dr. Amos tried to find the silver lining in the fact that his daughter was thrown out of the school. He told her, "If you're not going to play in a conservatory, at least be good at popular music." Of course, Edison Amos had a slightly different idea of the term "popular music" than his daughter. "The only thing he could equate with pop was Judy Garland, with cabaret performing. Mention Joni Mitchell and he'd say, 'What?' "[20] But his intentions were pure—Dr. Amos really wanted to understand his daughter's aspirations and be helpful. By the time she was ten, he had set her up to sing at the church, both in the choir and also to perform at weddings and funerals. Then, when she was thirteen, her parents would drive her down to nearby Washington, D.C., so that she could do a weekend gig at Mr. Henry's, a local gay bar, and at the Tiffany Lounge at Mr. Smith's, which served a "mixed clientele." She chose her middle name as her stage name, and suddenly Ellen Amos was a working pianist and singer.

"My parents chaperoned," Tori told the *Philadelphia Daily News* years later. "The experience was fantastic. I played standards—a little Gershwin and Cole Porter, your Billie Holiday stuff. I'd also do whatever was current—Zeppelin, Carole King, Billy Joel, Elton John. Gloria Gaynor's 'I Will Survive' was a biggie. You had to do 'Send in the Clowns' and 'Feelings' at least five times a night. Plus your Beatles and Stones catalog."[21] Over to the side, Reverend Amos would be sitting, complete with his collar. Amos has said that her father, with his mixture of slightly-older–James Dean good looks and the forbidden allure of the religious garb, seemed to fascinate the gay patrons, but they never worked up the nerve to approach him. Mrs. Amos also often stayed and watched her daughter play, fascinated, since she had never been into bars before in her life.

Ellen also had been working on her own songs since when she was only seven. She started off with a few instrumental pieces. She says the first song she wrote with lyrics had the unusual title "The Jackass and the Toad Song." By the time she was in junior high, her songs were a little more polished, like the song "More Than Just a Friend," which she wrote in 1976. That was written for a boy named John in her school that she had a crush on. He was a little older and was dating a beautiful cheerleader named Sylvia ("[She] should be on the front of a ship," Amos recalled.[22]) When she was invited to sing it for the school during an assembly, the boy threatened to beat her up if she played the song for everyone. She went up and nervously performed the tune. John did not live up to his threat of violence. In fact, he came up to her later and told her it was better than he expected it to be. Of course, this was junior high school, so this was not the start of something beautiful, of her fantasy schoolgirl romance. John never spoke to her again. This little childhood indignity became yet another inspiration for Amos, though. Her later song "Precious Things" was loosely based on the incident.

All was not always in complete harmony in the Amos household as far as the daughter's musical aspirations, though. In Dr. Amos's congregation, and in the other churches in the archdiocese, it became a bit of a scandal that his thirteen-year-old daughter was performing the devil's music. And in gay bars! Places where liquor flowed, where illicit acts and deviant lifestyles were happening in close proximity to a small child. She was the child of a man of God, no less. Dr. Amos heard the whispers and snickers and sometimes doubted the path that his daughter was taking. Luckily for Myra Ellen (and millions of future record buyers), Mary Amos often stood up to her husband on behalf of the girl's talent. Mrs. Amos reminded her husband that their daughter had a gift that most people would never have. She trusted her daughter to handle herself and not get seduced by the seamier aspects of the musical nightlife...the drugs, the drink, the partying. Dr. Amos believed, too, and despite his concern for his daughter, he stood up to the parishioners who questioned the wisdom of his young girl being exposed to this part of the culture.

On March 31, 1977, the local newspaper, the *Montgomery Journal*, had two pictures of community girls who had won a contest. Amos sang "More Than Just a Friend" to win the top prize. The pictures had the spectacularly alliterative title "Top Teens in Talent Test." (It's funny to imagine what the intelligently precocious singer must have thought about that corny headline.) The brief story read:

> The girl at the piano is thirteen-year-old Ellen Amos, first-place winner in the Thirteenth Annual Teen Talent Contest sponsored by the Montgomery County Recreation Department and the Kensington–Wheaton Jaycees. Ellen not only plays and sings, she is a talented composer. In fact, she wrote the song that she performed. Second place winner at last Saturday's competition was Barbara Hackett, shown at right putting body and soul into her oral reading from "The Member of the Wedding." Barbara played both thirteen-year-old Frankie and the family cook Berniece. Ellen and Barbara won $100 and $50 bonds respectively.[23]

In the summer of 1978, the Amos family moved to another parish again. Now they were in Rockville, Maryland, which would later be memorialized in the song "Don't Go Back to Rockville" by Amos's future friend Michael Stipe and his band, R.E.M. Dr. Amos moved the family to the parsonage of the Rockville United Methodist Church. Ellen was just about to turn fifteen and was beginning to find another artistic endeavor almost as interesting as her singing. She decided that she liked the idea of becoming an actress. This was spurred on by a sudden passion she had developed for old movies. She became fanatical about stars like Barbara Stanwyck and Bette Davis. Amos decided that her future may lie in the same direction. She won the lead in a high school production of the musical *Gypsy*.

She had roles in other productions at the school and the local Rockville Summer Theater. Amos also became director of the children's choir of her father's church, where she wrote some musical plays for the kids. She was getting more wedding gigs and other functions. This didn't even take into account her nighttime bar gigs. Ellen Amos was a very busy teen.

"When I was fifteen, my father stopped acting as chaperone," Amos told *The Concert News*. "I found myself working with women who were in their late twenties and chatting with gay men all night, interrogating them about their sex lives."[24] Gay busboys would teach her how to perform oral sex using a cucumber. Hookers would sometimes hang out at the bar, grabbing a drink between the evening's johns. Desperate traveling salesmen would pound drinks, trying to work up the courage to take the leap to talk to them. Amos took it all in, fascinated. For the daughter of a minister, all this nightlife was not seedy or sad—it was strange and exotic and sometimes just a little bit sexy. "Prostitutes would come into the bar and smoke or drink for a minute, and I would play them something. I've always felt protective of the Mary Magdalenes, the prostitutes, the porn B-movie actresses of the world. You begin to see that most people had a dream of themselves when they were younger, and at twenty-seven or twenty-eight, it wasn't going how they had hoped. That was the place I realized that everybody has a story."[25]

Amos's story was about to take a turn for the worse. It was about this time that Amos first started noticing a bone abnormality in her jaw. It was the cause of horrible headaches for her; she has compared the pain to that of having a tooth abscess. Of course, she was a dramatic girl and right away became sure that it was a brain tumor. It turns out that the condition was called chronic TMJ (temporo-mandibular joint). "Part of my jaw doesn't go into the bone—which is a hook and pulling my skull to the right," Amos explained to *Student Advantage Magazine*. "What happens is my right side goes into spasm and my neck and shoulder get almost paralytic. And so, I have braces at night I have to wear and I can hardly talk. I can't do interviews in the braces although they would help me. That's really where my handicap is—or because you can't say handicap anymore, it's my physical challenge."[26] The condition could not be fixed with surgery, and Amos had no interest in going through the rest of her life popping painkillers. It has been a continued source of pain for her for well over twenty years.[27]

One of Amos's early experiences in a recording studio came on a song called "It's a Happy Day." An aspiring songwriter named Camilla Wharton wrote the song's lyrics. However, she only had a vague idea of what the melody was to be, and honestly that snippet was from a Paul Simon song. Wharton contacted Simon for permission to build a song from the little bit of his melody, and surprisingly he agreed. She wanted to put together a whole tune and have a singer record it to shop as a demo. Wharton hoped that if the demo came out well enough, eventually she could use it to send out to agents, publishing houses, and record labels. Her big dream was to use the demo to get a big star to record her song. (If she only knew…) She called the local Hallmark Recording Studios. The people from the studio suggested Ellen Amos.

Wharton called her, and the fifteen-year-old brought some friends and went about finishing the tune, writing the arrangement, playing piano, and singing on it. The song was pressed as a single under the group name Contraband. Wharton had five hundred singles printed up and sent most of them out to various industry types, but none of them clicked and the song was soon forgotten.[28] This obscurity was probably deserved. It's not a horrible song; mind you, just very generic and a more than a little jingoistic. The song was a patriotic tale of romance between an Air Force pilot and his lady love. The tune is actually pretty good for a song essentially written by a fifteen-year-old. The lyrics were a little trickier. Not horrible, just very average. Some of the references are now a little dated, particularly the then-still-sort-of-topical throwaway line "Watergate has flown away." Honestly, it would have never become a hit. But it was another step in the musical maturation of Tori Amos.

The experience helped to inspire her to get a synthesizer to do even more work on demos from her home. Her eleventh-grade English teacher, Mrs. Barrett, also opened her eyes to her writing. At first Amos was upset because the teacher kept giving her C's for her work. Finally an upset Amos asked Mrs. Barrett why she kept getting bad grades. She was told that it was because she was capable of so much more. It was fine for Amos to aspire to be Pat Benatar, but she could also learn from Sylvia Plath, Virginia Woolf, and Arthur Rimbaud. Immersing herself in those artists, she learned that poetry and lyrics can work on levels that were both accessible and artistic. Mrs. Barrett came to see Amos backstage at a show in 2003, and told her that she now taught her students Amos's writing.

By the time she was seventeen, Amos had made enough of a name that she had regular gigs at places like the Capitol Hilton Bar in Washington. Her sights were still aimed high, and she was getting noticed. By day, Ellen Amos may have been just a bored senior in Richard Montgomery High School in Rockville, Maryland. At night she blossomed into a chanteuse. The *Washington Post* sent a reporter to talk to the young singer, and Amos confidently told the woman, "I want to be a legend." Still, she acknowledged it was a difficult dream to attain. "I was a star at Eastern [Junior High School], but I tell you, that doesn't get you on the radio." Dr. Amos was interviewed for the article as well, stating, "My concern is to get her into entertainment without entering her into a lifestyle that is self-destructive."[29]

In Amos's quest to find that illusive radio time, Dr. Amos financed the session where she recorded her first single. The A-side was "Baltimore," a tune that she had written with her older brother, Michael, for a contest for songwriters to come up with tributes to the local Baltimore Orioles baseball team, who had lost the World Series to the Pittsburgh Pirates the year before and were hoping to return to the Fall Classic. The Philadelphia Phillies ended up beating the Kansas City Royals that year. The Orioles would not win until three years later, beating the Phillies. Beyond the baseball connection, though, the song was a tribute to her beloved hometown. City mayor William D. Schaefer awarded Amos with a citation of honor because of the tune.[30]

Listening to "Baltimore" with twenty-four years of hindsight to go on, it is an enjoyable sort of faux-disco pop song, but miles and miles away from the type of music that Amos would come to record in the future. In fact, if you are quite honest, the song sounds like the theme song from some late-seventies situation comedy. You know the type of song, the perky pop-sized nuggets of tune that went under the opening credits of *WKRP in Cincinnati, Three's Company*, or *The Facts of Life*. I do not mean that as an insult. It's just a statement of fact. It may be totally different than what Tori Amos has come to be known for, but "Baltimore" is an undeniably catchy song. It skips along on a lively tune and has some lyrics that were evidently subsidized by the local chamber of commerce. In fact, it is undoubtedly the only pop tune ever to use the word *Baltimorean*. It is likable, though, in a jingle sort of way. (And you can't really call any song that repeats over and over in the chorus "I've got Orioles baseball on my mind," anything but a jingle.) It does not really give Amos much of a vocal workout. She does not stretch herself too much, just keeping her vocals smooth and easy throughout. You get the feeling she could sing this song in her sleep.

"Walking with You" is a little more of a glimpse into Amos's future songwriting style, though even it is also a long way from where Amos would eventually land as an artist. It is more of a piano-driven ballad, though much more distinctly poppy than you'd expect. The single was released on the family's own MEA label (which was short for Myra Ellen Amos). There are only ten copies of the single known to be available, and it has since become a highly sought-after rarity for record collectors. According to the *Goldmine Price Guide to Alternative Records*, a mint-condition copy of the single is worth at least $500.00.[31]

The "Baltimore" single was not the only thing that Amos was recording at the time, though. "I did a couple of other things around that period that were separate from that session," Amos told *Record Collector* magazine. "They were done in a church. Michael, my brother, was there—he's almost ten years older than I am—and I was about fourteen. Those were called 'All I Have to Give,' 'More Than Just a Friend,' there was a song called 'Just Ellen,' and I can't remember the other one. I can hear it. The point is that I recorded a lot of things at that time."

She also did some "live" wedding recordings, which were a lot more low-tech than her studio work. Unlike the studio recordings, these were just cassette recordings, usually made on crappy Radio Shack tape recorders, of Amos performing popular wedding hits like "Evergreen," "We've Only Just Begun," and "The Wedding Song (There Is Love)." Making a whopping ten dollars per gig, obviously Amos wasn't going to spend much cash to immortalize the performances. Much of the time the tapes were made by guests at the nuptials who were trying to get an aural record of the ceremony, not necessarily the young future star belting ballads with vaguely heard quiet conversation and cutlery clanking on plates in the background.[32]

In 1980, Amos also changed her name to the one that she has become known for. "I just hated my name," she told *Q* magazine in 1998. "If a guy even started to look at me and they heard my name was Myra Ellen, it just created a limp dick immediately. I couldn't bear it."[33] One night she was playing one of her bar gigs in Washington, D.C. At the lounge, she met a new guy who was dating a friend of hers. Amos recalled the situation to the St. Louis radio show *The River Lounge*. "My friend Linda McBride, who I was in high school with, and she's somebody that's still a friend of mine. She was dating, in one of her serial dating periods, this guy for a couple of weeks. And I'm just really lucky that she brought him down to hear me play, because I would never have had my name. She just showed up and said, 'I just wanted you to meet him, tell me what you think.' And, um, he just looked at me and said, 'You know, that's not your name.' "The guy looked at her and said that she wasn't an Ellen. She was a Tori. Amos thought about it for a few minutes and then said, Yeah, I am a Tori. "And I said, 'Well, Linda doesn't have to like you, but thanks for my name. Bye!' We got from him what we needed, so he served his purpose."[34]

Despite the fact that she always considered herself to be a bit of a nerd, Amos was named Homecoming Queen of her senior class at Richard Montgomery High School in Rockville, Maryland. As always, Amos has taken the honor with a grain of salt, insisting that she received the honor because she was able to harness the untapped ethnic and geek votes. She was underestimating her popularity, though; she was active in the drama club and also voted Choir Flirt and Most Likely to Succeed for the class. "My friends were very forgiving with me," Amos told *Seventeen* magazine. "Because let's face it, I stick out like a sore thumb. I mean in a fashion sense at least. But after high school, we all went our separate ways. I am still close with Cindy [Marble]. She is in Texas. Unfortunately, people fall. You drift apart and things are happening to you, and unless you keep up. It's hard to keep up."[35]

In 1981, Tori got a two-month gig at the Hilton Hotel, down in Myrtle Beach, South Carolina. It was great for her to get back into the Carolinas, where she had spent so much time as a girl with her grandparents. She also finally got into the legendary Washington, D.C. club the Cellar Door. She got a regular gig at the Sheraton-Carlton in Washington, which lasts for almost two years. Her club calendar was getting more and more crowded. However, as far as getting a record contract, the cupboard was bare.

Tori Amos had been sending out demo recordings since she was thirteen. She has said that she had received enough rejection notices that she could have papered the walls of her room with them if she had chosen to. When she was twenty, a producer finally took an interest. He was Narada Michael Walden (who often just went by the single name Narada), a rhythm and blues producer and performer. He is probably best remembered now for his work with Whitney Houston (he produced her first album and most of her second, as well as part of *The Bodyguard* soundtrack). He also produced Mariah Carey's "Vision of Love" and wrote Aretha Franklin's "Freeway of Love." As a performer, he worked with the Mahavishnu Orchestra and Jeff Beck's band, as well as doing studio work with such artists as Al Green, George Michael, Diana Ross, Ray Charles, Stacy Lattisaw, Steve Winwood, and Natalie Cole. He also had a few minor hits as a singer; "I Shoulda Loved Ya" was a Top 5 R&B single in 1979. A chipper duet with soul singer Patti Austin called "Gimme Gimme Gimme" and a dance track called "Divine Emotions" also made some waves on the charts.

Walden had seen Amos perform at a Washington, D.C., bar. Amos had been sending him demo after demo hoping to get him to work with her. Narada encouraged her to keep working on her music. If she sent him a demo each week, he would produce her when she was ready. Finally in 1983, he agreed to have her fly to San Francisco to record some demos. The songs, with provocative titles like "Rub Down," "Score," "Predator," and "Skirt's on Fire" were basically frantic dance-pop extravaganzas, which again bear little resemblance to the music that Amos would become known for. It was exciting to be able to record in a professional studio with a known producer, though. However, Amos was not happy with the way that Walden sped up her vocals on the recordings to make her sound younger. It was a dance trick that just sounded wrong to the singer, so she returned home to the bar scene. In an online message board on the Prodigy system, she said of the recordings, "The dance album was a demo, and if we need war weapons to torture our enemy, then we should give them cassettes of this."[36] But the experience had planted a seed, and Tori Amos wasn't just going to stay in the D.C. bar scene for long.

However, she spent almost a year regaining her footing in the safe area that she knew. There was something to be said for being close to home and family. She got a nightly gig at the Lion's Gate Taverne in the Marbury Hotel in Georgetown. Here again, the *Washington Post* tracked her down and wrote a brief profile on her, although reporter Roger Piantadosi only attributed one brief quote to her. He also described her with the somewhat offhand list of attributes, "Ellen Amos. Age: 20. Appearance: 10 (as in the movie). Energy level: 7.5 (as in Richter)." He did, however, speculate briefly that she might very well become a major pop star someday, so give him points for his foresight.[37]

Two occurrences finally pushed Amos to give up the safety net and make the leap into the great unknown. In that summer of 1984, she damaged her vocal cords. Not only couldn't she sing, she couldn't speak for a couple of weeks. Then in August she turned twenty-one. The future was here. It was time to take the chance. It was a big decision, but it was really the only one that she could make. Tori Amos was determined to be a professional singer. Not just a bar singer, mind you, a recording and touring musician. It was finally time to spread her wings and leave home.

chapter 2

Y Kant Tori Read

Ready for a big change in her life, Amos moved to Los Angeles in September 1984. The Narada Michael Walden sessions had given her a taste of the music business and she was ready to jump in with both feet. So after a little while back home going through the same merry-go-round of bars and cover versions she had grown tired of, it was time for her to make the leap. Washington, D.C. was a great town to live if you wanted to make it in politics. However, if she was going to make it in the music business, well, that just was not going to happen in the Capital Beltway. So three weeks after her twenty-first birthday Tori Amos was in Los Angeles.

She rented out a tiny—and I mean extremely tiny—guesthouse-cum-studio apartment, which was situated behind the Methodist Church on Highland Avenue in Hollywood. She set about acclimating herself to her new home. She wanted to know the best place to get a cup of coffee, the best place for a cheap meal, the cool bars and restaurants, and the cutest boutiques. She quickly became a late-eighties Hollywood girl. Tight-fitting pants made of unnatural fabrics, push-up bras, lacy tops, "hurt me" pumps, and bottles and bottles of hair spray became staples of her wardrobe. She had left behind the confines of being a nice little Christian girl, left it all back on the East Coast. She was ready for some experiences. She was ready for life. And, of course, she was ready to become a huge star. It was a time of high life and partying and experimentation in Hollywood, and Tori Amos at the very least wanted to take a taste.

Nevertheless, she never forgot the reason that she was there, the reason that she had done most everything in her life. The music was the most important thing. Within a few weeks of arriving, Amos had gotten herself together a band made up of musicians she had met. But it didn't quite work out as she had hoped; there were some big problems with alcohol, drugs, and absenteeism. The problem was, these vices all surfaced on the very first gig that she booked them for and basically ruined the experience for her. Amos realized that not everyone was as driven as she was. The one person in Los Angeles that she knew she could trust completely was herself. So she decided to be a solo artist again. She started taking gigs playing piano bars again, because she knew what to expect and it could become steady work while she pursued her career.

Amos also didn't completely abandon her former lifestyle. She still taught choir at the local church. Of course, now she was doing it in red leather pants. The kids didn't seem to notice or care; in fact Amos felt a kinship with the kids because she had come up in the same type of world. The kids appreciated that she really seemed to get them, so things were fine with her students. The same reaction did not necessarily come from the parents. Amos admitted that she did get some really weird vibes from the mothers, like they thought that she was going to attack their little babies at any moment.[1]

But Amos quickly adjusted to life on the West Coast. Sure living on her own wasn't always easy. Once, while on a date, Amos had to call her mother to find out how long she was supposed to leave the chicken in the oven. She dated some guys, including one who was eleven years older than she was, and another that she said was "a failed cat burglar." She made up a group of sexual rules to live by, years later she acknowledged that they were completely arbitrary, but they kept her from being indiscriminate.[2] In her music, jobs were hard to come by. Even the bar scene was up and down for her. She obviously had the talent and the experience at it, but she was usually going into a hotel bar wearing spandex pants and with her hair teased high. She admitted later that she got fired a hell of a lot in those days.[3]

However, Amos could never imagine the way that one of those jobs would change her life forever. It would throw her life off kilter and cause her years of mental anguish. In January 1985, Tori Amos was the victim of a horrible, violent act. It was an invasion that shook her to the core and sent ripples throughout her entire life. She was working a hotel gig one night and started to talk with one of her semi-regular patrons. They had always gotten along well enough, so she felt it was not a problem to offer him a ride home. While in the car, he pulled a knife on her and brutally raped her. She has, understandably, been notoriously reluctant to discuss the dreadful day with the press, preferring to let her song "Me and a Gun," which she later wrote as a way to deal with the trauma, tell the tale in starkly horrific terms. But she did go into excruciating detail about the ordeal in a couple of interviews she did in the early nineties with *Hot Press* magazine. She bravely told the magazine in 1994:

> I'll never talk about it at this level again, but let me ask you....Why have I survived that kind of night, when other women didn't? How am I alive to tell you this tale when he was ready to slice me up? In the song I say it was me and a gun, but it wasn't a gun. It was a knife he had. And the idea was to take me to his friends and cut me up, and he kept telling me that, for hours. And if he hadn't needed more drugs I would have been just one more news report, where you see the parents grieving for their daughter. And I was singing hymns, as I say in the song, because he told me to. I sang to stay alive. Yet I survived that torture, which left me urinating all over myself and left me paralyzed for years. That's what that night was all about, mutilation, more than violation through sex. I really do feel as though I was psychologically mutilated that night and that now I'm trying to put the pieces back together again. Through love, not hatred. And through my music. My strength has been to open again, to life, and my victory is the fact that, despite it all, I kept alive my vulnerability.[4]

Amos told no one about the ordeal at the time. More importantly, she never reported it to the police. "It's not that simple," she later admitted to ABC TV's *Prime Time Live*. "Sometimes you're in a situation where if you come forth, you're nailed. The law isn't supportive of violent situations for women. Come on, I was a nightclub singer. I dressed sexy. Look, let's not kid each other, my case was closed before [it] began....Violence is such a strange experience. If you feel that kind of hate from another person, it's like, it gets into your cells. It gets into every part of your being. And so I've been committing myself to becoming the phoenix out of the ashes, for myself, and 'Me and a Gun' has been a great teacher for me."

Amos further explained that having the song was both a blessing and a curse for her. It was cathartic, and yet it was also harrowing. For many years in concert she stood there, vulnerable and exposed, attempting to exorcise the demons of that one earth-shattering violation on her person. She doesn't always reach the plane that she is shooting for, but still she forces herself to confront one of the single most tragic events of her young life. "My commitment is to crossing over that river," she continued on the show, "the river of victimhood. But you have to be in that river. You will be in that river if you have been violated. I'm really at a place where I believe you can heal. You can heal, and yet not forget. And it's a new way of thinking."[5]

So, instead of reporting the crime, she retreated into herself. She holed herself up into her own apartment, her own world. She spent way too much time crying and depressed and shattered by her violation. Music, family, friends, all receded into the background while she tried to come to terms with this horrible experience. She had what she termed "not quite a nervous breakdown."[6] Eventually, though, she was able to return to the mainstream of life. Not forget or move past it, mind you, but she had bills and she was not going to allow this one horrendous man and his hideous act to define her life. She slowly eased herself back into the music. Also, being in Hollywood, she toyed with acting and went out on auditions for some commercial work. She didn't get many callbacks, but that was okay. Tori Amos was doing what was needed to make her way into show business.

One of the best gigs Amos got, strangely enough, was as a singing pianist in a commercial for Kellogg's Just Right cereal. She beat out her main competition for the gig, a young actress who already had more of a résumé than she did. Sarah Jessica Parker had been on Broadway in the hit musical *Annie*, had starred in the cult favorite sitcom *Square Pegs* and had just gotten a supporting role in Kevin Bacon's popular movie *Footloose*. She would go on to do many movies like *Honeymoon in Vegas*, *State and Main*, *L.A. Story*, *The First Wives Club*, *Life Without Dick*, *Ed Wood*, *If Lucy Fell*, and *Girls Just Wanna Have Fun*. Her greatest fame came from television, though, doing the critically acclaimed (but little watched) series *A Year in a Life* and *Equal Justice*, before hitting huge with the controversial HBO series *Sex and the City*.

However, Amos has often acknowledged that it was probably not any great talent as a pitchwoman that allowed her to beat out the future Carrie Bradshaw.

The advertising people needed someone who could play the piano. Tori Amos could do it. Apparently, Sarah Jessica Parker couldn't. So Tori Amos got the opportunity to be the perky woman with a short bob (she cut her curly red hair for the role), sitting at a piano with the cereal box painted on top. She sits and plays with a very yuppie-looking bespectacled guy. The two sing the immortal ad copy, "Taste. Nutrition. *Ooooh. Mmmmm. Aaaah. Mmmmm.* Just Right!" while a voice-over announcer praises the flavor and nourishment of the flakes. Amos acknowledges she had no interest at the time in becoming an actress or doing commercials. The job was just a good paycheck at a time when she needed one. She did also act as an extra on an ad for Crystal Light drink mix starring sixties screen siren Raquel Welch, but the experience was not a good one when the former *Kansas City Bomber* star suggested that Amos was a little too animated and was stealing the spotlight.

Surviving her traumatic experience had a bit of an unexpected effect, though. In some ways, she became braver and more reckless, barreling into situations without always thinking of the outcome. "I used to chase people down the road when they would cut in front of me at a light," she told Maureen Callahan of *Spin* in 1999. "They would be in, like, a pickup truck and I would chase them—I didn't care if they had shotguns. I was twenty-three. I didn't appreciate life then like I do now."[7] This new devil-may-care attitude may not have always been best for her personal safety, but it was necessary for her to jump off on her next step to musical stardom. She was finally ready to trust others with her artistic vision.

Amos formed a band in 1985, which she called Y Kant Tori Read. The name was a sly (perhaps needlessly obscure) reference to her experiences having the teachers try to force her to stop playing by ear and read music at the Peabody Conservatory. The band was a kind of ever-changing collective of musicians…in the press kit for the debut (and farewell) *Y Kant Tori Read* album, she acknowledged that the band was her and whoever happened to show up that night.[8] The group was together for about two years, all of which were spent practicing and recording demos. They only did two live performances during their short career. Amos has sometimes said in interviews that the band was already together before she came along. However, she quickly took over and became the group's creative focus.

The band came together when Tori met and became friendly with drummer Matt Sorum. Sorum would soon join the Cult, then superstars Guns N' Roses, and eventually help to found the supergroup Velvet Revolver. Amos and Sorum worked together on a few songs. The two started rehearsing and were looking for a guitarist. Sorum introduced her to guitarist Steve Caton, whom he had also been gigging with. Caton would go on to work on Amos's future solo projects, touring with her and playing on every album she would record up until *To Venus and Back*. Beyond his work in Y Kant Tori Read, Caton also had another band called Climate of Crisis, for which Amos often contributed backing vocals. Brad Cobb was also part of their club group.

Of course, the sense of roster flux that Amos described was not completely by choice. The demos that the group had made led to her being signed to a recording contract for six albums with Atlantic Records in 1986. Later, when she became an established artist, she would come to complain that the long contract was a bad deal for her, but at the time it was the only game in town, so she signed on the dotted line. The label loved Tori (on the liner notes and promotion for the resulting album, she did not use her surname, going only by her assumed first name), but they weren't too high on the rest of the band. Therefore, the label brought in a cadre of studio musicians to work on the album.

Matt Sorum, Steve Caton, and Brad Cobb did get to participate on the album. However, they were joined by about thirty outside musicians, a hodgepodge of talented musicians who may just not have been appropriate for Tori Amos. Toto member Paulihno da Costa did percussion work. Former Eddie Money sideman Steve Farris played guitar. Farris had just broken away from his then-popular band Mr. Mister. ("Broken Wings" and "Kyrie" were their biggest hits.) Former Poco keyboardist Kim Bullard not only played on the album but cowrote four songs with Tori: "The Big Picture," "Cool on Your Island," "Pirates," and "The Highlands." Jazz guitarist Peter White would soon come to work with Basia and record several acclaimed solo albums. Vinnie Caliauta had been part of Frank Zappa's band. Veteran soul singer Merry Clayton, who had previously worked as one of Ray Charles's Raelettes and sang with Joe Cocker on "Feeling Alright" and the Rolling Stones on "Gimme Shelter," added background vocals. Robin Zander, the lead singer of Cheap Trick, also added some backing vocals, under the not quite difficult to decode pseudonym Zobbin Rander.

Music biz veteran Joe Chiccarelli took on production chores. Chiccarelli has worked with varied and eclectic artists like Frank Zappa (he engineered the *Sheik Yerbouti* album), Pat Benatar, the Bee Gees, the Bangles, Sandra Bernhard, Bon Jovi, Rodney Crowell, Lone Justice, Ricky Martin, and American Music Club. "Joe Chiccarelli taught me a lot of things," Amos told *Record Collector*. "He had produced Pat Benatar and done a lot of groovy records, Oingo Boingo and stuff. [He showed me] a lot of simple fundamentals that you apply when you're in a producer situation, and that was a gift. Like, never do a take with the band right after they've eaten; don't do punch-ins because the tempo's going to slow down; or, if you're doing a substance, stick with that substance 'til you've done the overdubs!"[9]

Many of the songs that the group had been performing were thrown aside. Tori got together with Kim Bullard and Brad Cobb to write new tunes for the record. Once the record was ready for release, the record company pushed it to the wrong crowd. They touted Y Kant Tori Read as heavy metal, but it wasn't a metal group. It was a more pop-rock band. The marketing department got Amos into a tight spandex outfit and plastic pants and hair moussed to the ceiling, while she held a scimitar on the cover. The sword wasn't just an affectation, either. She was taking fencing lessons, totally immersing herself in the

New Romantic lifestyle and shopping at the kind of stores that she laughingly referred to as "retail slut."[10]

"I was a rock chick," Amos admitted when she first talked with me about the group. "I was in a band that was pretty progressive. We were never a metal band. It was just interesting and progressive music. [The finished album] really isn't representative of the band. First of all, all of the songs that we were doing as a band, none are on that record. And none of those songs [which made the album were ones] I did with them as a band. Matt Sorum played on the album, if you can see on the credits. [Note: she is referring to the fact that most copies of *Y Kant Tori Read* out there are bootlegs, which usually do not have the musician credits.] We were a band for two years together. We played mostly rehearsal studios. That's what we did," Amos said, laughing. "We played rehearsal studios. We just rehearsed all the time. Made tapes, wrote tunes and turned them in to record company. We did two gigs. Which is really funny, but that's what we did. We rehearsed three times a week. We were just dedicated to making music. Atlantic signed and then we brought in all sorts of different people. They changed hands many, many times.

"It really could rock. You know, if Matt's in it and these two other guys named Brad Cobb and Steve Caton—Caton played on 'Precious Things.' He can rock. He's played with all sorts of people over the years. [The band's melodic thrust] was just make lots of noise. It was pretty musical, and people who got brought into the project didn't think what we were doing was working, although that got us signed. Disputes and arguments tore us to pieces. All that was left was me. This forced me to go back to my piano. Writing with different people and changing things. Finally a different producer came in who was different than where it all started and tried to pull it all together and put out an album."

At the time, the Tori character was still a work in progress, though. She was profiled in her hometown newspaper, *The Gazette*, as the *Y Kant Tori Read* album was released. "Local rock 'n' roller shoots for stardom" trumpeted the headline. In the interview, she still went by the name of Ellen Amos and referred to Tori in the third person. "Tori is so fiery, so filled with passion, rebellious," she explained to reporter David Schwartz. "She's not rebellious just to be rebellious. She does exactly what she pleases. Tori is like Peter Pan in leather."[11] (Looking back on it, I'll bet she would wish that she could take that quote back.) The reporter was impressed by the album, but just a little baffled by the whole experience. For example, he couldn't figure out whether Y Kant Tori Read was Amos's stage name or the name of an old group of hers or just some weird mind fuck. All of which, of course, were the case. However, the journalist was able to report the good news that the album had become huge in the state of Idaho, which was being used as a test market. She may have struck a chord in the Potato State, but sadly, the rest of the country did not follow suit.

Still, she was enjoying the experience. A minister's daughter rarely gets the chance to really cut loose, so she was going to live her newfound lifestyle to the fullest. "To me, if you haven't been a rock chick, you haven't lived," she later told Jon Savage of *Interview* magazine. "I had some wonderful hair sprays. I teased my hair, I put on the lacy stockings, and I went out with gorgeous guys and talked about Shelley, poets. They liked my hair spray, and I made a record. What I had to deal with was being called a bimbo, after being a child prodigy. You wanna talk about a hard one to the face?"[12]

"She had these big boots on and her hair was all crazy," Matt Sorum recalled to VH1's *Behind the Music 2* in 2000. "She was sort of, I think, being put in a mold that they kind of saw would work for that time period. Okay, here we have this, this girl, we need a beat, and we're going to have her dance around in a video."[13] Steve Caton agreed that it was the wrong direction for her, acknowledging on the same show that one of her greatest talents was completely overlooked in the band. "Tori didn't play piano," Caton said. "She mainly stood there and sang and then had a little string synthesizer."[14]

Even Amos seemed to be fumbling forward, not sure how she was supposed to promote her own creation. In the original press kit for the album, Atlantic's publicity department explained the fact that Tori was not even the singer's real name with the following quote, "Tori came from 'notorious,' " she divulged, "for wearing red leather pants to my father's church on Sundays and directing the children's choir."[15] Perhaps this clarification had a basis in fact, however the really bad pun and the need to create a bad-girl mythos seemed just a little bit desperate. Then she goes on in the press kit to give a long and convoluted description of the album as her "decoding rebellious statement," whatever the hell that means. Again, the band name was causing confusion, with Amos cryptically suggesting that Tori may not read to be a non-conformist, maybe because all the news was bad, or maybe it was just a statement that even though Tori was supposedly illiterate, it doesn't mean that she doesn't deserve love.

"Everything was kind of diluted," Amos admitted to me in 1992, looking back at the eventual failure of the *Y Kant Tori Read* album. "I truly believe to this day that if that band would have come out as it was [originally], it would have been a different album you would have heard. At the time, if you would have had this conversation with me when that record was coming out, I would swear to you up and down that this is what it should be," she laughed. "I wasn't able to say maybe some mistakes were being made. Maybe we were doing this for the wrong reasons."

Perhaps, but listening to the finished product, the truth is, the *Y Kant Tori Read* album really wasn't half bad. Not great by any means, but there were little gems of talent and possibilities shining through. It was quite definitely a product of its times, but there are enough good songs and potential here to see what was coming in the future for Amos. The first song was also the debut single. "The Big Picture" is probably the most dated eighties-sounding song on a very eighties-sounding album, but it is not a half bad pop-metal jam. A ratcheting background guitar line (apparently inspired by John Parr's 1985 single "Naughty Naughty") swerves in and out of a snaky backbeat. Tori is in more of a Pat Benatar belting mode than she will be known for in the future, but the style works pretty well for her voice. No one could ever mistake this song for being from any time in history than the one that it was in, but it was a pretty good eighties arena anthem.

The second single was the more timeless sounding "Cool on Your Island," which sashays on a nice tropical beat and a much more laid-back vibe. Tori's vocals have a different, more sensual lilt to them than the previous track did, and a soft native drumbeat makes this song memorable. It also is nice how the song's ballad structure on the verses and chorus segues into an atmospheric mid-tempo sultry groove on the bridge, complete with a brief flamenco guitar solo. "*Y Kant Tori Read* was a pivotal point for me as a writer," she told *Performing Songwriter* magazine. "Some of the things on it work, some of them don't. 'Cool on Your Island' works more than anything else, and I wrote that, I think, with Kim Bullard, but you'll have to check the credits because I've been using too much deodorant lately."[16] Ironically, when "Cool on Your Island" was released as the album's second single, Atlantic packaged it on a radio promo single together with Phil Collins' soon-to-be number–one smash "A Groovy Kind of Love." In a way, pairing *Y Kant Tori Read* with the newest hit by one of their biggest acts showed that Atlantic wanted to support the song and the act. It also showed that they had no real understanding of what the group was all about, or how to market it.

Despite the self-consciously old-fashioned misspelling of the song title, "Fayth" was an okay-enough attempt at arena-oriented power pop. If the "suggestive" lyrics ("You took my love, you took my money, you took my sex") were a lot less subtle than the ones that would become her specialty later, it still was a way of working out her musical and lyrical direction. The song is somewhat memorable, if that is the word for it, for Tori's oddly exaggerated vocals. She draws out normal words and stretches and contorts them so that they're nearly unrecognizable. *Together* sounds like "too-geee-ther." *Sex* becomes "Say-ucks." The song also features squealing guitars and Tori doing a strange rap-inspired interlude.

Much more successful is the power ballad "Fire on the Side." It is actually a quite pretty song that is built on a delicate keyboard line and a powerful, emotional vocal. This song would have been a huge hit if it were recorded by Heart or Foreigner. Then again, is that a good thing? How many Tori Amos songs have ever sounded like they should have been recorded by Heart? Well, actually several songs on this album. "Pirates" is more uninspired light metal, which does have a pretty good choral hook, but it also has a bit of a pretentious lead guitar line reminiscent of Europe's "The Final Countdown." This instrumental break doesn't even have the courage of its cheesy convictions, downplaying itself into the production so that it seems almost an afterthought.

"Floating City" continues the stylistic pandering. It's not a bad song, it's just trying too hard to be "current." Of course, today this has left the song far behind, as the soft pop-metal sound it espoused has been pretty much overlooked ever since Nirvana's "Smells Like Teen Spirit" exploded out of Washington State in the early nineties. I love the wonderfully melodramatic title "Heart Attack at 23." Musically it is just fine, sort of like Pat Benatar circa 1983. Little touches like a brief sax solo prop up a song which otherwise would be kind of unspectacular. "On the Boundary" is further proof that the band was probably best at slow, devotional love songs. "You Go to My Head" is a little funkier than the rest of the album, but otherwise it is rather unmemorable. You may notice that many of the songs are compared to other artists. This lack of originality is probably *Y Kant Tori Read*'s biggest problem.

The album-ending "Etienne Trilogy" is the one place on the disc where Amos hints at her own musical viewpoint. It starts off with a brief instrumental passage. Then, for one of the too few times on the album, we actually are given the opportunity to hear Tori at the piano driving the melody. "Etienne" is a delicately pretty song where Amos imagines herself as a witch traveling the plains of Europe in search of her love. The trilogy fades out with a version of the traditional Scottish "Skyeboat Song" played on bagpipes.

Amos personally thinks that the "trilogy" was not so much a look forward as a look back. "It was more just me at the piano. You can't compare 'Precious Things' and 'Waitress' and 'Cruel' to 'Etienne Trilogy,' you know what I mean? Or obviously I wouldn't have made the four records I just made," she told *Performing Songwriter* magazine in 1998. "There is a bit of the balladeer in me, and that comes across on all the records also, but the records aren't just ballad records as you well know. But I do think that 'Etienne,' as a song, was more of what I was doing before I came to L.A."[17]

There was also a music video recorded for the premiere single, "The Big Picture." Marty Collner, who also made videos for Aerosmith and Whitesnake, directed the clip. It was a typical clichéd state-of-the-art, late-eighties hair-metal music video: lots of smoke, motorcycles, sports cars, graffiti, curtains blowing in the breeze, and hot, barely dressed women. (And, yes, Tori *was* included in that group.) The story—if you could call it that—had Tori's car being broken into. The thieves stole everything, including her panties. A cop comes and takes her story, and as he walks away at the end, we realize he has Tori's red panties in his back pocket. Not exactly sophisticated social commentary. However, it was a perfect bad metal video. In fact, if it were ever reviewed on *Beavis and Butthead*, MTV's parody music video series of the early nineties, the kids would have thought the video totally rocked, though it probably could use a fire truck to make it completely cool. Needless to say, the video did not get a whole lot of airplay (one estimate said it showed less than ten times on MTV), and when it did hit the airwaves, it just sort of faded into the *Headbanger's Ball* woodwork—a visual case of been there, done that.

To a large extent, Tori has divorced herself from the *Y Kant Tori Read* album at this point. She won't come out and say it's horrible, she just says that she bought into too many of the outside influences and made the album as she believed it was supposed to be done at the time in order to sell lots of copies…writing for focus groups, not as she would have done it just for herself. Ironically, in the handwritten thank-yous in the CD liner notes, she thanked Atlantic for allowing her to make the album in her way with no interference. Amazing what a little sales failure can do to a person's point of view. Because we all know it is unheard of for someone to say something insincere in an album's liner notes. Well, okay, maybe not.…

The *Y Kant Tori Read* album did not get reviewed in that many places. However, *Billboard* magazine actually gave it a relatively positive capsule review in their June 11, 1988, issue. "Classically trained pianist pounds the ivories on her pop-rock debut, belting out self-written material with a forceful, appealing voice. Unfortunately, provocative packaging sends the [inaccurate] message that this is just so much more bimbo music."[18] Of course, being a sensitive artist, Amos fixated on the negative, often referring in interviews to the fact that in the review of *Y Kant Tori Read* that *Billboard* called her a "bimbo." Which, as you read the review, you see they really didn't say at all. That didn't matter to Amos, though. It was all in her perception. *Bimbo* was the one word that stood out.

The *Y Kant Tori Read* album was only released in very limited quantities. It did get made in all three formats that were still available at the time. They printed up 3,800 of the CDs, 3,300 of the LPs, and 3,200 on cassette for commercial sale. (Additional versions were supplied as promotional and review copies.) The album was quickly labeled a failure by the label and was quietly slipped into the cutout bins of record stores. For the most part they stayed there untouched until a few years later with Tori's surprise success with her debut solo album *Little Earthquakes*. Fans started grabbing up any copies of the album that could be found, until it was soon nearly impossible to find an original copy.

Although there was a significant interest in the album once she hit it big, Amos has since refused to rerelease it, saying it was not representative of her work anymore. Because of this, a huge black market has sprung up around the album. It is one of the most widely counterfeited of Tori Amos's recordings, and she was arguably the most bootlegged artist of the 1990s. Tori has always been vocal about her disdain for the bootlegging of music (though her hero Robert Plant early on told her that when people start selling illegal copies of your music, you know you've really made it).

So if you are at a record store and see the *Y Kant Tori Read* CD, chances are you aren't just getting lucky and finding a long-lost copy of the mythic Tori Amos album. One good sign that a *Y Kant Tori Read* CD is a boot is if it has "bonus tracks." Most bootlegged copies of the CD stick on some later Tori odds and ends that they claim are from the *Y Kant Tori Read* sessions. These so-called bonus tracks include the song "Happy Workers" that Amos recorded for the odd 1992 Robin Williams film *Toys*, an outtake from her first solo album called "Song for Eric," a live version of the *Little Earthquakes* track "Happy Phantom," or a cover of Amii Stewart's disco classic "Ring My Bell," which she recorded for a 1992 tribute

CD called *Ruby Trax*, put together by the British music newspaper *New Music Express*. However, if you do stumble upon a legit copy of the original LP and it's in near mint condition, it is worth at least $125.00.[19]

But this after-life value of *Y Kant Tori Read* would not come to be for a few years. In late 1988, it slowly began to dawn on Amos that as the album had become a notorious flop; she was becoming a bit of a joke in the music community. She would run into old friends and acquaintances she had made in her years in L.A. while dressed up in full Y Kant Tori Read regalia and they would ignore her or mock her behind her back. Calls were not getting returned. People were all of a sudden very busy when she needed them. Suddenly, after a shockingly brief flirtation with the big time, Tori Amos was on the outside looking in, yet again. A friend had told her that getting a record contract and making an album was a nice first step—but it was only a first step. Many people never made it past that step. Tori Amos was determined that the gravestone on her musical career was not going to read "Y Kant Tori Read."

In the fallout from the Y Kant Tori Read failure, Amos was disheartened, but unwilling to give up her dream. She spent a bit of time feeling sorry for herself, holing herself up in her place, not seeing friends or doing work. She cried all the time, amazed that after working all her life to make it in the music world, she was already considered washed up before her twenty-fifth birthday. She has said that she spent most of the next months sitting on the floor of her kitchen, unable to think or move or do much of anything. She didn't work; instead Amos survived on her savings. She even got rid of her piano.

She had just met a producer named Eric Rosse as the Y Kant Tori Read debacle was going down, however. There was a spark, and soon they were living together in the tiny Hollywood apartment, which was essentially a little guesthouse. Rosse did his best to help her to deal with the record's failure. Before they became roomies, he'd come over and they would talk and talk. He encouraged her not to give up on herself. However, Amos had to come to terms with it in her own way.

It took her first love to pull her back from the abyss. The one thing she understood totally and that totally understood her. The piano. The healing began when she was talking with her old high school friend Cindy Marble. Marble was by then living in L.A. as the leader of a never-signed band called the Rugburns. Cindy could tell that Amos was in a bad way, so she told her to come over. When Amos got to her friend's house, she just sat down at the piano and began to play. And play. And play. She sat there for hours, feeling the music washing over her, performing improvised melodies. Not a word was said, Marble just sat in a corner and listened. Amos became so engrossed in what she was doing that she forgot that her friend was even there. Finally Cindy got up. She was crying. She said that they had known each other for years, but she had never *really* seen Tori before. This was what she was meant to do. And suddenly Amos realized that she was completely right. She had listened to others about what her music should be and it had been a disaster. She wasn't Lita Ford or one of the members of Vixen or Girlschool. She had spent too much time trying to pretend she was. It was time for Amos to listen to her heart and her intuition. Within a week, she had rented a piano to go into her tiny apartment. Tori Amos was going to return to what she knew.[20]

However, it took a while before she could bring herself to think of the next major step in her career. Instead, she took some musical side trips to pass the time. She worked with several artists. Amos's former producer Joe Chiccarelli remembered his old front woman and steered her into studio gigs when he could. For example, he produced a 1988 album by one-hit wonder Robert Tepper, who had a hit with the song "No Easy Way Out" a couple of years before from the soundtrack to the movie *Rocky IV*. Amos was brought in to sing backing vocals on Tepper's follow-up album, *Modern Madness*.

She also did a lot of work with British folk rocker Al Stewart. Stewart had several big hits in the late seventies, including "Year of the Cat," "Time Passages," "Song on the Radio," and "Midnight Rocks." Amos played keyboards on Stewart's 1988 comeback album *Last Days of the Century*. As well as playing on much of the record, she sang on two songs as well, "Last Day of the Century" and "Red Toupee." Amos has stayed in contact with Stewart over the years, also cowriting the song "Charlotte Corday" with him on his 1993 album *Famous Last Words*.

A few years after first appearing on Stewart's *Century* album, right before *Little Earthquake* became a surprise hit, Amos came out and played piano for "Year of the Cat" at Stewart's show at the Royal Festival Hall on April 24, 1991. Stewart introduced her rather oddly, though, as an entirely different, fictional pianist. "We've imported a pianist for the next song," Stewart announced from the stage. "We have Viliana Tchaikovskaya, who is a Russian pianist who knows not a word of English, and knows not much about English music, apart from the fact that she's learnt one of my songs. Will you please welcome Miss Viliana Tchaikovskaya!"[21] Amos came out and sat at the piano and played.

Years later in 1999, when she finally played the Hall as the headlining act, she told the story to the audience, explaining the alias was her own doing. "I don't know if you all know this, but I've played this place before. But I didn't play it as me…," she told the crowd. "The thing is, in 1991, I think. And I got a phone call from somebody and he goes, 'Tori, my piano player is sick. Will you come to the Festival Hall and fill in?' And I said, 'Um, well, I do know the song?' I said, 'Definitely, I'll come. Just make sure he doesn't get better….It's a long train ride for me, so I'm coming in, don't fuck me over.' So I show up and Al Stewart said to me, 'You know this "Year of the Cat" song?' I said, 'Of course, I'm born the year of the cat—I know all about it….There's only one problem—I can't play as me because I, um, have a passport problem.' And he said, 'Do you really think that anybody from Passport Control is concerned about what you're doing tonight?' I said, 'Well, maybe, you know, just maybe. I'm playing this big gig at the Mean Fiddler, and I'm opening for seven people and I can't blow that.' And so he said to me, 'Okay, well, you'll be Viliana Tchaikovskaya.' And that's who I was."[22]

In 1988, under the fake band name Tess Makes Good, Amos was hired to re-cord a song called "Distant Storm" for the long-forgotten, straight-to-video mar-tial arts movie *China O'Brien*, starring Cynthia Rothrock. The song played through the first few minutes of the film. Amos only did it because she needed the money (she has recalled that she was paid $300.00 to do the vocals) and told the produc-ers that she did not want to be credited for the song anywhere, hence the group name. She even drew up a contract forbidding the name Tori Amos to be used in conjunction with the song (she couldn't afford to go to a lawyer). She just didn't want the song to come back and haunt her when she made it. In fact, years later, Amos admitted that she recalled recording it, but was surprised to hear that the song was ever used for anything. The song was done under the fake band name, but even though Amos sang the lead, the credits did list "Ellen Amos" for backing vocals.

Amos really did contribute backing vocals on a version of Prince's "Little Red Corvette" by hip comedienne Sandra Bernhard. The song was recorded for the 1989 album version of Bernhard's one-woman show *Without You I'm Noth-ing*. Y Kant Tori Read producer Joe Chiccarelli produced the album. A few years later Amos spoke with Bernhard for *Interview* magazine. Amos acknowledged she added "oohs" to her song and Bernhard recalled, "They're great oohs." Ber-nhard then recalled running into Amos soon afterward, when she was working as an "usher-waitress" at a party for Steven Spielberg. "I knew you were already doing something," Bernhard continued. "But I meant, When is someone gonna do something for you? I think it's a woman's responsibility to her friends and to other women who are real artists and real sufferers to say, 'I believe in you, and I know it's hard, but it's gotta come together.' That's why when I saw your success, I thought, it's just so great and weird and perfect."[23]

Amos also did backing vocals on three songs by Stan Ridgway, the former lead singer of eighties pop group Wall of Voodoo, which is best remembered for the early MTV hit "Mexican Radio." The songs "Dogs," "Peg and Pete and Me," and "The Last Honest Man" appeared on Ridgway's 1989 solo album *Mosquitoes* al-bum and featured Amos. The album was recorded and mixed by Chiccarelli. An-other album that her former producer brought her in for was *Phantom Center* by Canadian folk troubabour Ferron. Amos sang backing vocals on all the songs on the album. The record came out in 1990, and when it was re-released five years later, after Amos had established herself, the songs were remixed to make her vo-cal contributions much more prominent.

All this time, Amos had not forgotten her own work. She was putting to-gether songs with boyfriend Eric Rosse for a planned solo album. It wasn't exactly high-tech; many of the demos were recorded in their tiny apartment. Rosse said later that their place was so small that when they started recording together, they had to take all of the clothes out of the closet in order to be able to play guitar. Tori Amos had spent enough time being a piano and voice for hire. It was time to go back to her personal vision. It was time to see what she could do.

chapter 3

Excuse Me, but Can I Be You for a While?

After the disappointment of *Y Kant Tori Read*, Amos took a little while to collect herself. The execs at Atlantic told her that they were willing to hear her do something different. They just weren't sure what it was going to be. So Amos decided that maybe it was time for a reinvention. She would stop trying to be someone else. She was going to write for herself. "That record," she told journalist Ken Sharp, "was the catalyst for me to go back and write at the piano. Before that, I just wasn't ready. I finally faced up to the fact that since the age of seven I had been trying to please other people rather than myself."[1]

She had worked her way past the whole idea of being a rock chick. "There was a part of me that really wanted to be in snake pants—although they were plastic—and walk around feeling like a bad girl," she told Mat Snow of *Q* magazine in early 1992. "But now my insides are strong and I don't need my hair sprayed out ten inches and my bra showing through."[2] In fact, she said other times that she almost felt a need at that time to dress down and limit the mascara and blush. It was like penance for past indiscretions. Say twelve "Hail Mary's" and try to look plain. "I had to go through a phase of wearing big bags," she told *Vogue*, "absolutely no makeup, completely disclaiming anything female, because I felt I had so abused it."[3]

Luckily, she didn't stick to this act of contrition. Amos had gotten enough guilt in her childhood. Tori Amos was a woman meant to stand out. She couldn't avoid that simple, natural fact. So while she never again quite tried to sell the sexiness vibe as blatantly as she did on *Y Kant Tori Read*, she still projected a certain aura. Now she was just finding the sensuality in herself instead of in accessories. In many ways this opening up was even more dangerous than the way she had displayed herself in the old days. Some people bought into it, some people didn't. (She once said the only review she read that ever truly hurt her was when the writer called her "unattractive."[4]) But she was no longer going to let herself be judged as hair metal Barbie. Now she would show who she really was.

Amos stopped writing with different collaborators. Instead she decided to trust her own songwriting abilities on what would become her breakthrough album, *Little Earthquakes*. Even at the time, fresh off the disappointment of her band debut, Amos said that she did not do the album to make a big hit. She did it simply because she felt like she had to write some songs. Not just wanted to, she needed to. If there was an audience out there for it, that would be a great bonus. However, it wasn't necessary. Amos was birthing her songs and bringing them to artistic life. Atlantic, her record company, kept coming to Amos asking about the solo album. Amos turned in the tunes that she was working on, but this just confused the execs, who were expecting Billy Joel or something. In particular, label co-chairman and co-CEO Doug Morris seemed unsure how he was going to get any of this stuff onto the radio and into people's homes.

She gave them a ten-song demo version of the album. Several of the songs that were on the demo would end up on the *Little Earthquakes* album, but the Atlantic execs quickly rejected this early version of the album. The demo was made up of the songs "Russia" (which would be renamed "Take to the Sky" by the time *Little Earthquakes* reached record stores), "Mary" (which ended up with the European CD single for "Crucify"), "Crucify," "Happy Phantom," "Leather," "Winter," "Sweet Dreams" (which did not make it onto the album, but showed up as a bonus track on the "Winter" maxi-single), "Song for Eric" (which was only released as a live performance on the *Little Earthquakes* video), "Learn to Fly" (which has never seen the light of day), and "Flying Dutchman" (which has only been released as a live version on the "Past the Mission" EP).

So Amos holed herself back up in the studio and recorded more songs for the album. This new batch included "Little Earthquakes," "Girl," "Tear in Your Hand," and "Precious Things." These were also met with a scratched head and collective shrug from Atlantic. Eventually the label decided that they needed to get her in touch with a producer who could reel her in. Someone who could extract music from her, music that they thought might actually get on the radio. "I kept turning in these songs," Amos said, laughing to me after *Little Earthquakes* was finally released. "They'd hear 'Leather' and go, 'You're out of your mind. We're not interested in this.' I said, 'Well, this is what I'm doing.' Eventually, after a few years, I finally hooked up with Davitt, who told everybody, 'You guys are missing the point. This is what she really does. It is what she's been doing since she was two years old.' And nobody knew."

Davitt was producer and former rock journalist Davitt Sigerson, who had at the time just produced the Bangles' third album, *Everything* (which included the smash hit "Eternal Flame"). Sigerson had also recently worked with the critically acclaimed folk-rock band David & David (*Welcome to the Boomtown*) and Olivia Newton-John (he produced *The Rumour* album). Sigerson ended up producing six songs for Amos's debut solo album, and was promoted to the executive offices and had become the president of Polydor Records by the time that *Little Earthquakes* was released. In the years since, he has also tried his hand as a novelist, releasing *Faithful: A Novel* in 2004.

"The best thing about what I did as a producer is to give Tori permission to express herself in the way that she really needed to," Sigerson told *Billboard*. The label had been making her try to fit a square peg into a round hole. They wanted her to conform to musical standards, to make an album that would be easy to sell, like it was an appliance or paint or something. Sigerson acknowledged that he got her into hot water with the execs because he told her just the opposite was true. She had to be faithful to the voice inside her. The music she created was a part of who she was; it should not be diluted for anyone. "Be who you are!" he told her. "Fit everything else around you and your music and people will come to terms with it because this is great and should not be changed."[5]

The finished *Little Earthquakes* album seizes the listener from the very first moment. Over a calm and beautiful piano line, a hushed and delicate vocal lets go the words, "Every finger in the room is pointing at me. I want to spit in their faces, then I get afraid of what that could bring." It's quite a grabber of an opening. It is full of anger, confusion, insecurity, desperation—all of these emotions bubble underneath the languid piano line and unobtrusive percussion. "Crucify" is a stark exploration of a woman who is trying to balance lust, religion, and self-doubt in her life. The song may have first gained notice because of the somewhat controversial nature of the title, but it rewarded repeated listens.

It was a stunning example of the early-nineties youth-angst culture that led to Nirvana, the movie *Singles* and the changing political values of the Clinton era. What had been bad was good, what had been right was wrong. A new generation of artists and politicians were not afraid to show that they were hurt and bleeding. And here was Tori Amos, taking one of the most sacred images of the Catholic Church and showing that sometimes it could just be self-mutilation. "Crucify" as a song was not overtly religious, however, other than its evocative central image. It was more an unblinking look at the panicked lack of self-esteem and, sometimes, outright self-loathing that people can feel. It is a search for love or even any kind of feeling in areas that they were nearly impossible to find. The spiritual imagery is used to dramatize the problem, not as a cause of it.

Amos continued to explore the gap between what is expected of women and what they need in the second song. Despite the fact that the song had a deceptively appealing and somewhat cheerful tune, the chorus of "She was everybody else's girl, maybe someday she'll be her own" was a simple and powerful indictment of how women were expected to sublimate their wants and needs for others. The funny thing is, "Girl" came very close to never being recorded. It was just a musical doodle that Amos had worked on when visiting her parents' farm in Virginia. She got as far as writing the chorus and then just filed it away, pretty much forgetting the song. In the tour book for *Little Earthquakes*, Amos said several months later she was cleaning the apartment (which she acknowledged was a shock in itself) when Eric Rosse ran across the tape and asked what it was.[6]

The first single from the album was "Silent All These Years." The track is a quietly mesmerizing look at a relationship that has gone bad, featuring what was quite possibly the best vocal hook in a chorus of that year. Lyrically it was about a woman who struggles to assert herself and her needs upon a straying lover.

Again, the dramatic lyrics are somewhat at odds with the delicate piano line and tasteful orchestral arrangements. She told *Keyboard* magazine that the song "has a certain story line going on musically that's really the antithesis of what's going on verbally. It's counterpoint, pure and simple."[7]

Of all the critics who were moved by "Silent All These Years," perhaps the most important one to Amos was her first supporter, her father. A proud Dr. Amos told the *Washington Post* that the song was "about the structure of a culture that has encrusted your soul to where you are not who you should be. There's no ephemeral writing from Tori, it's all out of experience or meaning. As a philosopher and theologian, I think there's a lot of great wisdom about life in her songs."[8]

Amos took it a lot more lightly. On the radio show *World Café*, she had this to say about her breakthrough song: "Yeah, this is 'Silent' and this is about a lot of things. I started it with this bumblebee riff. You know we all grew up playing…you know that bumblebee song? I decided that that song tortured me so I'm going to pay it back."[9] Ironically Amos did almost not record her "bumblebee" song. During her performance on *VH1 Storytellers*, Amos admitted that at the time she wrote "Silent All These Years," she had actually been hoping to sell songs to other singers because she simply needed the money. The songs that she had submitted for Cher and Tina Turner had been rejected, so she started work on this song for Al Stewart. Stewart told her she should keep it for herself. Needless to say, she is happy that he did.[10]

Even though most of her songs aren't strictly autobiographical, Amos does use her songs to work through the problems and concerns she feels are somewhat universal. This is quite obvious in her writing. Amos's songs are a gloriously human mixture of intense strength and a crippling insecurity. In the song "Precious Things," Amos can be powerful enough to chide a man with the line, "So you can make me cum, / that doesn't make you Jesus." However, in the very same song, she is also vulnerable enough to admit that a man who was seducing her told her that she was an ugly girl. Amos was even more shocked by her own reaction, of thanking him. The song is musically much more aggressive than the previous songs on *Little Earthquakes*, with stabbing keyboard, thundering drums, and Amos's primal screams emanating from the vocals.

"It's like when you have honey and garlic together," Amos explained. "When you have different spices that you wouldn't normally put together, they don't always work. But when they do work, they really work. It's the subtext. We're not one-dimensional people. We can hate something and at the same time be turned on. We can really be hurt by somebody and want to hit them, but if they would give us a hug, we would just hug them back. There are so many things that go on. At the end of the day, most of us don't think we're enough. We do just want to be accepted."

A strong sense of nostalgia and melancholy suffuse the lovely "Winter." The tune is an exploration of the complicated but close relationship between a father and a daughter. The daughter as an adult looks back upon the safety that she felt when he was there for her, and remembers the gradual realization that he would not always be able to fix everything in life for her. She recalled the inspiration for the song in a club show in Fort Lauderdale, Florida, in 1998. "My father's here tonight," Amos said from the stage. "I remember he took me for this walk in the mountains, and it was snowing and it got inside of my boots and made my feet cold. But I'll never forget it because it was the first time in a long time that we had connected. I wrote this for him."[11]

Far more upbeat is "The Happy Phantom," which actually bounds off playfully on a skipping piano line that belies its somber opening line about dying today. The lyrics are full of odd non sequiturs about Confucius doing the puzzle in the *Sunday Times* without benefit of an eraser and Judy Garland skipping hand in hand with the Buddha. The song is a nice little island of lightheartedness on a sometimes-serious album. "China" is a lovely portrait of a relationship in decay. Amos uses the title word as two separate yet lovely pieces of symbolism. (Which is probably why she changed the title from its original name, "Distance.") The marriage is developing little cracks just like the ones in their delicate, expensive plates. At the same time, the two people are constructing emotional barriers that rival the Great Wall of China.

In "Leather," Amos strips herself literally and figuratively for the audience to gaze upon, warts and all. Then she asks the simple question of them, "Don't you want more than my sex?" The song is at least partially a response to the experience with her former band, where Amos felt she had whored herself out for popular acceptance. Amos had written "Winter" for her dad, so it only seemed fair that she also record a song called "Mother." Again, it was not so much about being with her parent as it was the eventual realization that she would have to leave the warmth and safety of home and venture out on her own.

Though it is not all that similar musically, Amos has said that "Tear in Your Hand" was also inspired by the classic Simon and Garfunkel ballad "Scarborough Fair/Canticle."[12] In the song, she mentions a friend that Amos cultivated in California. Neil Gaiman was the author of the comic strip *The Sandman.* They met through mutual friends and quickly there was a bond. In an online chat on the Prodigy system, Amos called him perhaps the most important writer currently working. She went on to write the intro to his graphic novel *Death: The High Cost of Living.* Gaiman in return has used many of Tori's attributes in a character of his called Delirium, who is a tall redheaded woman. The character is not specifically created for Amos. Gaiman had introduced her before they met. However, since then, she has taken on many of Amos's traits.

The most nakedly confessional song on this album full of private statements is in many ways the simplest one. On "Me and a Gun," in an a capella voice, Amos relives and tries to come to grips with the rape that nearly destroyed her life years before. The story is told in a whisper and she recounts the thoughts, emotions, rage, desperation, and resignation she felt when she was violated. She tries desperately to forget what is happening to her by thinking of the things she has done, like eating her grandmother's biscuits in North Carolina. She also thinks of the things she has never had a chance to do, like taking a vacation on the island of Barbados. Only an unorthodox talent like Amos could write a song as devastating and personal as "Me and a Gun" and then right in the middle drop in a sly joke about Mr. Ed, the talking horse from a sixties situation comedy. Honey and garlic mixed together yet again.

Is this song the whole story of that horrible night? Of course it isn't…not exactly. Tori Amos is a writer first and foremost, and a writer's job is to take her truth and make it interesting and tenable, passionate and accessible to her audience. Although many of her songs are strongly rooted in her own experiences, Amos says that she always mixes some truth with some fantasy in her lyrics. For example, she was raped at knifepoint, not at gunpoint as she said in the song. She says it is important to expose herself in her music, but she never wants to be considered a completely open book. Nor does she want people to know how much of her song is real and how much is just part of her fertile imagination. That, she explains, is just for her and her therapist to know.

It did have a very important and very pointed message to convey, though. "I hope attackers as well as victims are listening," Amos acknowledged to *Glamour* magazine. "As well as judges, as well as lawyers. I want you to taste in the back of your mouth what it was like to be in a car with that pervert."[13] The song came to her somewhat out of the blue as well. She was in London, and had decided to see the movie *Thelma and Louise*, starring Geena Davis and Susan Sarandon. When it came to the scene where Sarandon killed a man who was trying to rape her, Amos was shocked by the way it moved her. After years of trudging through life with this horrible night as a constant weight, she finally felt that she could breathe again. She hopped onto the Underground to her gig that night at the famous club the Mean Fiddler. She wrote "Me and a Gun" on a couch in the parking lot of the venue before going onstage. She tried the song out as a work in progress that night and polished it up the next day.

It was cathartic to get out of her system, but it also opened a door that Amos never expected. Over the years, when meeting female fans, she was made privy to the women's stories of their own victimizations. At one point, Amos estimated one in every four women she talked with told her about their own dark moments of abuse. She was flattered and moved to be invited to share something so personal. At the same time it was somewhat painful to her—writing "Me and a Gun" had been her way to try and close the book on that passage of her life. It was her way to not have to talk about being attacked. But it kept returning. She wanted to be there for the women she met, because she knew what it was like to be alone and dealing with such a trauma. This was a rare and special connection that she did not take lightly. It set the wheels in motion for Amos to help found RAINN, the Rape, Abuse & Incest National Network.

The final song on the album is the title track. It is buoyed by a thudding drumline, and Amos's vocals seem to be slightly distorted to give the tune a strange, dreamlike quality. Her vocals are multi-tracked so that her voice seems to be pulling at the edges of the song, doing battle with a doppelgänger of her voice. It is disorienting and strangely seductive. Amos said that she wanted to have three bridges in the track. By the time the martial drums lead to primal screeches, she seems exhausted. Her voice is a hoarse whisper on the final verse, completing the atmospheric tour de force.

When she finished the album, Amos knew that she had created something that was special to her. What she couldn't say for sure was if it would connect with the rest of the world. She was okay with that, though. Amos had come to feel that she had betrayed her own sense of art with the *Y Kant Tori Read* album, so it felt good, if nothing else, to know that she had finally been completely true to her musical vision. "After *Y Kant Tori Read*, I had a huge dose of what it's like to be on the precipice…," she told the *Illinois Entertainer*. "Bloody hell. I had no idea that *Little Earthquakes* would get heard. It was such a dose of humility."[14]

Though the Atlantic execs could see that they had a viable piece of art in the album, they were still baffled about how to sell it. Finally, label exec Doug Morris decided that European audiences would probably be more open to the subtle charms of *Little Earthquakes* than Americans. "When I first heard this record, I didn't get it at first because it was so eclectic," Morris admitted to *Billboard*'s Melinda Newman. "But then I fell in love with it and realized it wasn't a record that could be handled in the normal way by going directly to radio."[15]

Morris suggested that Amos move to London and they would release the album there. If the disc built a following overseas, then they would see about getting it into the stores in Amos's home country. Amos had worked too hard and put too much of herself into the album to do it halfway, so she packed up and went to her potential audience. Actually, she soon told *Interview* that she had been hoping to go to England for two years before it happened. She said she had been sending mental messages to Morris to get her there and she was happy that he finally picked up on her vibes.[16] She got a regular gig at the famous London club the Mean Fiddler. Early gigs were nearly empty, but the word of mouth was good and little by little Amos's crowds blossomed. Soon enough, she was selling the Fiddler out. She also was doing well at other London acoustic clubs like the Troubadour and the Borderline.

She loved it there, but it was also a real culture shock for the young pianist. As she said on a Westwood One radio interview, "When I moved to London, that was a huge step, when you leave a country. It's a whole new culture. Just because they speak the same language, they're very different people, let me tell you, trust me, folks. I love it over there, but…they're much closer to the Europeans, they're much closer to the French, and they will readily admit this, than they are to the Americans. We're just very different."[17]

There were some adjustments to the European lifestyle. For example, in what Amos has called the dumbest move she ever made in her life, she and a girlfriend were nearly arrested on drug charges at the German border. "In the early nineties, a friend and I were stopped at the border at Aachen, Germany," Amos told *She* magazine. "She had cannabis on her, so the sniffer dogs came to the car. The police searched us, and they wanted to pump our stomachs for drugs. Thankfully, they changed their minds."[18] However, she felt connected with Europe as well. She loved Scotland. She also felt a great connection and spent a lot of time at the great rock formations in Avebury and Stonehenge. She believed in the power of the places (she referred to Stonehenge as a transmitter) and soaked up their energy. These monolithic slabs were miraculous in the fact that they had somehow had come to be in a way that no one could quite explain. Now, centuries later, they still stood. It made Tori Amos feel a little small sometimes, but it also made her feel at one with the universe.

Amos may have felt small, but the buzz over her music was growing bigger. The British press had really embraced her, writing glowing stories about her music and her shows. The venues and gigs were getting bigger and bigger. Soon she was touring colleges across the country. Word was spreading. Amos was pleasantly surprised to see that the European men were as into her music as much as the women. Back home she had been led to believe that it might be seen as a bit "girly." However, crowds were building everywhere she went, and the listener's sex was not a contributing factor. Quality music was.

Amos got the opportunity to open for singer and pianist Marc Cohn, whose career was cooking thanks to his smash hit single "Walking in Memphis." Cohn told an interviewer to keep an eye on Amos—she was going to be great. In November 1991, a couple of months before *Little Earthquakes* would be released in England, Amos got her first live television gig. The performance was on the venerable BBC show *The Jonathan Ross Show*. She did "Silent All These Years," and though she later recalled that she was so scared that she nearly froze up in the middle, she was able to pull it off.

By the time that *Little Earthquakes* was officially released (on Atlantic's sister label East West) in Europe in February 1992, Amos was already becoming a name to be reckoned with. The release of the album just fanned the flames. Both "Silent All These Years" and "China" had previewed the album and become popular singles. Sales for the album were brisk, too. Brisk enough that word was spreading back to her home country. Doug Morris's plan had worked better than he could have even imagined. Tori Amos created a buzz in Europe, and it was crossing back over the ocean.

In the years since *Little Earthquakes*, Tori Amos has been responsible for much truly brilliant music. However, still, to this writing, she has never quite topped the solo debut as a whole piece of her wonderfully eclectic art. It is the most brilliant distillation of her talents. She would experiment in more styles later in her career, but the record is even now the strongest and most clear-eyed view into Amos's beautiful and peculiar musical world. *Little Earthquakes* was, and deservedly so, voted to be one of the fifty best albums of the 1990s in several publications, including *Mojo* and *Spin*. "No one else this side of Prince during his golden age had climbed so far down into sex and so far up into heaven at the same time," *Spin's* Joshua Clover announced in the magazine's decade-closing roundup of the ultimate musical statements of the era. "The final version of the album, with its expressionist clothes and naked feeling, offered an alternative to the alternative scene's boys 'n' guitars monopoly."[19]

Tori Amos had finally gotten the notice that she had been craving since she was a little girl at the Peabody Conservatory. She had reached a height that she had been striving for and preparing for almost twenty years. Now that she had found her audience, she was not going to take it for granted. That not to say that she couldn't take a little time to appreciate the view from up there. "It's been a long and difficult road leading to the place where I am today," Amos told Larry Flick of *Billboard*. "I'm thoroughly enjoying this moment in time, and all of the attention I am receiving. I know how it feels to sit on the tip of the label's kicking boot. Believe me, where I am right now is highly preferable."[20]

Right then Tori Amos was on top of the world. She was nominated for Best New Artist at the MTV Music Video Awards, eventually losing out to Annie Lennox, who had released her first solo album, *Diva*, after a decade of topping the charts as the voice of the Eurythmics. But this did not happen until after a well-known popular musician (who Amos has always refused to name) hit on her hard in front of Amos's companions for the night, her parents. She won't say who the Lothario was, but she often told the story of the experience in concert.

Entertainment Weekly and *Rolling Stone* named her one of their faces to watch. Perhaps most exciting, at the *Q* magazine music awards, she actually got to meet her hero (and childhood fantasy) Robert Plant. "Silent All These Years" may not have gotten that much radio airplay (at least on mainstream stations; the alternative stations jumped on it), but it did become a heavy-rotation video on MTV. She performed "Crucify" on *Late Night with David Letterman*, *Top of the Pops*, and *The Tonight Show*, and "Silent All These Years" on *The Arsenio Hall Show* and *The Dennis Miller Show*. Suddenly those days of crying on the kitchen floor in her tiny Hollywood apartment seemed very far away. Tori Amos was finally becoming a star.

One of the many people whose eyes were opened by the debut album was a young piano player from the San Fernando Valley outside Los Angeles. John Ondrasik went on to be the voice and musical focus behind the popular band Five for Fighting, whose hit single "Superman (It's Not Easy)" became the unofficial lament of a grieving world after the terrorist attacks of September 11, 2001. He also had a big hit with the 2004 single "100 Years." But, at the time, Ondrasik was just another aspiring musician. He really had only Elton John and Billy Joel to look toward as proof that a pianist like himself could become a pop star and hopefully make an artistic statement at the same time. "People forget that when Tori's first record came out, it was at a time of huge productions," Ondrasik recalls.

"She had a piano, her voice, a few strings, and words that touched your heart. What a wonderful relief."

One thing that Amos had learned from living in England was the importance of the single. It was common practice for British acts to release bonus tracks as part of their singles. This was a nice way to give back to the fans and offer some additional music that would not see the light of day otherwise. The B-sides of the two *Y Kant Tori Read* singles had both been just album tracks, "Heart Attack at 23" and "You Go to My Head." This was the common practice in the States. Tori Amos embraced the idea of extra bonus songs, and from *Little Earthquakes* on, she made sure that all of her singles had bonus tracks that were unavailable anywhere else. Over the years, Amos has recorded enough non-album single tracks to make three or four albums all on their own.

The best known of these were on the *Crucify* EP, which was released in July 1992. Actually, the songs were originally recorded as the second disc of a limited-edition two-disk U.K. maxi-single for "Winter." It was made up of the album version of the song, plus three interesting cover versions. When it was time to release *Crucify*, they just added a remix of the title track to the four songs on the "Winter" maxi. As discussed before, the originals were lovely examples of her songcraft. The real eye-openers to people who had already digested *Little Earthquakes* were the cover versions, though. "It's kind of tricky," Amos said. "For a lot of reasons. Normally the stuff I do has been done very well. I don't pick covers that I think haven't been done well. I pick covers because they excited me. If it's been done well, the question that I ask myself is, there's no point in doing this unless I give this a different read, and, is that read valid? Sometimes it is. Sometimes it works."

The real stunner of the bunch is Amos's version of Nirvana's then-recent rock smash "Smells Like Teen Spirit." The idea of changing Kurt Cobain's yowl of adolescent torment into a piano and vocal ballad was an inspired act of revisionism. Without really changing the tune, just slowing it down a hell of a lot, the song becomes just as haunting as Nirvana's throbbing angst-ridden howl of anger. Somehow the fact that you can actually distinctly hear the lyrics, which were somewhat muddled by Cobain's screeching style and the tune's pounding power chords, adds to their desolation and disorientation. The little strangled yelp of "Yeah" at the end of the third verse captures the fear and confusion of the age much more convincingly than the original's raving, and there is a genuine feel of panic to Amos's voice as she fades out repeating over and over again, "Oh, denial."

"Smells Like Teen Spirit" was the one that got the most notice. Nearly unheard of at the time, as a non-album bonus track, the remake got a good amount of radio airplay itself. Atlantic even had the cute promo idea of buying a whole bunch of Teen Spirit deodorant sticks and mailing them out with stickers on the top of the box that read "Smells Like Tori Amos." Nirvana heard the version, and apparently approved, taking it with good humor. According to freelance journalist

Dave Cavanaugh on the Nirvanaclub.com Web site, he was interviewing Kurt Cobain at a show in Belfast for *Select* in early 1992. "When they came on-stage that night, Tori Amos's cover of 'Smells Like Teen Spirit' was playing on the PA, and they pirouetted to their places like ballerinas. Very funny. It was a great show."[21]

The other two covers were also worth listening to. The read that Amos did of the Rolling Stones' "Angie" was much more faithful to the original, but it had a quiet, lovely, and vulnerable power. The song was always one of the Glimmer Twins' more thoughtful, emotionally exposed songwriting moments. Amos boiled it down to the bare bones, just a hushed (and rather husky for Amos) voice propelling the song forward over a fragile keyboard arrangement. Led Zeppelin's "Thank You" took the folksy mid-tempo song from *Led Zeppelin II* and mined it for the bare bones of the melody. (One critic referred to the version as Chopin meets Led Zeppelin.)

All of them are very impressive takes on the tunes, and showed off an interesting ability that Amos had to reinvent well-known songs in her own style. It was a trick that Amos would continue to mine over the years. In these early years, she also played a good amount of similar covers in concert, such as "Whole Lotta Love," another Led Zeppelin song (well, if you get technical, it was a Willie Dixon composition that Zep claimed as their own). Amos also regularly performed "American Pie," Don McLean's epic exploration of popular culture in the aftermath of the plane crash that killed rock pioneers Buddy Holly, Ritchie Valens, and the Big Bopper. Cover versions would continue to be a staple of Amos's live performances over the years.

Amos also dipped her toe into tribute and soundtrack albums, upon which she would periodically drop cover versions over the years. Amos recorded a slinky fuzz-toned version of the disco-ball classic "Ring My Bell" for *Ruby Trax*, a three-disc set of remakes released by the British music newspaper *New Music Express* to celebrate its fortieth anniversary. Some of the other rethinks on the set included Blur's take on Rod Stewart's "Maggie May," Tears for Fears channeling David Bowie on "Ashes to Ashes," Marc Almond doing Madonna's "Like a Prayer," Boy George's redo of George Harrison's "My Sweet Lord," and Manic Street Preacher's rock-up of "Suicide Is Painless," the theme from *M*A*S*H*. Amos also recorded "The Happy Worker" for the Robin Williams movie *Toys*, but that was only a remake in the fact that she hadn't written it. It was actually written by British producer Trevor Horn (the band Yes and Frankie Goes to Hollywood), who she would work with again eleven years later on another soundtrack, *Mona Lisa Smile*.

Amos had finally become widely accepted now. Critics championed her as the latest in the line of great female singer-songwriters that had been coming out steadily in those years, such as Suzanne Vega, Sinéad O'Connor, and k. d. lang. The influence that was pointed to most for Amos, particularly in her early years, is Kate Bush. Much like Amos, Bush was a child musical prodigy, playing the piano naturally from a young age and writing the songs that became her debut album, *The Kick Inside*, starting when she was only fourteen years old. Bush was a star right out of the chute in her native England. Her debut single was "Wuthering Heights," a delicately beautiful ballad based on the classic Emily Brontë novel. That song became a number-one hit all over Europe. In the years that followed, she recorded several well-respected albums, including *Lionheart*, *Never for Ever*, and *The Hounds of Love*. The last of those albums was the one that finally broke Bush to America, where "Running Up That Hill (A Deal with God)" gave Bush her first Top 40 hit.

Bush was always a notorious perfectionist, though, and her albums kept coming further and further apart. Two albums in one year, then two years for the next, then three years, then three more, then five. It was twelve years between the album *The Red Shoes* (1993) and her most recent album, *Aerial*, which was released in November 2005. Her fascination with dance and choreography has limited her live performance as well, after her respected 1979 tour of England, she has never performed live again except for occasional appearances at charity concerts. Due to a fear of flying, she has never played live outside of Europe, except for one appearance on the TV series *Saturday Night Live* in 1979. So by the time Tori Amos was coming up, Bush's star was fading.

Amos has tended to downplay the Bush comparison in interviews when it came up, saying that some music reviewers feel a need to put female artists in a box. Because they were both women who played the piano and wrote about their feelings, they have to be grouped together. However, Amos does seem to acknowledge the similarity sometimes. The most blatant nod probably came by posing on the cover of *Little Earthquakes* inside a wooden crate, just as Bush had done on the American cover of her 1978 debut album, *The Kick Inside*. (The extremely phallic–looking mushrooms on the back of the CD case have also been said to be vaguely reminiscent of the cover of Bush's *Never for Ever* album, although I think that one is really a bit too much of a stretch.) Amos has also occasionally performed Bush's 1985 hit single "Running Up That Hill (A Deal with God)" in concert, even once on a radio performance. "Well, if you're going to be compared to somebody," Amos said in a radio interview. "She's wonderful. She does what she does incredibly well and I've always admired her."[22]

Amos told *Q* magazine about her late introduction to Bush's work. "I'll never forget the first time I heard about Kate. I was playing in a club, I was eighteen or nineteen and somebody came up to me, pointed their finger and said, 'Kate Bush.' I went, who's that? I wasn't really familiar because Kate didn't really happen in the States until *Hounds of Love* [in 1985]. I was shocked because the last thing you want to hear is that you sound like someone else. Then people kept mentioning her name when they heard me sing, to the point where I finally went and got her records. When I first heard her, I went, wow, she does things that I've never heard anybody do, much less me. But I could hear a resonance in the voice where you'd think we were distantly related or something." The writer asked her if she was saying that she was not directly influenced by Bush, to which Amos responded, "Well, I must tell you that when I heard her, I was blown away by her. There's no question....But I knew that I had to be careful, so I didn't voraciously learn her catalogue. I left the records with my boyfriend at the time, because I didn't want to copy her."[23]

Bush, on the other hand, has mostly stayed mum on the subject of Amos's music. In fact the only quote I could find attributed to Bush about the music of Tori Amos was when she was interviewed by *Rolling* Stone about her 1993 album *The Red Shoes*. When asked if Bush had heard any of Amos's songs, Bush acknowledged that she had heard a little about her. "I heard one track and I thought it was very...uhh, nice," she said, diplomatically.[24]

Other interviewers have asked Bush about Amos, and she has been even more noncommittal, as journalist Simon Reynolds acknowledged in his 1993 interview with Bush for *Pulse* magazine. "[Bush's] bursting, exultant style is unique and unprecedented, and, as is the way with originals, it's been a big influence on subsequent female singers. Not that she appears to have noticed [indeed, she makes like she doesn't listen to much contemporary music]. She's noncommittal when she hears a roll call of the indebted, which include Tori Amos [whose piano-based melodrama owes a lot to Bush's early style], Sinéad O'Connor, 'kooky' Canadian singer-songwriters like Mary Margaret O'Hara and Jane Siberry, and even a few post-punk chanteuses [ex-Sugarcube Björk, Liz Fraser of the Cocteau Twins]."[25]

Even the press kit released by Atlantic for the album acknowledged certain similarities, but they also noted the spin-off into Amos's originality and her own particularly personal quality. "For the first few seconds of her debut album, *Little Earthquakes*, you're thinking Kate Bush, maybe," the press kit reads. "Then out comes the knife. The veneer is torn away. Imagine biting into a pea and it turns out to be a chili. Better still, imagine you just picked up a hitchhiker in the middle of the night along the highway that runs past the forest. She seemed like such a nice girl, but now you're starting to worry....That's Tori Amos."[26]

Many other people pointed to Joni Mitchell as an influence. This is more for the highly personal and poetic lyrics than musical or vocal similarities. Maybe because they *were* rather different stylistically, Amos is happy to acknowledge that when she was growing up, Joni Mitchell was the one female singer who most inspired her. On an interview with National Public Radio, she was asked who she most wanted to be when she was young. "Joni Mitchell. Always, always," she answered and played and sang a few lines from Mitchell's classic "A Case of You." "Always Joni. You know, I'd listen to her and go, 'God, she said things I would give anything to say.' You know, you'd want to give a tape to somebody and go, 'This is what I've been trying to say for four years.'"[27]

Amos *has* been known to perform "A Case of You" in concert, and she recorded it as a special non-album track used on a limited-edition British "Cornflake Girl" maxi-single. There was a very simple reason she chose to cover the song. "I could name five songs, right off the top of my head, that I would have given my right arm to write. 'A Case of You.' You don't get it any better. A better song hasn't been written. I don't care what female singer-songwriter you throw up in my face: None has done anything in the league of 'A Case of You,' me included. I sing 'A Case of You' almost every night in concert because of that. For a woman to be able to say what that says, with that kind of addiction and yet that kind of grace, is just not done. Even Zeppelin and those guys listened to Joni. They were totally influenced by Joni."[28]

However, in the end these comparisons are all way too confining—Amos has a distinctive talent that cannot be explained off with rote terms like *female singer-songwriter*. "I believe in a balance," Amos explained to me in late 1992. "I believe you have to hear from the women. You have to hear from the men. You've got to hear from different cultures. This is how you get perspective on things. We need it from all sides. That's how you get clarity. Everybody needs to be listening to a bit of all of it. If you cut yourself off from Ice Cube and Ice-T and all those guys, then you're going to cut yourself off from their perspective of what truth is. You cut yourself off from Pearl Jam and Nirvana and those guys, you're cutting yourself off. If you cut yourself off from Neneh Cherry, or from me, or from Sinéad, then you're also closing yourself off. So it's about a balance of all of these things."

Sinéad O'Connor was a singer that Amos could relate to on more than one level. The striking Irish singer with a shaved head had released a critically acclaimed first album and had a minor single hit with "Mandinka" in the late eighties. Her second album, *I Do Not Want What I Haven't Got*, made her a star. Her hushed and emotionally open remake of an obscure Prince song called "Nothing Compares 2 U" became a smash hit all over the world. (Prince had originally written the song for the Family, a group made up of some former members of the Time.) However, soon the music seemed to take a backseat and O'Connor was in the midst of a series of odd media stories. An odd war of words broke out between O'Connor and Prince, in which she said that he tried to beat her up. There were rumors she attempted suicide. O'Connor started an uproar when she refused to allow "The Star-Spangled Banner" be played before one of her shows. Many Americans didn't take that well, including septuagenarian crooner Frank Sinatra, who threatened to kick her ass. She refused to appear on the television series *Saturday Night Live* with notoriously chauvinistic stand-up comedian Andrew "Dice" Clay.

While *Little Earthquakes* was finally reaching the charts, Sinéad O'Connor was very much in the news because of the incident that happened when she did finally appear on *Saturday Night Live*. O'Connor performed an a capella version of Bob Marley's "War." At the end of the song, she tore up a photo of the Pope to protest policies of the Catholic Church. As someone who has been very vocal about her own religious upbringing, Amos felt sympathy for O'Connor, although she thought that O'Connor might not have considered the outcome of her act.

"I don't think that what Sinéad was doing was hype," Amos said at the time. "I think she really believed in what she did. [But] I don't think she was aware of how it was going to be perceived. When you do something like that, you have to take responsibility for it. That's the main thing. You have to do it without being afraid of the consequences. And there are consequences. One of them has been that the Pope has been made a martyr. Which is the last thing that was her intention. It's not just this one Pope. This is about all of us dealing with responsibility. This is all of us dealing with suppression in ourselves of what we're really thinking, and hiding behind any kind of institution. And how the institutions have to be held accountable.

"When you do something like that, what happens is you just become an extension of the institution—of what they've done for thousands of years. You don't mean to be. What happens when you're a dog pushed in the corner and you're hit so many times. You start biting back. Then what happens? They go shoot the dog. They don't say the master was beating the dog. Just the dog bit somebody. Shoot it. That's what has happened. You know what? She felt she needed to do that. You've got to honor that. I don't think that it's right for artists to attack other artists in any way, shape, or form. We have to respect the fact that others need to express it. Now, if we want to personally say something to them, that's our business. Sometimes artists have used other ones to move their own ahead."

Amos was not immune to this type of television censorship herself. When she appeared on *The Late Show with David Letterman* on June 28, 1994, she performed a song from the *Little Earthquakes* song "Precious Things." Amos wasn't even originally set to be on the show, she was a last-minute replacement for a musical act that had bailed on the show. Amos was in town doing a concert, so she agreed to be a stand-in. At the insistence of the CBS television network, she had to change the line "So you can make me cum, / that doesn't make you Jesus" to a less fiery "So you can make me calm, / that doesn't make you Jesus." (Sometimes when the story is recounted, it is said that the execs told her to change the word to *calm*, sometimes it is *hum*.) She told *Esquire* magazine about the whole experience several years later, "When I performed 'Precious Things' on the *David Letterman* show, I couldn't say *cum*....I said, 'I'll give it a diphthong and you won't know what it is. I'll sing it as though I've got a dick in my mouth.' "[29]

As respected as her album had become, what really sold Tori Amos to the world were her live shows. They were about as low-tech as a concert can get. Amos traveled light; it was just a woman and a piano. No band, a minimum of sound and lighting guys. Tori Amos became known for giving a heartfelt, personal show. "You know, there is a level where your intestines kind of fall to your feet," she told journalist Ken Sharp about concert performing. "But you have to make a choice for yourself. If you go out there and strip in front of everybody, then you have no quarter, because you don't strip and say, 'Is it okay?' Because if you're doing that, then you have given all your self-worth away. It can't be 'Is it okay?' It's okay that I'm a bit under the microscope. I want to take it so that it's not just me under the microscope. It becomes the whole room, so that everybody else feels that they may see themselves. Then they can see their own experiences."[30]

Amos helped spread the word by tirelessly (okay, she did get tired, but she kept soldiering through) doing concerts all around the world in 1992. The *Little Earthquakes* tour was a monster trek. It lasted from January 29 in London, England, to November 30 in Auckland, New Zealand. She played over a hundred and fifty dates in over a hundred cities (many of them twice). It all seemed a little overwhelming sometimes. "I've done about, my goodness, about a hundred twenty dates already since January," she told John Norris at the 1992 *MTV Video Music Awards Opening Act* in September 1992. So we're on a world tour and we're on the U.S. leg. We finish in December. Then I'm going to have some Mexican food."[31]

I saw her twice on that first tour, and I remember feeling at the time that a Tori Amos concert was not like anyone else's. No band, just a woman and her piano. This added a sense of closeness to the proceedings, which worked well for Amos's strengths. In the long run, Amos seemed to be all about intimacy. The audience almost got the feeling that they are spying on Amos as she practiced alone. Amos has an unusually seductive voice, and she used it to lure you into her world. She rode her piano bench like a lover. Amos let you in on her secrets, her desires, and her feelings. Most musicians hoard their hits, refusing to play them until the end of the concert (or the encore) for fear that the audience will leave once they've heard the songs that they've heard on the radio. Amos, on the other hand, started many shows playing the two first singles, "Crucify" and "Silent All These Years," back to back. For Amos, her voice is another instrument. The a capella "Me and a Gun" was an incredibly naked performance; almost disturbingly intimate. Tori Amos is an artist that works without walls. If she feels it, she will let you know. After the show was over, I had an enormous urge to have a cigarette. I don't even smoke.

When the tour finally wound down and she was able to have that Mexican food she'd been craving, Tori Amos had become one of the biggest new names in music. She had finally reached the audience that she craved. She had embraced her muse and was pleasantly surprised to see how many others embraced it as well. Now she needed some time off. "I need to get away from music for a little while," she told *Spin*. "I've been on output so much. I need to be on input."[32] As far as her future, she had taken the leap from no expectations to great expectations. The world was waiting to see what she would come up with next. The question was what would she do for an encore? Even she wasn't sure. "Maybe you could go somewhere deeper," she told *The Concert News* in November 1992. "If you're so involved with the pain, it can be dramatic. Or melodramatic. I know because I can be a real drama queen. I think it'll be interesting what I come up with next, because I really have no idea what I'm going to come up with."[33]

chapter 4
Past the Mission

"I'm getting better at not having to make friends with everyone. It's okay if we don't agree. It's okay if you walk out of here and don't understand, or I don't get you," Amos told Brad Balfour of *The New Review of Records*. "I'm not going to do anything now that doesn't feel good. When before I would just go numb and think, 'What are they going to think of me if I don't do this or that?' I now have a better handle on it and I'm not a sweetie pie; I'm more awake. There are compromises in life, but not if you have to become something you aren't."[1]

This viewpoint was not just on how people would look at her music—it extended to how she did her work and with whom she did her work. Amos decided not to collaborate with Davitt Sigerson and Ian Stanley on the follow-up album. She had enough confidence that she and boyfriend Eric Rosse were going to do this one themselves. Atlantic wanted to bring in a new producer to work with Amos on the album. The label still couldn't quite get behind the fact that the music they were hearing was not quite what they saw as commercial, even though they had been pleasantly shocked by the popular acceptance of *Little Earthquakes*. Amos wasn't interested in the interference even in the least. The label tried to negotiate a settlement with her, but Amos angrily told them if they tried to make her work with a different producer, she would torch the master tapes of the album.[2]

"We musicians have turned our self-worth over to those who listen to our music," Amos told *Musician*. "The troubadour thing was that if they didn't like you, you'd hope you didn't lose your head and then move on to the next castle. But these days, we turn over our music like puppies....Not all of us do that, but I know I've had that tendency in me."[3] This time she wasn't going to let it go without a fight. Confronted with her passionate belief, the label backed down and allowed Eric Rosse and Amos to continue working on the album. Amos was not going to let the executives run roughshod over her artistic vision, or who would help her to realize it. "I'm not a part of this business," she told journalist Brad Balfour in 1993. "I was playing music before [these] people were peeing in their beds. I've been doing this for twenty-seven years, twelve hours a day, and that hasn't changed."[4]

However, she also knew where to keep clear the boundaries between their personal relationship and their physical one. "I'm only monogamous in bed; I'm sharing my thoughts with everyone. I have a very deep imagination: I don't have to do it with somebody to be emotionally involved. It's beyond the penis and vagina. How many dicks do you have to suck before you realize that you have to draw the line somewhere when you're sharing molecules with someone?" Also, no matter how close their relationship was, Amos said there was no plans to marry Rosse. "I don't need a church to sanction anything I do," she explained to Balfour.[5]

Amos decided that she also needed a change of scenery for this new album. The songs just weren't coming to her in London. She loved her new European home; she had an apartment in the hip, charming, and eccentrically diverse neighborhood of Notting Hill (which would be immortalized on film by Hugh Grant and Julia Roberts five years later). In fact, Amos fully planned to buy a house in London when she was finished—but this album somehow felt like it needed to be created somewhere different. Specifically, she decided, it was time to move to Taos, New Mexico, for a while.

Not that she chose the place at random. The Wild West was calling to her. Amos wanted to be near the Indian lineage she so treasured, though she went to the home of the Pueblo Indians rather than her ancestral Cherokees. She could just feel that was where this album needed to be created. So she and Eric and her musicians all made the pilgrimage. Amos and Rosse rented a house in Taos and got to work on their follow-up. The change of scenery worked, and the writer's block that she had felt while promoting *Little Earthquakes* and touring faded into the desert sun. Songs were sprouting like cacti in the sand.[6]

As she had on the last album, she wrote many of the songs on keyboard. But not all of them could be called "piano songs" as before. Some of the songs were written specifically to find a different musical timbre. Amos had earned the right to shake things up a bit. Not that she was in any way interested in abandoning the sound that brought her, like she mostly did on *Y Kant Tori Read*. It was still her first passion, her strongest musical identity. "I love piano, from blues to classical," she told the *New York Post*. "I'm not a great piano player, but I *understand* it."[7]

The writing and piano were important, because soon she temporarily lost access to her most important instrument—her voice. One day, while dusting the place she was renting in New Mexico, Amos mistakenly breathed in some of the Pledge furniture polish that she was using. This caused a lung infection, rendering Amos unable to talk—and, more importantly, sing—for a few weeks. The experience led to a dark night of the soul for Amos. She was frightened. What if she could never sing again? What if her vocal cords were damaged? Did she even have any worth or value without the ability to be a performer?

Amos acknowledges that she went through quite a bit of worry and more than a bit of self-pity during those weeks. She truly did feel that without her voice she had very little to offer the world. Her music had been the focus of her life for as long as she could remember. How would she go on if it were gone? She had to work with a vocal coach by telephone to try to get her vocal cords back into shape. Needless to say, the condition was not permanent. However, Amos remembered the weeks of uncertainty and fear long after the condition was healed.[8]

For one song she wrote for the album, "Past the Mission," which sported a reggae backbeat, Amos decided she needed a male voice as counterpoint to her own. She knew right away who that voice would be, too. Amos imagined the man as Trent Reznor, the one-man band also known as Nine Inch Nails. Amos loved Reznor's work, to the point that she name-checked Nine Inch Nails in her *Little Earthquakes* song "Precious Things." She would also go on to refer to the band's album title *Pretty Hate Machine* in the song "Caught a Lite Sneeze" on her next album, *Boys for Pele*. She first learned of Nine Inch Nails when she was living in L.A. writing songs for the first solo album. The boyfriend of a girl who she had babysat for when she was younger in Rockville was crashing at her place for a while, where he introduced her to *Pretty Hate Machine*. (This same guy was the one who had also brought Neil Gaiman's *The Sandman* to her attention.) Soon she was hooked on the album.

Reznor learned of Amos's music when the rest of the world did, with the release of *Little Earthquakes*. Reznor told *Axcess Magazine*:

> I really liked her first album, which is not the kind of thing I'd normally listen to. Someone had given it to me and said that it sounded like Sinéad O'Connor. I fucking can't stand Sinéad O'Connor, so I ignored it. Then I saw the video for "Silent All These Years" and it struck me in a way where I wasn't sure if I liked it or not. But it was interesting. I was pleasantly surprised to find someone who I thought was taking chances. Not playing it safe, and also writing good songs, melodies, and good lyrics. I thought I should try and get in touch with her, just to try and say, not that I normally do this either, I think your record's really good. I relate to her work a lot, on some level, in an opposite of a Nine Inch Nails arrangement kind of way. I really think that it works. She approaches things with a totally different aesthetic than I do, but it's good.[9]

So when the opportunity to have Reznor sing on "Past the Mission" came up, Amos had no alternative. In fact, she said on a radio interview that she was commanded to use him by the song itself. Reznor just made sense; he fit her idea of the tune. "The choice for ['Past the Mission'] had to be somebody that represented rage and anger because this is all about a girl trying so hard to work through being a victim," Amos told Sue Smallwood of the *Virginian-Pilot*. "I felt like for a guy to be supporting her, it had to be a guy that could rage, because then it would really mean something if he could be tender. Trent is…well, you can't be in all that much rage and pain unless you have a very big heart."[10]

So Amos packed up a bag and left New Mexico to visit Reznor in a Beverly Hills mansion that he was renting to record the next Nine Inch Nails album, *The Downward Spiral*, which would become his popular breakthrough. The rented residence was infamous on its own—it was the same house where the Manson family murdered actress Sharon Tate and several others. At different points, Reznor has contradicted himself on the subject of the house. He has said that he rented the house to pick up the disturbing vibes of that horrific experience; at other times, he's maintained that he really just didn't know the house's violent history until he was already there.

Amos was happy with the finished product that would be her second album, *Under the Pink*. (The title *God with a Big G* was considered for the album, but ultimately rejected.) The title *Under the Pink* referred to getting beneath the skin. She felt that it was a different vibe from the first album; she wasn't just foisting

Little Earthquakes: Part Deux on her fans. She had grown and changed in the over three years since she started working on the debut album. She had experienced things she had only dreamed of, and acceptance beyond even her wildest flights of fancy. She felt confident to lead her fans down a new path. "You have to dig a little deeper," she told Larry Flick of *Billboard*. "There are not just naked flowers coming to woo you like the last record. This is very raw stuff. You have to get on the elevator and go—and the elevator is going down."[11]

Amos described the inspiration for the song "Pretty Good Year" in concert. It seems that she was sent a letter while on the *Little Earthquakes* tour. It was passed from assistant to assistant for a few months, no one was quite sure what to do with it. Finally, Amos was at the British offices of the record label and someone just slipped the letter into her bag, telling her it had been around the office for quite a while and she should probably have it. Amos forgot about it for a few days, when she ran across it inside her bag, so she read the note. It was from a guy named Greg.

"He's from the north of England," Amos told the crowd of a show in Seattle on the *Under the Pink* tour. "I guess I could tell you some letters that would like curl your toes and stuff. This is not one of those letters. But this letter inspired this next song. He's from not quite Scotland, but in the north and it's where the working people live. Most people work their father's mine and stuff. They have a harder life than people in the south and then they kind of hate them. Anyway, it says, 'Dear Tori, my life sucks. . . .' He's twenty. And he goes, 'I don't know what you girls expect of us. I can't figure it out. First you want us to be a provider and then once we do that, we've got to take like art classes on Thursday nights. And then, you got to cum four times first. Then we have to have the quiche in the oven. I don't know what you want!' and I was like, 'Guys, I know it's really rough, but no pity.' "[12]

She may not pity Greg and guys like him, but she does understand where they are coming from. She does empathize with them. "I care about Greg, you know I do," Amos told *The New Review of Records*. "But there's no pity in the song. If I pitied him then that's really condescending. I got this letter from this guy Greg and he thought his life was over. And he drew this picture with drooping flowers and glasses and hair to here; he was from the north of England. And he was a very good writer; I've found so many guys twenty-three years old that thought their life was already over."[13]

"Pretty Good Year" was a luscious piano ballad that would have felt right at home on *Little Earthquakes.* From the opening notes of "God," the second tune on the disc, she starts delving into uncharted territory for her. It springs out of the speakers, the traditional Amos piano line is garnished by a snarling, squealing swirl of fuzzed out industrial guitar and huge booming percussion. Of course, as you can tell by the title, Amos hasn't completely changed her stripes, exorcised her demons, nor her quarrel with the church. "My father says, you're so lucky," she told New York's *Newsday*. "What if I was a doctor? What would you be writing about?"[14]

Not that she was trying to be antireligious. In fact, she felt the song was rather sympathetic to the Almighty. He's got a tough job, lots of worries, and lots of stress. He needs to relax a bit. "God's problem is he needs a babe; hey, I'm not busy Tuesdays and Thursdays," she told Brad Balfour.[15] No one could find that idea offensive, could they? The church was constantly talking about the sanctity of marriage. Man is supposed to be created in God's image. So shouldn't He be getting a little bit of lovin' too?

"On my second record I thought that way," Amos told *Rolling Stone* a few years later. "Like with the song 'God.' Why don't people want to hear about God getting a blow job? I thought those born-again Christians would love that. But then I realized that even my sister wouldn't buy my records if I wasn't her sister—to her, I sound like the psycho in *Reservoir Dogs*, Mr. Blonde. She says, 'Why do I want to listen to that on my way to work?' "[16] Luckily, Marie Amos had come to understand her sibling's artistic license. More importantly, other people were buying into it as well. "God" was the first U.S. single from *Under the Pink* and also the first Tori Amos song to break into the U.S. singles chart. It wasn't a huge smash—it peaked at seventy-two on the charts of *Billboard*, that same magazine that six years earlier didn't quite call Tori Amos a bimbo. But "God" would continue to open doors for Amos in radio and sales and open the eyes of listeners.

In the press kit for *Under the Pink*, it says, "While *Little Earthquakes* was about coming to grips with victimization, *Under the Pink* describes taking control of one's life and one's being."[17] This is certainly true, but the album has another underlying subject matter, that of duplicity. The record is about how to survive being let down by people that have done you wrong, how to react to it without driving yourself mad. There is an even more specific topic that emerges several times, the treachery toward women by other women.

"There is a triangle on this record," she told Brad Balfour. "The songs 'Bells for Her,' 'Cornflake Girl,' and 'The Waitress'—a triad about women betraying women. That's a kind of theme here. We women have to deal with the patriarchy first, but then, what's the alternative? Do you need a woman to look after you? I'm here to apply for the job. But when you say patriarchy, you don't have to be a man to be part of the patriarchy. After I read *Possessing the Secret of Joy* by Alice Walker, about how mothers sold their daughters to the butchers; that kind of floored me. One always feels safer when there are good guys and bad ones. But there are no good guys out there. And it's not as if one sex can make it okay."[18]

If you think that "Bells for Her" sounds a little off, musically, it isn't just your imagination. Eric Rosse has said that in order to capture the dissonance that they were searching for and that would translate to the off-kilter feel behind the lyrics, they deconstructed their own equipment. First, they took Amos's piano and purposely undid its tuning. Then they nearly destroyed the soundboards by pounding on them mercilessly. Therefore, the piano has a muted tinkly thudding sound, almost as if the song was played on that tiny little toy piano she posed with in the crate on the cover of *Little Earthquakes*. This dinky backing provides a counterpoint to Amos's heartfelt vocals tracing a longtime friendship on a sure collision course with impending doom, due to one friend refusing to humor the other and blame men for the her problems.

"Cornflake Girl" is a pop song, or at least as close to pop as Amos is ever going to get. In it she rails against "girls that fuck you over."[19] Over a sprightly, barrelhouse piano line, she tries to find a middle ground, a meeting place between two distinctly different types of women, which she refers to as "cornflake girls" and "raisin girls." The cornflake girls are narrow in mind and body, hard and brittle. The raisin girls are more well rounded, a bit soft in the middle but with a tough skin.

"Now with 'Cornflake Girl,' the idea was that I always had this sisterhood and it was just blown to bits," she continued. "I was betrayed by someone…a girlfriend…who gave me a pretty shitty deal. Her opinion was [that] I'm a shit. It depends on whose table it is that you're having arsenic at. I think the disappointment of being betrayed by a woman is way heavier than being betrayed by a man. We expect it from you guys. It hurts, but I'm not shocked."[20]

This sense of betrayal is revisited in "The Waitress." The song was inspired by a real altercation Amos had gotten into, though of course she was unwilling to go into the specifics of it. She preferred to have the words and mood of the song speak for itself. "I was mad," she acknowledged to Balfour. "I wanted to throw her up against the wall. She did something—one day I'll tell you—that made me want to kill her. My reaction was a bit extreme. I was ranting and raving. I've had this feeling about being a peacemaker. Why can't we sit down and talk about it: and here I am throwing this bitch against the wall, having no problem with annihilating her cell by cell. But the issue, I know, was in my head and she was calling it up in me."[21]

Despite the quiet, solemn intro, complete with a subtle dance backbeat, the rage is palpable in the song. From the whispered first line, "I want to kill this waitress," to the primitive-scream chorus of "I believe in peace, bitch," there is simmering fury boiling over throughout the track. Musically it changes from a calm piano line with a stuttering drum track to a pounding, aggressive swirl of piano, bass, and thundering percussion.

Not that all of the songs were about women hurting other women. "Baker Baker" is a view of the battle of the sexes that is as old and true as time itself. Amos has said that in many ways she feels the tune is tragic. There is such a difference between what men and women want from each other. Then there is the added chasm, she admits, between what women want from men and what they expect from them. The song is an acknowledgment that her relationship with Eric Rosse was coming apart. Surprisingly, Amos shoulders the blame herself in the song. "I was the one that wasn't emotionally available," Amos told the *Los Angeles Times*. "We're always blaming the guys, saying, 'You're not sensitive enough; why can't you just be more understanding?' And then when they are more sensitive, we kick 'em in the face and go for the hockey player. It's like 'Dominate me, just dominate me. Not long—I'll time you—just a little!'"[22]

On the other hand, there is a quaint, old-fashioned, oompah-beer-hall-pi-ano feel to "The Wrong Band." Musically, it wouldn't feel totally out of place in an old-time Broadway hit like *Oliver!* However, the subject of the song was just a bit more risqué—the song was about coming to terms with the prostitute in oneself. The idea was brought to Amos's mind with the scandal of the Hollywood Ma-dame. "There was this hooker in D.C. that I knew, and she'd been having a fling with one of the governors," Amos told *Illinois Entertainer*. "She got in too deep and thought her life was threatened, so she fled to Japan, where she was protected by one of the hierarchy over there. I never heard from her again. It just all came back to me when the Heidi Fleiss thing hit and I started thinking about what that world is about. People don't think of hookers as people, but I quite like them. I find their story really interesting, and when people start judging [them], they should just shut up because they have no idea what it's like to be on the other side."[23]

From prostitution to self-pleasuring, in the song "Icicle," Amos writes about a woman who "masturbates to survive a repressive atmosphere."[24] In it, a woman tries to balance inside herself the divine and the profane, the need to be one with her God and the needs she feels as a woman. Amos used to feel that way as a teen, touching herself as her father and his fellow religious scholars were downstairs debating the Scripture. As a confused teen with hormones raging, she was having trouble sorting out what was more vital, her rapture or the Rapture. It came down to one of her earliest problems with religion, that in order to be a good, divine be-ing, you must be willing to sublimate your desires, your needs, and your passions. Or as she put it while introducing the song in concert once in Las Vegas, "This place inspires me. It reminds me of my grandmother, who would burn every one of you to a fucking crisp….This is for all you tortured Christians."[25]

The delicate, wispy tendrils of "Cloud on My Tongue" and Amos's hushed vocals create a sense of vulnerability and sorrow. " 'Cloud on My Tongue' [is] deal-ing with Eve…dealing with feeling inferior, that somebody else has something that you want."[26] It is a sparse, quiet song, featuring just Amos's piano and vocals combined with the tasteful backing of John Philip Shenale's chamberlain. In the long run, despite the openness, it does show great strength and, in Amos's view, is a positive statement. She told the *Baltimore Sun* it was all about acceptance. "There's a wonderful acceptance in 'Cloud on My Tongue,' an acceptance of being in circles and circles again. That's its whirlpool vat. It all leads to that."[27]

There is a snaky groove channeled in "Spacedog," Tori Amos's closest ap-proximation of a David Bowie glam rocker. "Space dog is one groovy cat,"[28] she told *B-Side* and, hallelujah, that's the truth. It rides forward confidently and safely, almost like it is in a musical womb. The song came from a very surreal place for Amos. She wrote it while visiting Mexico, and she saw this dirt drawing, which resembled a dog. Later she was flying to Chicago from New Mexico, reading a bodice-ripper book and she was suddenly she felt a presence. "Most people think that I'm nuts," she acknowledged in concert once, recounting the story. "But the truth is, things just like happen to me, I don't like dream them up. I was busy read-ing a romance novel; I was way more interested in what was going on in my book.

And all of a sudden I hear this voice. It's this dog talking to me."[29] Some people would ignore a vision like this, or write it off to a really bad airline ham sandwich, but Amos found the idea kind of comforting. "We've worshiped everything else, why not him?"[30]

"Spacedog" was not the only song on *Under the Pink* inspired by a visitation, either. Amos told the *Independent* (London) that the song "Yes, Anastasia" was based on the infamous Anastasia Romanova, who was the daughter of the czar in Russia when the country fell to Communism in the 1920s. The decision to write about the girl came to her through a mixture of botulism and spiritual intervention. On the *Little Earthquakes* tour, before a concert in Richmond, Virginia, Amos became violently ill after eating some bad crabs. While Amos was feeling sick and feverish and just essentially wanting to die, she suddenly sensed a weird hazy light. She found it to be the ghost of the young princess, who told Amos that she would learn and grow if she were to write about her. Whether it was really Anastasia's ghost or just a fever-dream hallucination brought on by bad shellfish is anyone's guess, but the important thing is that Tori Amos believed it.

"The funny thing is that Anna Anderson, who claimed to be Anastasia, died very close to where I was playing, an hour or so from there in the eighties," she told Sandra Garcia of *B-Side*. "The feeling I got that Anna Anderson was Anastasia Romanov. She always tried to prove it and a lot of people believed her and some people didn't want to believe her, because of what that would have meant.... And again, it's really working through being a victim. 'Counting the tears from ten thousand men, and gathered them all, but my feet are slipping.' You can't blame the men anymore; there's always you. It comes back to us; it comes back to me."[31]

After spending weeks working on the album in Taos ("I drive myself nuts the way I get a very specific eye on something"[32]), Amos headed back to her adopted home. As the plane touched down, she was glad to be back. She had the best of both worlds. She felt at home in England, but there was still enough American in her that she loudly and angrily rebuked a woman who tried to cut in front of the line at customs. After a couple of days of no sleep, she had trouble remembering how to negotiate the locks and alarm at her flat (she had forgotten the code, causing a screeching cacophony that lasted a half hour before her landlord could be tracked down).

The heater and the washing machine were broken. Each was more than bit of a problem—the first since it was late November and freezing, the second because she'd gone six weeks without doing laundry. A Laundromat solved that problem. Amos was able to rest a bit, catch a movie (*The Piano* with Holly Hunter, Harvey Keitel, and Anna Paquin), and hang out with friends like Cindy Palmano (who did all of the photography for both albums and directed the four music videos from *Little Earthquakes*). On a sad note, she found out an old friend had contracted the HIV virus. Eric returned from the States a day later to work on finishing the master tapes. She got a Thanksgiving call from sister Marie and made plans to return home for Christmas.[33]

Already the promotional machine was switching back on. Atlantic had big hopes for *Under the Pink*. The execs got the publicity revved up to push it and push it hard. They pulled out all the stops on getting the word to radio, retail, and the press. For the U.S. and U.K. branches of the label, they put on a "live interactive satellite showcase" in January 1994. More than just the normal listening party, Amos appeared via satellite from London. Amos was in her own home, playing some of the new tunes to people from all around the world. She also fielded questions from reporters.[34] "I dangle carrots to get the meat for my next carnivore experience," she said.[35]

Under the Pink was a success out of the box. "Cornflake Girl" became a hit in England when it was released in January 1994. When the album came out the next month, it debuted at the top of the U.K. charts. It also opened at a high spot on the U.S. album charts, debuting at twelve on the *Billboard* album charts. Despite the fact that American radio was somewhat resistant to the first U.S. single, "God," the album was a grassroots success. Word spread among Amos's growing fan base that the new album was not a disappointment; in fact, it was a step forward.

It was a turn of events that pleased and relieved Amos. She knew all about the sophomore-album syndrome, where a songwriter has his/her entire life to prepare for his/her first album and just a year to get ready for their second. Many artists fail to pass this important career test, fading away after one big splash. There were examples of it all around, people like Terence Trent D'Arby, Soul II Soul, EMF, Tanita Tikaram, and Jesus Jones were just a small sampling of the artists that had fallen victim to it in recent years leading up to Amos's follow-up. "I'm glad that the exposure isn't all because of one album," she admitted. "There is a sense that the sophomore record can really trip you up. There are a lot of people whose second record doesn't get heard, and I was aware of that. So I am breathing a little sigh of relief, to be totally honest, and I can go on with it now. I don't have to worry about the sophomore jinx anymore. I've passed that, so I've got a career!"[36]

Under the Pink deserved the success. It is a very good album, full of interesting ideas and fine singing, but the problem is it doesn't quite catch that certain *je ne sais quoi* that made Amos's debut, *Little Earthquakes*, so effective. The songwriting and performances on *Under the Pink* were uniformly good, and Amos sounds very well adjusted to life and fame. Still, there is nothing on *Under the Pink* as immediately shocking as "Me and a Gun" or as pastorally soothing as "Winter" from the debut. It's probably unfair to hold heightened expectations against the album, which is strong. *Under the Pink* charted the maturation and psychological growth of Tori Amos. Too bad she was sometimes more interesting when she was neurotic. Amos herself acknowledged the change in tactics with the new album, saying that she could only be completely naked before the listener for so long, on this album she felt it was time to wear clothes.

For a cover story, *Q* magazine asked Amos to get together with two other female-alt rockers, Björk and P. J. Harvey, to have a little coffee klatch discussion of music, sex, drinking, touring, and turn-ons. Amos did it and enjoyed spending time with the other artists, though she did think that the grouping was a little arbitrary. Just because they were women singers who were a little off the beaten path, it was no reason they should be pigeonholed together. "It's funny for women because journalists pit women against each other," Amos told the magazine. "If you think about Jimi Hendrix, Jimmy Page, and Eric Clapton, they were all much more similar to each other than we are. We have tits. We have three holes. That's what we have in common. We don't even play the same instruments."[37]

However, those comparisons were always there. At the same time as *Under the Pink* was catching on, Canadian singer Sarah McLachlan was releasing her third (and breakthrough) album, *Fumbling Towards Ecstasy*, which featured the hit singles "Possession" and "Good Enough." Their careers had been going somewhat on parallel tracks, and they were often equated. McLachlan's debut album, *Vox*, had been released about the same time as *Y Kant Tori Read*, and like that album, sales were nearly nonexistent. However, unlike Amos's band effort, *Vox* had received very good word of mouth. Her follow-up, *Solace*, came out the same year as *Little Earthquakes*; although it had a couple of minor radio hits in "Into the Fire" and "Terms (The Path of Thorns)," album sales were a little sluggish.

McLachlan told me as her *Fumbling Towards Ecstasy* album was being released that she did feel a bond with Amos:

> I know with Tori and myself, we both write personal songs, generally from an emotional point of view. Maybe that's needed in our society today. Maybe not enough people are addressing that. I sense a lot of rage in songs these days, in the music scene. Like Nirvana and Pearl Jam are a good thing for that and a lot of the heavier industrial alternative bands that have now become mainstream. You go to those shows and you sense so much rage from the audience. A lot of times that's very male-based, too. There's a lot of young guys sort of pounding around and stuff. Raging testosterone. But that's sort of getting off the subject. I really don't know what to attribute it to, except that there are an awful lot of people with a lot of diverse tastes. Actually, also, radio has opened up, that kind of helps. Before, music like mine, there wasn't a market for it. There wasn't a format of radio that we would be accepted on. We would have to remix the songs and change them to pigeonhole them into something it would fit into.
>
> A lot of musicians, such as myself, who have written songs out of the radio format. But what has happened, stations—like triple-A stations, as far as I can tell—have really opened up a new door for us, like me or Tori Amos, who before might have gotten a little play on modern rock but none of the songs really fit anywhere unless you really bastardize them and change the sound of the mix and change the instrumentation and arrangement so it would fit into the format, or you wouldn't get played. Which I refused to do. So I wouldn't get much airplay. But since triple A, I don't have to do anything. My songs finally fit into a format without me writing them for any particular format.

McLachlan also mentioned Amos when discussing artists she liked. "Peter Gabriel is a master. I love him. I don't love him, I love his music," she says with a laugh. "I don't know him. I'm sure he's wonderful. I met him once, but I really like some of what Tori Amos does."I mentioned to McLachlan that Amos was going to be playing at the same venue we were doing the interview at later that same week."Oh, she's going to be here? Oh, so she is on tour. Right on. I hadn't heard anything about whether she was touring or not. I'll write something on the wall for her." I doubt that Sarah McLachlan is a vandal, but if you're ever in the dressing-room area of the Keswick Theater in Glenside, Pennsylvania, you may want to check the walls to see if there is a personal note from Sarah McLachlan to Tori Amos.

In the irony of show business repeating itself, just two years after Amos had people comparing her music to other singers, suddenly she was the one being compared to. Actress and model Milla Jovovich released her debut album, *The Divine Comedy*, in 1994 to strong reviews, but it was often compared to *Little Earthquakes*. She told me that while she thought Amos was a good artist to draw comparisons to, she didn't really see it."Not really Tori Amos,"Jovovich said. However, she was quick to acknowledge that,"[*The Divine Comedy*] definitely has a Kate Bush influence."

The music world was dealt a serious blow on April 5, 1994, when grunge figurehead Kurt Cobain of Nirvana climbed up into a small garage apartment on his Seattle compound, pointed a rifle to his head, and pulled the trigger. Immediately fans and well-wishers migrated to the Pacific Northwest to mourn a man who was arguably the most important rock and roll voice of the 1990s. Whether the world had lost the voice of a generation or just a very talented, deeply disturbed musician is up for debate. Both claims have been made and both have a great amount of validity. It's probably a little bit of both.

The death of Cobain hit Amos hard. After all, her cover version of Cobain's signature tune "Smells Like Teen Spirit" had played a big part in her getting noticed on the alternative airwaves. Soon after, she performed the song again in concert, this time as a mark of respect."We all know that Jesus is at a Nirvana concert right now,"she said at a show in Germany a few days later.[38] She did the tune as a medley with Don McLean's seventies classic"American Pie,"which was about the tragic plane crash in 1959 that killed Buddy Holly, Ritchie Valens, and the Big Bopper. The night that she heard of Cobain's suicide, she said that the song about "the day the music died"played in her mind over and over.

Amos was on a European tour at the time; she had been in Paris on the day it happened. Days after the suicide, Amos was playing a show in Dublin and did her tribute to the singer. As Amos came to the chorus, she later told *Blender*,"All of a sudden, in perfect pitch and very quietly, as only the Irish can do, [the audience] started singing it like a hymn. It was like they were sending his spirit off. It was an honor to play his music that night."[39]

Cobain's widow, the famously unhinged and drug-addicted rock singer Courtney Love of Hole, did not necessarily appreciate the honor. Love is said to have once cruelly said that Cobain killed himself because of"that awful cover that Tori Amos did."There was also speculation that Love came between Amos and Trent Reznor, damaging a budding friendship. Amos always tried to avoid discussing her problems with Love in public or in the press, usually simply stating that they had mutual friends and she was not going to get them in the middle of something. There were rumors that Amos wrote the song "Professional Widow" on her next album about Love, but Amos refused to acknowledge that, usually saying it was about herself. Love once posted on her Web site that she thought Amos wrote good lyrics, but she found her boring. By the year 2000, Love had changed her tune on Amos somewhat. In an online chat on her band's Web site, Hole.com, Love acknowledged, "Yeah, I like Tori Amos more and more—is it cos [sic] I'm getting older?"[40]

When planning the tour for *Under the Pink* in March 1994, Amos's personal assistant and tour manager, John Witherspoon, suggested they hire a sound engineer for the tour named Mark Hawley. Like Amos, he was a child prodigy. He was drumming when he was four. He started playing guitar at ten. By the time he was eleven, he was taking personal lessons from the drummer for British musical icon Sir Cliff Richard's band. He'd built a studio in a barn when he was still in his teens. At the time, it was just business. He was the front-of-house engineer, and Tori Amos relied on him to be aware and open to her musical twists and turns in concert. She probably had no way of realizing that just a few years later, Mark Hawley would become her husband.

Of course, at the time, she was still together with co-producer Eric Rosse. In many interviews Amos stated that she was ready to have a baby, but she was always cryptic and not at all forthcoming when the interviewers asked the logical next question: who was going to be the father? She'd just say something like, "Yes, there will be a father," and leave it at that. However, things were starting to unravel between her and Rosse, and they came to a head during the tour in August 1994. After seven and a half years in each other's lives, Tori and Eric Rosse broke up.

It was a difficult, devastating thing. Not just personally, which was hard enough, but professionally as well. "It was mutual," Rosse would later explain to VH1's *Behind the Music 2.* "It was a mutual agreement that we needed to do that in order to grow as individuals."[41] As was her way, Amos used the pain to fuel her muse. She started writing songs about her feelings about the split, most of which would appear on her next album.

Amos also finally came up with a way to have a positive effect on all of those girls who were telling her horrifying stories backstage of their rapes and abuses. She had always tried to be a sympathetic ear, but she realized that she could do more. In June 1994, Amos and Atlantic Records helped to create RAINN, the Rape, Abuse & Incest National Network. RAINN was a telephone hotline, with people on duty twenty-four hours a day, for victims to call. It is a toll-free call (in the U.S. the number is 1-800-656-HOPE) where women can get counseling or just tell their story to a sympathetic ear. "I got so many letters from so many young women," Amos told L.A. radio station KSCA that summer, "They didn't choose to . . . go seek out help. I felt like they needed to have something easy, that if they just needed to talk to somebody, that it could be there."[42]

Some people questioned her motivation, but Amos felt that RAINN was a necessary and important thing, both for the victims and for herself. "I get these guys who are suspicious from the get-go, asking, 'Why are you doing this? What are your motivations?' " she told *Spin*, "and I'm like, 'How can I not do anything?' When I'm getting bags of mail from girls who are saying they can't go home because their fathers are abusing them. I've got to do something besides just saying I'm sorry."[43] Over the years she has, whenever possible, given her time and money, and contributed performances to make sure the network is able to continue doing its important work.

chapter 5

Putting the Damage On

In 1996, Amos released *Boys for Pele*, her third solo album. With eighteen songs and at seventy minutes, *Pele* was significantly longer than the first two solo albums, but it still mined the depths of Amos's hopes, dreams, and sometimes controversial beliefs. Basically, it runs on the loose concept of the power and pain of womanhood. From the single "Caught a Lite Sneeze" to the nostalgic beauty of "Horses" and the sadness of "Blood Roses," Amos was inviting the audience to share her worldview. "I don't think you move people when you're a hired gun," Amos explains. "You're not going to touch people's hearts."

Boys for Pele was also the first album that Amos produced completely herself. All of her previous work had been done with her co-producer and former boyfriend Eric Rosse or other producers suggested by the record company. But Amos felt strongly that this album had to be a more personal statement. This would be particularly important because many of the songs dealt with the dissolution of her relationship with Rosse. "I had to do it because of the subject matter," Tori explained. "I really had to live what I was singing about. Producing it on my own was a way for me to grow up and not wear little girls' clothes anymore. Of course, they're in the wardrobe, but it's only just a part of my repertoire now, instead of always turning it over to other people. I was really fortunate to work with some exciting people, Eric being one of those."

Boys for Pele is best experienced, she told *Break*, "when you know what it is like to crawl." She added, "You have to know what it is like to feel desperate for somebody else's fire to really understand this record."[1] Amos admitted at the time that her songs about relationships tended to be sad, but she explained, "It has been my experience. So, maybe, one day I'll write from the perspective of a relationship that is not falling apart." Also, she says, just because she was inclined to write serious songs, it didn't necessarily mean she's an unhappy person. "You can write songs that have sadness in them and still enjoy a giggle and a margarita."

Boys for Pele was named after children sacrificed to the Hawaiian goddess of fire by being thrown into a live volcano. (Amos has said often that she meant no disrespect to the world-famous football [soccer] star also named Pelé. She just really didn't know much about him other than the fact that he had some very strong and sexy-looking calves.) Amos didn't want people to think she relates to this vengeful goddess, but then again, she didn't feel like one of the poor village boys who meet their death, either. In fact, Amos admitted, "I relate more to the fire. The fire aspect of what Pele means. The flames. The independence of feeling your own fire. As you walk outside that day and you have access to this feeling, this passion, just because you're alive. Everybody has that right, but we were never taught that."

As always, Amos used the opportunity of a new album to stretch herself artistically, to redefine what she has been doing as a performer. As she said in the press kit for *Boys for Pele*, "Musically, I always allow myself to jump off of cliffs. At least that's what it feels like to me. Whether that's what it actually sounds like might depend on what the listener brings to the songs. But, to me, this album sounds like the biggest cliff yet."[2] She put it even more succinctly in *Diva*, "*Earthquakes* was my diary. *Under the Pink* an impressionistic painting. This record is a novel."[3]

The sonic novel that she was penning was one of the most heartfelt, and most disturbing, that she had recorded yet. Breakup albums have a tendency to place a microscope on the artist and *Boys for Pele* is no different. While the death of her longtime relationship with Eric Rosse and the sudden loud ticking of her biological clock certainly contributed to the album's stark power, this was only one dimension of the record's self-analysis. The collection also continued *Under the Pink*'s fascination with womanhood, causing her to question her own place in the world and women's place in general. She had recalled a traumatic experience when she was only eight, when a girl who was slightly older than her had forced her to lie on the bathroom floor and undress. She felt that the experience had colored all of her relationships with women afterwards...she could love them and be with them, and yet she would often keep them at a certain distance.[4]

On a broader spectrum, she tried to come to terms with the places of men and women in the larger scale of things. Surprisingly, since *Boys for Pele* and the rest of her music deals so strongly with the empowerment of womanhood, Amos did admit that she thought that the whole idea of feminism was dead. "Feminism was based on a filtrating hierarchy, which it had to do. It was a hugely important step, to break this program and pattern of male domination. However, at a certain point, the tide shifted—once women infiltrated. In truth, in many cases it became a part of the domination. I speak for myself as much as anybody else, because I had that experience. Therefore, the whole concept of feminism, it was important and it should be honored, but now it's about the feminine honoring the feminine—in men and women. And really not wanting to be a part of the whole domination cycle, whether that's to dominate or be dominated."

But, as was her nature, Amos was not being controversial just to be controversial. That is way too easy an explanation of Amos's distinctive songwriting power. She likes to challenge preconceived notions, widen the horizons of her listeners. Everything was a way of opening people's eyes—from her deeply felt lyrics to the notorious picture inside the CD jacket of Amos with her shirt open suckling a baby pig. "I enjoy making people kind of turn their heads to one side and look at it from a different perspective. I don't like regimented concepts. I don't see how they help anybody. So a lot of times I go after structured ways of thinking, with something I say or in something I do, that pushes the regiment of structured thinking. A little like Pisa. . . ." Of course that picture may have made some people turn their head a little too much. A man in Los Angeles claimed that a giant bill-board with the picture had so distracted him on the road that he wrecked his car. So he sued Amos and Atlantic for causing a public hazard, but the case was eventually dropped.[5]

As was quickly becoming her habit, Amos decided that the album needed to be recorded in a different place. This one was calling to be recorded at two distinct and different areas—it was split between a studio in New Orleans, Louisiana, and a church in rural Ireland outside of Dublin. It was the perfect blend of the ecclesiastical and the profane. In New Orleans, they were close to both—for every church there are several bars in the French Quarter. The city is world–famous for the linking and blurring of religion and revelry; the Mardi Gras celebration alone epitomizes the deep marriage and divide of the heavenly and the earthly. The Irish sessions were actually recorded in a huge box that the band constructed in a local church, and they had to make this easy to deconstruct to keep out of the way of the worshipers and their services.[6] The box had a harpsichord on one side and a piano on the other, and for hours on end Amos would sit in the box unable to see anything else but the keyboards. Amos was determined these changes of scenery and disparities could only help to enrich the final work. "I think everything that you do affects what you write," Amos said. "If you spend time in other places, it can't not [influence the music], you know what I mean?"

Of course, to Tori Amos, it wasn't so much a case of writing the songs as leaving herself open to them and channeling their energy. "To take credit for them," she told *Entertainment Weekly*, "would be like taking credit for the sunset if you're a painter."[7] Many of the songs had come to her before the recording process, either on tour for *Under the Pink* or at her new home that she had bought in North London right on a canal. In a speech that she gave on creativity at the University of California in Los Angeles (UCLA) in early 1995, she told about her new life on the water. "There's this hole right underneath the piano, and if you go underneath the canal, in the boats, you can wave to me and I'll wave back. . . .I take all the mail down to the boats. Because I live in the little canal house, and I take it down, and it's great, great being the mail girl."[8]

So between delivering letters to the docks and delivering songs from the faeries and being a completely single woman for the first time in years, Tori Amos had a backlog of songs that were just itching to be created. The songs that she had written while on tour had been patient, but the incubation time was coming to an end. "Not because I didn't have anything better to do," she told *Billboard*, "but because of what was going on in my personal life. . . .I was separated from my soul mate. Just feeling that shock when half of you walks out—the songs just started coming to me."[9] It was time for them to see the light of day. The first stop was that church in County Wicklow, Ireland, where Amos started to stray from the piano and experiment with the harpsichord. The final songs came to life in New Orleans.

And come they did. There are eighteen songs on *Boys for Pele* (nineteen if you count the medley of "Beauty Queen" and "Horses" individually.) To continue the birth analogy, to a certain extent there were labor pains with each one of them. Amos was in a particularly unsettled place in her life and the songs showed it. Even just two years later, she was able to look back on the whole process with a little more objectivity. "That record was very much about trying to understand a serious breakup that I had with someone I had been with for a long time," she told RollingStone.com. "I was trying to find parts and pieces of myself that I had never claimed. I'd been living through other people in my life, particularly the men in my life. So it was a really tough record, very depressing, but in the end it gave me a lot of strength. It was a real tough journey—one of those where you think you're going to bite your own arm off. And you just hope somebody is there to put a muzzle in your mouth. But nobody put a muzzle in my mouth and I made *Boys for Pele*."[10]

Or as she put it in a 1998 concert in Boulder, Colorado, "I turned in the record, and, um, I've never really had such a moment in my life. I mean, things were kind of better when I pooped in my pants. I walked in and, you know, I'd sold millions of records for this company…and I walked in; I'd had some pizza and a nice glass of wine, and I was like, 'Well, I'll meet the new girls.' I know it's a little dark, but you know, everybody needs a good bottle of wine and some depressing songs every once in a while. And so I walked in, and this is what I met." She imitated the execs by sitting stone-faced with her arms folded in front of her. "So, basically, after this record went platinum, I said, 'Well, we didn't do it, because of anything you all did.' I'm just saying that it was because of you guys. Record companies, radio had absolutely fuck-all to do with any of this whole year. And that's the truth."[11]

The record that had the Atlantic execs a bit stone-faced was probably Amos's densest, most difficult to penetrate album to date. This can be a good thing or a bad thing, of course. The label people were probably wondering—possibly with legitimate reason, because they are ultimately in a business to make money—how are we going to get this on the radio? With the likes of Mariah Carey, Celine Dion, TLC, Hootie and the Blowfish, R. Kelly, and all the other acts that were topping the charts at the time, *Boys for Pele* certainly stood alone. The answer, of course, was that they weren't going to get it the airplay they wanted, so no point in even losing sleep over it. Tori Amos had become a prestige artist for the label, someone who would never hit the *Top of the Pops*, but whom the label could point to proudly when explaining that they also had a good barometer for artistic expression.

It leaves the gate quietly, demurely, with the double feature of "Beauty Queen/Horses." "The record starts off with the horses from 'Winter' taking us and we ride," she told Sandra A. Garcia of *B-Side*. "Going into that program of the beauty queen. She's a beauty queen, and that's not enough because it never is. The idea that beauty is our answer when we are four years old, 'Oh, isn't she pretty'—that's the first thing that you hear. So it's going after those programs of the feminine, going after them, going after them."[12]

Amos told *Musician* magazine that she was trying to capture something even more specific in "Beauty Queen." The song snippet was a snapshot, a flash of time captured for all to view:

> When you hear "Beauty Queen," you are hearing this girl in that moment: She's standing in that bathroom, watching those girls put on that lipstick. I don't want us to be talking to her fifteen minutes later about what she realized in that bathroom. I want her to go back to that moment in the bathroom: It's white. It's that funny fluorescent light. It's that tile, with the green crud in between. It's those old toilets with the beautiful handles. You can hear the sound of the water dripping. Time doesn't exist in that moment. I wanted you to feel that kind of swimming, where you're almost coming back from fifteen feet under water, and you're coming up, and you're almost up. That's what it's like in that bathroom, when you're looking and you're realizing what's really going on at your table. That's what I want to catch. This is not a confident girl. You are not at acceptance level. You are in her brain, getting triggered. The little windshield wipers are going, and you're starting to see it from the other side.[13]

After that pastoral but slightly disturbing Polaroid comes "Horses," which is again deceptively idyllic musically while harboring a hidden sense of darkness. This partially comes from the lyrics, partially from the fact that it was played live in one take on a Leslie keyboard speaker. The Leslie was a big old thing that couldn't even fit in the church, so they had put it in the graveyard beside it. Created by Donald James Leslie, who had died at age ninety-three on September 2, 2004, the Leslie refined the sound of the Hammond Organ and other keyboard instruments.[14] For such a large thing, the song has a very hushed, delicate feeling; the quiet tinkling of Amos's Bösendorfer piano accompanying a hushed vocal that seems to be about to shatter into a million little pieces at any moment.

The harpsichord makes its first appearance on the next track, "Blood Roses," a dark meditation on relationships of the sexes. The song was originally supposed to be the first track on the disc, and it was one of the last recorded. It makes musical the realization that one is being mistreated and then the extreme and unhealthy depths one might take to get back at the person who caused the pain. It was a look into the depths of Amos's soul. She wasn't necessarily thrilled with what was down there, but she did take a certain pride in it. It may not be pretty, but it was all part of her. Once when she was starting to play the song in concert, a guy in the audience yelled out that he wanted to marry her. She looked at the audience somewhat crossly and told her indistinct suitor, "You know you don't want to do that. No, you don't. Just listen to these words, sweetheart. You don't want to go there."[15]

The next song on the album had the scintillating title "Father Lucifer." It was all played to a somewhat spirited piano ballad, complete with an occasional *Sgt. Pepper* horn bubbling up to the top. As she has done so often in her career, the song is an exploration of good and evil and the definitions that have been placed by society and religion. Was it sacrilege to compare the Prince of Darkness to a man of the cloth? Was it romanticizing evil and darkness, making him a dashing figure? Or was that the point? Wouldn't it make sense for the devil to appear in the most impressive light? Where is the temptation without the sense of reward? Is he just the ultimate example of the bad boy mystique?

"I wanted to marry Lucifer. Even though I had a crush on Jesus. Lucifer was the brother holding the space for mankind/womankind to act out their fears and hidden secrets, things they won't acknowledge," she told *Spin*. "Some of my girlfriends—liberal London girls—had a problem with the idea that I was writing a song called 'Father Lucifer.' One of them heard it and cried and said, 'You made him so beautiful,' and I said, 'What if he is beautiful?' Shadow defines light. The shadow is where I hang out a lot because I like chasing and diving with those forces."[16]

As discussed earlier, there have long been rumors that "Professional Widow" was based on Courtney Love. Amos has always refused to answer them, but there was a weird triangle thing going on between Amos and the lead singer of Hole and Trent Reznor. Love fueled rumors that Amos's relationship with Reznor was more than just friendly, telling a story in her biography about being at Reznor's New Orleans homestead when a female alternative rocker showed up and tried to get in with a key. The locks had been changed, as had his cell phone number, so a security guard would not let her in. Love never officially said that it was Tori Amos, but the description in the story certainly seemed to point that way.[17]

Amos won't talk about their relationship, nor will Reznor, who only did acknowledge vaguely that his relationship with Love got in the way of his relationship with Amos. However, the jagged instrumentation and raw-nerve lyrics of "Professional Widow" fuel the speculation that it is indeed about Love, though Amos has said that she wrote it about herself. Lyrics like "Honey, bring it close to my lips / Yes / Don't blow those brains yet" could definitely be taken to be a reference to Love's late husband Kurt Cobain's suicide. Also, the idea that Love glommed on to the more famous late-singer could be read into the chorus line, "Starfucker / just like my daddy / selling his baby." That could probably refer to Love's absentee father, Hank Harrison, who famously lived off of the Grateful Dead for years in different positions (from roadie to biographer) without ever being a member of the group. It certainly makes it harder to believe it is about Amos. No one could ever call Reverend Amos a hanger-on. Ironically, Reznor recorded a song that he called "Starfucker." It was also said at the time he might be writing about Love. But rumors that Nine Inch Nails song was about Love have been pretty much dismissed. It is widely agreed that his song was Reznor's rebuke to his former protégé Marilyn Manson.[18]

The next song, "Mr. Zebra," is a short little song snippet with an old-fashioned vaudeville show tune vibe, complete with a calliope piano, emphatic horn charts by the Black Dyke Mills Band, and somewhat inscrutable words. Amos told the radio show *World Cafe* in Philadelphia:

Lyrics to me, when they become references so that Mr. Zebra can be who you want it to be. Although you know that there are certain clear words: "Strychnine, sometimes she's a friend of mine." And you get a sense of the characters, of who they are. And I'm sure the person, women that you know that are Ratitouille Strychnine, and we can kinda love those women, but you have faces that are different from the faces that I see when I sing about um, that cute little babe that's poisoning the muffins in the kitchen. But we love her, too. And that was important in this record. This is really the hidden sides of the feminine, the ones that get a little wicked, and the reasons that they're wicked. That's what is being said also in the story, the reasons, 'cause they haven't been recognized, that they kinda have to mutiny for me to listen to them so that we can get to the heart, and that's really the core of the record.[19]

"Marianne" is a tender tribute to Marianne Curtis, a girl Amos had known when she was growing up. She had died of a drug overdose at fifteen. The stories were that she killed herself, but Amos refused to believe she would have or could have done that. In concert Amos called Marianne "the most beautiful human being." Then Amos laughed. "That's hard to believe isn't it? We women can have a real mean streak. Another pearl can enter the room and we are ready to go…and your boyfriend will say, 'She's so nice.' But that's okay, guys. We women have been killing each other in the harem for years. But Marianne was truly nice." She angrily recalled hearing from her mother that Marianne had committed suicide. " 'Fuck you, Mom!' That's your first reaction, you know. Somebody so wonderful that gave everyone such a gift. No!"[20]

Relations with men formed the spine of the first single, "Caught a Lite Sneeze." This song is much more of a trip into an alternative musical pathway, complete with clicking drum tracks by Alan Friedman and guitar swells by old friend Steve Caton. It sort of sticks out a bit from many of the other songs, a more eccentric vibe and instrumentation and yet at the same time it is more catchy than many of the denser tunes on the album. The song is a intimate look at the inability, or unwillingness, people often have to terminate relationships that obviously no longer work. (The reference to Nine Inch Nails' *Pretty Hate Machine* has led many to think it was about Trent Reznor.)

Sometimes, she acknowledges, it is easier to stick with what is familiar, even when it does not work. It is very hard to do, so you keep sifting through the muck, hoping for something that will bring you to believe that it can be saved. "The whole current of 'Sneeze' is doing anything so that you don't have to face yourself," she told *Aquarian Weekly*. "Nothing is enough—you don't feel that you have the tools. I couldn't get to this until everything was falling apart. I couldn't get to this until things were being flung back in my face. When you're being gushed and gooed over, and all that stuff in a relationship, it disgusts you."[21]

"Muhammad My Friend" sprang from a trip back home with her parents for the holidays. In a 1996 London concert, she told the story. "My father dragged me to Christmas Eve service," she said. "Not this past Christmas but the one before.

He didn't get me this past because I was with a boy. Ha. But anyway, this was the first time he's never got me to Christmas Eve. Last time I went I had this idea because…you know the little kids were singing this song. You know"—she did a line of the carol "Away in a Manger"—" 'The little lord Jesus lay down his sweet head…,' so he's going, 'Go ahead. Sing, Tori Ellen, you gotta sing something.' And I'm like, 'They both know it was a girl, yes. . . .' "[22]

Amos saw "Muhammad My Friend" as a harbinger of a change in direction for the album. It had been about a woman stumbling blindly, trying to find herself, but now she was starting to look at everything from a different perspective, a different viewpoint. However, as this song closes, you can sense the woman righting herself, and with the following song, "Hey Jupiter," she starts to find her way. "'Muhammad My Friend' is me looking for the seed of that idea: How did I come to think that guys gave me my own worth?" Amos told the *Dallas Observer*. "'Hey Jupiter' is me just saying that's it—I've had enough, I just can't continue."[23]

"Hey Jupiter" was Amos's reaction to bottoming out in a hotel in Oklahoma City on the last tour. It was after the breakup with Rosse, and suddenly she felt a devastating, helpless sense of complete loneliness. She'd never felt this way before. She desperately wanted to call Rosse, but knew she couldn't. She wanted to call anyone but had no one to call. "That's where I was literally at the bottom," she told the *New York Post*. "It was like I was thinking, 'Just you wait, Henry Higgins,' and as I sat there on my knees in Oklahoma City, waiting for the phone to ring, needing to feed. I'd reached the end of my rope."[24]

However, from this low point, Amos started to resurface. You feel the heaviness still in the piano and gospel chorus of "Way Down" and the swampy Southern gothic murder mystery of "Little Amsterdam." She was working her way forward, not going to be a victim anymore. So even when she referenced a famous victim in "Talula," it was one who was known for her strength of character. "Anne Boleyn, the second wife of Henry VIII," she told *Seventeen*. "She gave him one daughter but wasn't giving him any sons, so he chose to get rid of her [she was beheaded]. I make reference to her on my new song 'Talula.' "[25] The song isn't one of mourning, though, in fact it is a mid-tempo dance track where Amos experiments with styles like jazz scat singing. Amos has called the song a nursery rhyme and a riddle, but it works in the context of the CD as more of a healing moment.

The healing continues in the next song as we touch upon what Amos has often referred to as a "moment of compassion." The song "Not the Red Baron" seems in the broad sense to be a tender benedictory for wartime pilots, however, it is meant in a more as a peace offering to the men in her album, in her life. The song was actually recorded as a B-side, but Amos says it insisted upon being on the album. Another short musical snippet was "Agent Orange." "With 'Agent Orange,' I was hoping you could see this orange-bodied muscle man," she told *Aquarian Weekly*, "and give yourself a giggle so that we'd transform this being from a mutilated skin person to Orangina. It's the idea of becoming Tang—transmuting the chemical effect. You can't forget that happened—you can't forget the warfare."[26]

Another song that was almost a stowaway on the album was "Doughnut Song." It was late one night in Ireland and the band was just about to go to a local pub called The White Lady, but the music had other plans. "This record was almost finished and this little song began creeping through," she told a concert audience. "This meant the guys couldn't go and get Guinness. And they thought it was all over and I said, 'Excuse me, I hate to break the party, but this girl has to come now.' And they went, 'Okay, fine, good…fuck. . . .' But she came and she's like my favorite right now."[27]

The song "In the Springtime of His Voodoo" opens with quiet, unintelligible murmurs, for nearly a minute and a half, finally picking up the script with the line "Standing on a corner in Winslow, Arizona," which is a quote from the seventies hit "Take It Easy" by the Eagles (cowritten by Eagles singer Glenn Frey and fellow Southern California songwriter Jackson Browne). The song has a more confident gait than many of the songs that proceeded it, riding on an almost bluesy guitar line by Caton.

She finally tries to reconcile herself and her life and her losses in "Putting the Damage On." It is a very quiet but subtly gorgeous song, with delicate horn lines that sound vaguely like the work of Burt Bacharach. " 'Damage' speaks for itself," she told *B-Side*. "The song, being herself damaged, is trying to teach myself about graciousness, and I have such a hard time with that….'Damage' was so essential for me to sing, it's one of the most difficult ones for me."[28] The album closes out with the lullaby "Twinkle," which has a sweet, beautiful piano line and a hushed vocal imparting some slightly less-than-tranquil lyrics, but it still eases the listener out of the album on a balanced, even keel; it is musically a tonic for the soul even if it alights upon the hurt that preceded it.

The release of *Boys For Pele* was an event for the record label, so they went all out to make sure that it got as much notice as possible. "Caught a Lite Sneeze" was one of the first songs ever to be posted on the Internet over a month before the album's release. "God, what a schmoozy thing to say…on the 'Net," Amos said, laughing, in an interview with Toronto radio station CFNY, which, by the way, was aired "on the 'Net."[29] In fact, the Internet was playing a larger and larger role in her career. Dozens of Web sites were sprouting like flowers, slavishly devoted to her career and finding the minutiae of her life and career. The fans who created them called themselves Toriphiles, and individual sites like A Dent in the Tori Amos Net Universe, Here in My Head, and Toriphoria all offer an astounding wealth of information on their goddess. This is made all the more impressive because they were labors of love from devoted fans. They are not cynical money-making ventures. A fanzine called *Really Deep Thoughts* also delves deeply into Amos's work and her world.

By now it was becoming obvious that Tori Amos's fan base was especially rabid, and I mean that in a good way. They were an extraordinarily devoted bunch. Tickets for the 1996 Dew Drop Inn tour were gobbled up in under twenty-four hours. *Boys for Pele* debuted at number two on the U.S. album charts and made it to the top in the U.K. and continued the upswing of her album sales. The single "Caught a Lite Sneeze," while still getting little or no radio airplay, made it a little higher up the *Billboard* singles chart, making it to number sixty in January 1996. Then an acid house remix of "Professional Widow," done by a DJ named Armand Van Helden (with Amos's blessing, of course), took Amos into a different venue. Another remixer named BT had her sing his song "Blue Skies," which also became a dance hit. For a brief heady time, Tori Amos was queen of the dance floors. Amos released a photo album-cum-biography called *All These Years* and the Toriphiles snapped it up. She did an episode of MTV's then red-hot concert series *Unplugged* and was a musical guest on *Saturday Night Live. People* magazine even named her one of "The Fifty Most Beautiful People in the World," though Amos gave credit to good genes. "My great-grandparents were doing all sorts of things in the bloodline."[30]

The fandom could be taken too far sometimes, one Toriphile decided to make his body a canvas for the goddess, determining to cover himself head to toe with tattoos of the flame-haired singer. But, for the most part, they were just a well-adjusted, extraordinarily faithful following. Strangely, a just as determined anti-Tori faction also popped up, smaller but just as vocal. A guy once told me that he hated Tori Amos because she reminded him of his suicidal ex-girlfriend, who was a huge fan. Trying to explain to him that he had a problem with the fan, not the artist, was useless. He wasn't going to budge from his position any more than a Toriphile would if you said that you thought one song kind of sucked. People don't seem to have measured reactions to Tori Amos. It often seems like you're either all in or all out.

Amos also refused to pander to radio just to expand her base. While she had still never had what anyone could ever call a "radio hit," she was content to spread the word in a little more unconventional way. The fans and the good press had been working for her so far. Amos had seen so many musicians who had subverted their art just to get airplay. She even felt she had sold herself out back in the Y Kant Tori Read years. To her, it just hurt the music and the integrity. "If it becomes your common denominator, of course it can, because you will write different work if you're trying to write for that medium. That medium will embrace you or won't embrace you. You can't calculate that wish for too long. You can maybe get away with it for a little while, but in the end it'll be very unfulfilling, anyway."

Instead of buying into the radio flavor of the week, Amos felt you just had to experience the album. Either it would speak to you or it wouldn't—it was that simple. Not to say that she wasn't willing to hedge her bets a bit. Amos was willing to sway the listener's appreciation with outside forces. "I'd get them all a really good bottle of red first," she laughed. "I'd make it mandatory." While a good bottle of wine certainly couldn't hurt, the record got a good following, even from teetotalers.

And how did Tori Amos feel with the direction her career had taken at that point? That her career has put her on a fast track of hit records and sold-out tours and the fact that people are moved by her work? "I look around and kind of smile and say, Hey, no complaints," Amos said, contentedly. After all, living well is the best revenge. However, it turned out that all was not quite as placid as she claimed. Truth is, her life was in quite a bit of turmoil. There was the breakup with Eric Rosse. She got pregnant, but had a miscarriage. She had a cancer scare and nearly lost her voice in the past couple of years. Her relationship with Trent Reznor had flamed out. Life seemed to be rushing by her eyes, out of control. In the years since recording *Boys for Pele*, Amos has come to find it hard to listen to the album. "I was really in a bad way," she told *Blender* magazine in 2002. "I was finding out what I believed in. What was my ideology? What was the woman I wanted to be? What was sexy to me? What was exciting? I was breaking away from a lot of things and people, and they were breaking away from me as well. It was a low in my life."[31]

However, things were starting to look up. On the plus side, she was getting to know soundman Mark Hawley, a relationship that would play a huge part in her world. She has said that her first reaction to Hawley rather mirrored her reaction to Pelé (the soccer star, not the goddess). She noticed that Hawley had strong, sexy calves. She also dropped little hints of Hawley in the songs and in the interviews that she did for *Boys for Pele*. In an interview that she did with longtime friend Terry Gladstone on Los Angeles radio station KSCA, she admitted, "I got into nerds. I got into techies. I'm into techies now. I'm not into rock stars."[32] While Hawley may not appreciate the nerds comment, he certainly filled the techie bill.

They started a serious relationship, although Amos did her best to keep it out of the press. Not that she was embarrassed in any way (although an European magazine did later jokingly chide her for fucking the help)[33], but after the high-profile breakup with Eric Rosse and the rumors of a relationship with Trent Reznor, she wanted to give it some time to grow and blossom. Amos and Hawley became pregnant in September 1996. Perhaps the lowest point in her life came when she miscarried the baby in December 1996. Amos had been three months pregnant with a girl. She had already decided to name her Phoebe. However, when getting a scan, the nurse told Amos with tears in her eyes that the baby had been miscarried. Amos said years later that she had a feeling that something was wrong, but it still didn't prepare her for the loss. About five months later, she had yet another miscarriage. This time, she didn't even know that she was pregnant, which may offer some cold comfort, but still had Amos worried that she could never carry a baby to term.

But they say it is always darkest before the dawn, and Tori Amos would come to be further proof of that. The shared tragedy brought Amos and Hawley even closer. After the first miscarriage, they would stay up all night—neither one could sleep—and just talk about their lives and their experiences. They worked through their grief together, at first not even wanting to leave the house during the day, but eventually allowing themselves to try to work past their loss. Their bond grew closer and closer. Tori Amos finally had found the man that she would marry.

Eventually both realized that the most important thing in Tori Amos's life was her work—her music. So Amos decided to throw herself back into her art. Songs started to well up from the sorrow, and Amos channeled them and put them on paper, getting together the songs that would become her next album, *From the Choirgirl Hotel.*

Beyond her own work, Amos had started collaborating with many of her musical peers, putting together a group of wide-ranging all-star collaborators, including Peter Gabriel, Michael Stipe, Robert Plant, Trent Reznor, even Tom Jones. Amos said working with these people opened her eyes, but mostly it helped her put it all in perspective, because they are all so human. Amos said that what was most interesting about it was that with these people who she respected so much, you could still sit down and have a cup of tea and just hang out.

But she did more than hang out—she learned as well. For example, she has said that Peter Gabriel gave her the single most important piece of business advice she ever received. He told her to build her own studio. That way, if her relationship with a record label ever went south, the label couldn't collect up her master tapes, because they had to go to the owner of the studio to get them.[34] Plant, her childhood hero, approached her to record a duet of the Led Zeppelin song "Down by the Seaside" for *Enconium,* a Led Zeppelin tribute album. She was thrilled by the opportunity.

"I was asked if I would do a song," Plant told the *Baltimore Sun,* "and I said, 'Yeah, I'd like to do a duet. I'd like to do 'Down by the Seaside.' I'd like to do it in E minor, and I'd like to do it as slow as humanly possible.'...I'd met Tori a few times, and I really, really love her.... She flew into London, and we just busked it for about half an hour. I played guitar, and she played piano, Michael and Charlie played brushes and upright bass. It was cool."[35] Their version of the song was certainly a departure from the original; in fact it felt more like the country-gothic dramatic ballads of Chris Isaak.

Amos also added backing vocals to Tom Jones's lovely comeback single "I Wanna Get Back to You." She was out on tour, so they were not able to record together, so she went into the studio to record her vocal. "It was a wild session," she said in *Attitude.* "It all got very out of hand because Diane Warren had written this song with this background part they wanted me to do, but it was something that I just couldn't say. I really wanted to be a part of Tom's project so I changed the words and it worked much better. He's really been a musical force, whatever you think of him. Especially with all those Christian women and those leather pants, I mean, you just have to give ode to Tom. After I recorded it, Tom's people asked if I changed it. And I said, 'Yes, and I'm not charging the royalties. And it works!' They were nervous because Diane had written it. I never met Tom, but he did send me a nice Cartier clock."[36]

Michael Stipe, the lead singer of the popular band R.E.M, was impressed by a complete rethink of a cover of his hit single "Losing My Religion" that Amos recorded for the movie *Higher Learning*. They had previously met backstage at an Amos show in Georgia in 1994 and ended up becoming good friends. The two later recorded a duet called "It Might Hurt a Bit" slated to be the theme song for the Johnny Depp and Marlon Brando movie *Don Juan DeMarco*. The track also featured contributions by Flea of the Red Hot Chili Peppers and Dave Navarro of Jane's Addiction and the Peppers. Unfortunately, the producers of the film decided at the last minute that they wanted to have a more commercial song as their theme, so they replaced it with Bryan Adams's flamenco ballad "Have You Ever Really Loved a Woman." Adams's song did top the pop charts, but the Amos and Stipe duet has never seen the light of day. It was also considered for, but eventually left off of, the soundtrack for the Liv Tyler film *Empire Records*. At the time, Amos said someday she would like to remix the song and release it, but it still has never happened, making the song the one that got away for the millions of fans of both artists.

So with the "Losing My Religion" cover, and a cover of Leonard Cohen's "Famous Blue Raincoat" for a Cohen tribute album, *Tower of Song*, Amos was continuing her reputation as a terrific interpreter of other people's songs. She had also hit the interesting point in her career where she had enough of a body of work to have other people considering recording *her* music. When I asked her in 1996 what would be the ideal cover choice of one of her songs, she didn't even have to think about it for a second. "Metallica. 'Silent All These Years.'" While that cover version never came to be (at least not yet, are you out there, Mr. Hetfield or Mr. Ulrich?), the first few Amos remakes started to surface. An artist named Bimbetta did a version of "Leather" and a jazz combo called Nite Flyte recorded "Professional Widow." Popular progressive rock act Dream Theater has been known to play "Winter" in concert.

It was flattering, but it also seemed to Amos to be a similar position to what she had learned from getting to know her heroes. She had no more interest in being romanticized as a person than she would with any other singer. She had found out, thankfully, that even the most talented performers were still *just people*. "From Peter Gabriel to Trent to Michael to Robert," she acknowledged. "I never met Tom. I was on the road, so the tapes flew out themselves.… It really kind of takes the myth away a bit, which is wonderful. Because, again, we go back to this concept of hierarchy and leverage. It's easy to put people on a pedestal, but I don't think pedestals are healthy. Admiration is one thing, but pedestals again, it's those that have and those that don't. I'm not finding that very interesting, and I don't think that's truthful. I don't think there are those that have and those that don't. I think that there are those that have developed a skill or ability or certain traits and those that haven't. But, everybody has the ability if they want to."

That ability was out there in spades. Contrary to some popular belief, Amos felt there was a whole world of great artists out there. There were singers and songwriters who had interesting things to say and offbeat ways of presenting them. They were willing to subvert the musical traditions that had led to them or, just build a better version of what was being done. All of it was available to the discerning listeners, or even ones who just stumbled upon something that moved them. "Yeah, loads," she said. "I mean, it's endless. We start naming them [the artists], I just feel like I'm going to leave people out. There's a lot of good music out there. I mean, you might have to search for it, from the underground, but you have to put your ear to the ground and search."

As one way of helping with that search, in November 1996, Amos decided to try her hand at being a record executive on her own. At the time in the industry, it was considered a pretty standard perk for an established artist to start a boutique label of their own, but only a few ever had any success, such as Madonna's Maverick label, which introduced Alanis Morissette, the Prodigy, Michelle Branch, and Candlebox; Prince's Paisley Park, with Sheila E and the Time; or Trent Reznor's Nothing, with Marilyn Manson and Pop Will Eat Itself. Sadly, it was much more common for these labels to be money pits for the major labels, with imprints like Luaka Bop (founded by David Byrne), Crave (Mariah Carey), or Real World (Peter Gabriel) gaining a certain amount of acclaim or sales but rarely paying for themselves. So by the late nineties, the practice would shut down for the most part. However, Amos was able to sneak in on the tail end of the trend, cofounding the Igloo label with her manager, Arthur Spivak, and Atlantic Records.

Igloo's first signing was a group called Pet. Spivak had actually found the band and played it for Amos, and that inspired the two of them to work to get the group heard. "I've never heard a girl scream like that and have such a beautiful range of fluidity," Amos told the Gannett News Service about Pet singer Lisa Papineau. "There is a tear in the soul of the band, like they refuse to be victims." Amos also recognized a kindred spirit in the band. They were a group of people who had been through hard times and were able to convey that in their recording. She knew the band's individuality would be stifled in the normal artists-and-repertoire process. "I thought it would be sad if another label tried to change that."[37]

Amos went into the venture with high hopes, planning to nurture ten to fifteen bands on her label within five years. Amos was executive producer of Pet's self-titled debut album, which surfaced and disappeared without causing much of a ripple. The group also performed a cover of Olivia Newton-John's "Have You Never Been Mellow" on the charity tribute album, *Spirit of '76*, but then broke up within a couple of years. Another band, the self-proclaimed California "post–New Wave–cow-punk" group the Uninvited also released a self-titled album on Igloo, but it received even less fanfare than Pet. Soon thereafter, the label seemed to just fade away. If any other bands were ever brought into the fold, it was never announced and albums were never released. After a brief series of interviews about the label to promote the Pet CD, Amos has never really mentioned the project again. This silence has left it open to speculation about whether she just lost the passion for the idea or if Atlantic simply shut it down, which was a rather regular occurrence in the late nineties as record sales decreased due to the digital revolution.

In the summer 1997, Amos's compatriot Sarah McLachlan decided to put together a tour celebrating the diversity of female artists. Sometimes the best ideas in life come from the simplest places. Unlike the movies, there's not always the snap of a lightbulb and the violins swelling to a crescendo in the background as history is made. Life is almost never that dramatic. For Sarah McLachlan, the genesis of Lilith Fair, her festival uniting some of the world's best female musicians, was rather anticlimactic. McLachlan and some friends were looking at the lineup for the past year's testosterone-laden Lollapalooza tour and realized there was very little in the festival any of them really wanted to see. The heavily male-skewed focus of Lollapalooza and other festival tours were shutting out a whole galaxy of great artists.

McLachlan certainly wasn't the first person to have a realization like this, but it occurred to her that she was one of the few who could do something about it. Her singing career had been steadily picking up steam since her 1989 debut album, *Vox*. McLachlan's album sales, concert tours, and venues all have become steadily bigger, reaching the giddy heights of double-platinum sales for her 1994 smash, *Fumbling Towards Ecstasy*. Her single "Possession" had gotten steady airplay for over two years. She was about to release *Surfacing*, which would be a multiplatinum hit.

"I just thought it would be a great opportunity to get a bunch of women together. It's very selfish. I wanted to see all these people play," McLachlan said while planning the tour. "I never get chances to, and I never get an opportunity to talk to any of them, either. As women in the music industry—or in any industry—it's great to get a chance to get together and to talk with your peers about what's going on in your life and the industry and how you cope with it all. It's an opportunity for all of us to form a sense of community that hasn't really existed yet. And of course, to offer people in the summer an alternative to tours like Lollapalooza, which at this point are very male dominated. The summer tours weren't representational of the music that was out there."

The proceeds from the tour were all going to charity. They would be split between local philanthropic groups in the tour stops and national charitable groups such as Lifebeat, an AIDS organization, and RAINN, Amos's organization that supports rape and incest victims. McLachlan had put together a wish list of female artists she wanted on the tour. The Lilith Fair was already shaping up to be the biggest tour of the summer. McLachlan was pleasantly surprised that almost everyone approached for the tour was very receptive, from established stars like Sheryl Crow, the Indigo Girls, Tracy Chapman, Susanna Hoffs, and Suzanne Vega to then up-and-comers like Jewel, Paula Cole, the Cardigans, Joan Osborne, Juliana Hatfield, Fiona Apple, Victoria Williams, and Tracy Bonham.

McLachlan tried to get as many diverse musical acts from as many genres as she could find. Very few artists who McLachlan approached did not sign on. However, there were some that could not work it out. "I wanted a lot of diversity on the tour," McLachlan acknowledged. "I wanted singer-songwriters. I wanted pop music. I wanted folk music. I would have liked R&B. Some of the acts were a little tougher to get than others. Some just simply said no. They looked at the bill and went, This isn't my scene. We got about ninety percent of who we wanted, I think that's a pretty amazing act. I would love to have Björk, Garbage, and Sinéad O'Connor. Ani DiFranco. There was a bunch of women who for one reason or another couldn't do it, mainly because their schedules. They were either in the studio, like Tori Amos, or had just totally had enough of touring. I totally respect that."

While Amos was recording her next album, which would become *From the Choirgirl Hotel*, that was only part of the story. The Lilith Fair continued for a few years after that, and Amos would never sign on. Amos later acknowledged that she didn't think that she would really fit into the Lilith vibe too well. Her performances were a little too intimate and complex to pull off in half-hour-to-forty-five-minute chunks in huge sheds. Also, she acknowledged, she liked a little testosterone on her tours. She did not want to be in a tour that wrote off the importance of male energy and vibe.

Early on, McLachlan had said she would eventually allow men to be on the Lilith tour. "I think right now there's almost a reverse sexism going on in the industry," she told me soon before the first tour. "There's such a growth spurt of women in the industry and there's a lot of really fantastic male artists who are sure falling through the cracks right now. At least within radio and within the touring element, because there's kind of nowhere to put them. Ron Sexsmith is an obvious example. He's a beautifully sweet, talented singer-songwriter who, if he was a woman, he'd be huge right now, I'm sure of it. People like that, I definitely want to have there." However, as the tour quickly became a huge groundbreaking entity in the U.S. touring scene, the idea of including men was written off. And, like the men, Tori Amos never ended up on the Lilith stages, though this was to be her choice. Amos said she would love to get together and have dinner and maybe a nice bottle of wine with McLachlan, but she couldn't quite bring herself to be on her tour.

Amos wasn't going to allow Lilith to be the only concerts adding money to the Rape, Abuse & Incest National Network's coffers. Amos did amp up her activity for RAINN in 1997. She gave a special concert in New York at the theater at Madison Square Garden on January 23, 1997. Designer Calvin Klein helped her put together the benefit, signing up to help RAINN for a year with a campaign that they called "Unchain the Silence." They hoped to earn $500,000 from the show.

Her good friend Maynard James Keenan, from the bands Tool and A Perfect Circle, who Amos has often referred to as her unofficial brother, came onstage and performed with her on "Muhammad My Friend." Keenan was happy to do the favor for his friend, as he told *Us* magazine, "The music industry does strange things to people. People trot out their cuts and bruises like sales points in a marketing campaign. Tori's managed to embrace her whole life experience without compromising and using it cynically."[38]

The concert was also shown on the cable television network Lifetime the day after the concert and later released on videotape, with the money going toward the aid organization. Amos also re-released "Silent All These Years" as a single, with all the proceeds for the benefit of RAINN. On the CD single, she offered both the original song and the live version from the RAINN concert. On Friday, May 15, 1997, Amos asked every radio station in the United States to play "Silent All These Years," followed by a public service announcement about RAINN.[39] Obviously, it was a very audacious plan, and of course not every one did it, but lots of stations did play the song. Five years after the song had originally caught the public's notice, it finally hit the *Billboard* Top 100 singles, peaking at number sixty-five in May 1997 and earning a decent amount for her beloved charity.

chapter 6
Tori's Strength

Amos's fourth solo album, which would become *From the Choirgirl Hotel*, was born of personal sorrow and calamity for the singer. "I got pregnant at the end of the last tour," Amos told Sylvie Simmons of *Mojo*. "It wasn't planned, but I was very ready at that point in my life to be a mother. Then, when I miscarried, the music just started to come. You know when you have this emptiness—internally, literally—your hormones are crashing and everything is happening? When I'm in some kind of trauma, the songs usually tear across the universe to find me."[1]

The two tragic miscarriages had Amos feeling introspective and horribly distraught. Many people would write about the loss in their diary. For Tori Amos, her music is that diary. So she funneled all that she was feeling into the lyrics; the heartbreak was terrible to live through but it was bringing to life some of her most personal, heartfelt songs yet. Her life was changing in so many ways. She was in love, but she was also touched by misfortune. Tori Amos's life never ceased to be complex, for better or for worse.

Amos went to Florida to facilitate the song-birthing process, while back at home in Cornwall an old barn next door to her house was being converted to her own personal recording studio, which she would call Martian Engineering. Amos had it built to be able to use herself as well as to rent out as a professional studio to visiting artists. As it points out on the studio's Web site, the building may look like an old barn from the 1800s, but the studio is totally state of the art, with accommodations both for recording and for being comfortable while the artist is there.[2]

Amos bought a huge estate in the Sewall's Point area of Stuart, Florida, back in 1995, where she went to write the music while her new recording facility was being brought together. Amos has done her share of construction work on this home as well, including having "a full-sized tree house" built in the living room. This was a place for recharging her batteries, visiting her family (it was not far from her parents' new home, where they had moved upon retirement), and relaxing. The area is surprisingly star-packed, although it is not quite as vocal about its famous residents as Palm Beach and Miami to the south. In the neighboring area, Burt Reynolds, Bernadette Peters, Gloria Estefan, Celine Dion, country singer Alan Jackson, designer Ralph Lauren, former Monkee Davy Jones, football star Joe Namath, and golfer Greg Norman all have homes (or had—Dion sold hers, when she got a three-year contract to play in Las Vegas), and actor Mel Gibson has also been known to visit. "I come to write there, and I come to get away from it all," Amos told a local newspaper, the *Stuart News*, about the vacation home. "But [Mark Hawley] won't allow a studio system in the house—it's more of a creating space and a rejuvenating space."[3]

As well as rejuvenating, it also gave Amos the opportunity to explore a new passion, which was a boat. The sea has seduced many people by its enormity, unpredictability, and seeming indifference to all other things. The sea is simply a force of nature, one that can be excessively beautiful and at the same time it can be horribly dangerous. It creates and sustains life and at the same time it can destroy it. Tori Amos's new boat was something that she truly loved, but it was also something that had her feeling rather philosophical.

"I've been racing my boat lately," she told *Magical Blend*. "It's really small, fourteen feet. I'm trying to learn the skill of taking waves and weaving in and out of the water. I just love being out on the water and having all of these massive boats pass by and get me all wet. I did something a couple of days ago that was totally humbling. I went out into the big ocean in my tiny little boat because it was very calm. And it was such a good feeling. I'm a bit cynical about religious deities right now, but sometimes you go out to the ocean and it's really simple, 'Ocean…big.' In a sense, your faith gets restored because if a storm kicks up, then a storm kicks up. It's not personal. With religions, I was taught if you do X, Y, and Z and you confess and you pray and you ask to be absolved and you do all these things, then God will respond. And that's a lie. There's no guarantee that God will do anything. I'm really learning it's a free-will planet and certain things are going to happen to certain people. No matter how loving you are or giving you are, you might face loss tragically. And there's no 'get out of loss free' card, just because you go to church."[4]

After the time away, it was a nice thing to get back home. Martian Engineering was ready for its maiden voyage—the recording of a new Tori Amos album. Leading up to it, Amos recorded some songs for a new film: a modernization of the Charles Dickens classic novel *Great Expectations*, starred Ethan Hawke with Oscar winners Gwyneth Paltrow, Robert DeNiro, Anne Bancroft, and Chris Cooper. She recorded the songs "Siren" and "Finn," which was referred to as an instrumental vocalization. The two songs also opened the movie's soundtrack album. A separate album was released with the film score, and Amos contributed to that as well, with both "Finn" and "Paradiso Perduto," another similar wordless vocal track. Amos was excited to work on the film after seeing a rough cut, although she admitted that the final version of the film was rather different than what she had been shown. But she was happy to play a part, though it ended up causing some stress due to behind-the-scenes trouble.

"I didn't enjoy doing *Great Expectations* in the end because it got politically weird and people weren't forthright anymore," Amos admitted on an Internet chat with America Online. "You have to understand something—having a studio tell me what to do, after we'd made an agreement, isn't what I considered having integrity. So, in my world, we have a team of people and we talk about things and we make decisions based on the creativity. And we sometimes have our hiccups and stuff, but musicians are sometimes just extraneous for film people and I don't see writing songs as extraneous. Obviously, it's not the center of the film, but there needs to be a level of respect and some film people forget that. When I remind them of that, they seemed quite shocked. When in actuality, I call it just bad manners."[5]

In October 1997, Amos was back at her brand-new studio and ready to work on the next album. One problem was that she needed another drummer and was having trouble finding one. It was ex-boyfriend Eric Rosse who suggested that she give a percussionist named Matt Chamberlain a shot at the job. Chamberlain had previously played on albums by Fiona Apple, Edie Brickell & the New Bohemians, Chris Isaak, Sam Phillips, and the Wallflowers. They hit it off right away and Chamberlain quickly became a staple of Amos's band. It was a great situation for him, particularly working with an experienced artist soon after being a part of Fiona Apple's breakthrough debut album, *Tidal*. Though he loved working with Apple, too (and did play on her follow-up album), he felt that Amos was "a lot more experienced in dealing with people. Definitely a lot more expressive—she knows how to tell you what she wants."[6]

Amos and the musicians settled in to work on the songs, though she acknowledges that this album came to life fitfully. They would hit points when the vibe just wouldn't come and the band would just sit around for days at a time waiting for the inspiration to strike. Other times, the feeling of the song would gush over them, and it would come together quickly and naturally. It made for an interesting recording dynamic, boredom followed by frenzied activity. Amos was intrigued with the idea of changing up her style as well. The hit dance remix of "Professional Widow" had her thinking more about electronic dance beats, different instrumentation, and sturdy grooves.

Her shift from the traditional piano ballads that were her stock in trade on *Little Earthquake* to more experimental, alternative music had been coming over the past two albums. She certainly was not going to give up on the traditional-sounding Amos fare, but now more than ever she was going to tweak the world's notions of what a Tori Amos song was all about. "I'd taken the 'girl and the piano' thing as far as I could, and I really wanted to be a player with other players," she told *Billboard*. "It was very important for my growth as a musician to play with other musicians instead of having them play around me."[7]

Not only that, she was willing to change the world's point of view on her in general. Tori Amos had finally met the man she was going to marry. She wanted to become a mother. She had been through two miscarriages. Perhaps it was time to put aside some of the young girl beliefs and—dare we say it—seem more of an adult. Amos told British music magazine *Vox* that the whole "kooky" Amos persona was just that, an act. She does have her flaky side, but she is also much more centered than people gave her credit for. Particularly in the U.K., they loved to paint her as a kooky redhead, and she was willing to oblige. However, that wasn't all that she was about.

"The record is really about the life force," she told *Columbia House*, "and that no matter what you go through, there are days that are going to be really bad days. To tell yourself there aren't any, I think, is the cruelest thing you can do to yourself.... I found a beauty in sorrow because I got to know her. As I got to spend time putting my feet in the water next to her, and listening to her, I realized, she likes a giggle and a high heel and probably a rave on Friday nights. It's not as if she doesn't have giggles in her world. She just understands where tears come from. More than anything, she's not afraid of them. As I really got to know this, there was a calmness that started to happen inside myself after I'd lost the baby. This record isn't about loss, but there's a thread of that in there, whether it's lovers or dreams you had or people."[8]

Musically the change was obvious in the direction of the songs she was recording. "I developed this record around rhythm," she explained in the press kit for the album. "I wanted to use rhythm in a way that I hadn't used it before; I wanted to integrate my piano with it." Therefore, she and the band took a live-in-the-studio approach to the new songs. It was much more of a band effort than ever before, much more a shifting of sounds and pulsing rhythms and massive beats. Amos felt that she had to bring her best work in just to keep up, and this sense of uncertainty and adventure was bringing out the best in her. "The piano player knew her head was on the chopping block with this one," she continued. "She really had to practice hard to be able to play with these guys."[9]

So practice she did. It paid off, because *From the Choirgirl Hotel* turned out to be her most adventurous album yet. The free-falling frenzy of the recording process brought out a whole new side of Tori Amos, one more way of showing us that we were just plain wrong if we thought that we had Tori Amos figured out. Of course the lyrics were some of the most heartfelt and saddest of her career. Being based on the tragic loss of a child, even an unborn one, it could not help but be introspective on the meaning of life. It also touched upon all of the stages of grief, the anger, the helplessness, the depression, and the confusion. The songwriting process as a whole had turned out to be rather therapeutic to Amos. People had trouble talking to her about her miscarriages, and she, too, felt uncomfortable discussing them. So Tori Amos did what she always had done—she dealt with the feelings by turning them into music.

The album may be sad, but at the same time it was not as somber as the preceding album had been. She came out on the other side with hope, and in general her life was more settled than it had been just a couple of years before. If she'd called her previous albums diaries and impressionist paintings, the current one was more of a short story collection. It was a significantly autobiographical one, but a short story collection nonetheless. Amos said that she believed this was her most complete collection to date. Any of the songs worked as an individual entity, a separate piece of a picture that did not need the others to be whole. That the songs worked well together, got along, and could learn and play together was a nice bonus.

The first song on the album was also the first single. "Spark" was a stark and desolate reliving of the loss of her unborn child, with soul-baring lyrics like "She's convinced she could hold back a glacier, / but she couldn't keep Baby alive." However, instead of playing the song as a depressing dirge, musically Amos gave it a sense of life. It was sad, but it was beautiful at the same time. The swirling piano over the chorus made the song surprisingly catchy. The song became the latest and highest charting yet of Amos's American almost-hits, reaching number forty-nine on the *Billboard* singles chart. That is to this day Amos's highest chart peak.

Pretty good for a song built upon such loss and sorrow. Amos told *Deluxe* that the miscarriage had made her mad at life and at God. She had been so ready to be a mother, and now she was seeing all of the injustices of the world and motherhood. "Going into a shopping mall and seeing some woman knock the head off her child, I'm going, 'So this is fair?' I don't know where the spirit went, whether she picked another mummy, like, 'Okay, choose her, then! Hope you're tone-deaf!'"[10]

The dance beats came out in force in the second song on the album, "Cruel." Full of odd instrumentation and strangely metronomic percussion by Chamberlain, it shows clearly that Amos's adventures in the dance world created by others had not fallen on deaf ears. In fact, it became a song that she felt stood out on the album. "I think 'Cruel' is my favorite. Whether anybody gets it or not, I demanded that it have its day in the sun. It's one of those ones that's really that underworld thing."[11] Amos returned to the more traditional sound in "Black-Dove (January)," a beautiful piano ballad.

The real change was pointed out with the next song. "Raspberry Swirl" was a dance track, pure and simple, as far away from Amos's piano-based fare she had ever dared to delve. This was music for a rave, a celebration of beats and textures. Contextually it was about Amos's relationships with her female friends. Amos felt it was interesting that she could love them and want to be there for them even though it was not a sexual thing. But the song could be perceived to have sexual overtones. However, Amos considered it to be more of a look at the roles of the sexes. "I wrote it, for one of my girlfriends who just had a streak of men who really didn't get her," she explained to the *Louisville Observer.* "Sometimes I play the role of the man in my relationships with my female friends. I'm not talking physical; I'm talking on an emotional level. And so this is about being understanding. That if I were six-foot-four and had one less hole and a couple more round hairy things, there's no way that these men would be able to compete. Because I really think that they miss the beauty in the women that I find really attractive. They really miss it."[12]

Two different things inspired the song "Jackie's Strength." The fact that Amos was getting married had her thinking about the whole institution and the leap of faith that it took for anyone. In a more abstract way, the widowed former First Lady Jacqueline Kennedy Onassis, who died a few years before, brought about the song. "The songs just grab me by the throat sometimes and say, 'We're coming in,'" Amos told *Rolling Stone*. "I saw Jackie as a bride, and I used to think I would never be a bride. I started to look at Jackie and how that woman held the country together after she watched her husband get cut down right in front of her."[13]

The guttural-sounding (and strangely titled) "i i e e e" was a song that celebrated Amos's Native American roots. Musically it was very significantly Old West (except of course for the blistering guitar solo in the middle), a respect for the wide-open vistas and plains and the sacrifices one must make to appreciate them. "'She's Your Cocaine' and 'i i e e e' came out of a sense of loss and sacrifice," she told *Performing Songwriter*. "And other songs celebrated the fact that I had found a new appreciation for life through this loss."[14] The song "She's Your Cocaine" was also one of the most blatantly rock and roll tunes that she has recorded, with a screeching vocal and a throbbing undertow that pulls the listener in, leading up to a quiet bridge that lulls you before the song pounds back in.

The drumbeat sound and quiet piano of "Liquid Diamonds" made this song, too, a throwback to the Tori of old; however, her sexy and hushed alto on the song was strangely reminiscent of the R&B group TLC. "Northern Lad" feels like an outtake from *Little Earthquakes*, an introspective tune with Amos's piano tinkling and Chamberlain's tasteful drumming being used as the only adornments to Amos's heartbreaking vocal.

The atmospheric ambient tones of "Hotel" return us to the discotheque, with a series of not-quite-natural beats leading into a more tactile feeling on the chorus. Amos says that the song is a remembrance of past loves, a realization of how even when you are happy in your current relationship they will always be a part of you. You may still care for some, you may still love some, and yet you can allow them to fade into your background. They may no longer affect you physically, but they will always play a part emotionally. Amos told *Alternative Press*, "My heart goes out to where that song comes from. It's very much about thinking you were loved for who you were, and realizing you weren't, and realizing maybe you don't love yourself. The line 'I guess you go too far / When pianos try to be guitars' is just about never being enough. I felt that with my instrument sometimes, wanting to be Jimmy Page. You can only be you. A lot of times it's never enough for people."[14]

"Playboy Mommy" was another song that sprung from the heartbreak, but it did not come out whole. She had most of the song formed, but the first line still eluded her. A trip to France with her good friend Nancy Shanks (nicknamed Beenie) and an accident finally pried that loose for the song. She was a little drunk on good local champagne and had fallen down a flight of stairs in her suite. As Beenie rushed down to help, she told Seattle radio station KNDD: "I'm lying flat and my nose is like taped to the rug and I said, 'Oh, Beenie, I need more champagne, this is so horrible.' But I laid there and I go, 'Oh, my god, Beenie, oh my god, I have a first line.'"[15]

The album closes out on the first song that Amos wrote after her miscarriage, finding it hard to come up with good reasons to get out of bed. The reason came to her naturally, as it always had, in the form of a song. "I didn't become a mother," she told the *Baltimore Sun*. "Although I owned life, I couldn't go back to being that person [I was] before…. I knew that there was some primitive agony of women losing their children that I had to dive through. And believe it or not, 'Pandora' took me by the hand and came first…. It took me by the hand, drug me under, and all of a sudden, we were off."[16] It makes a certain amount of sense for the first song to arrive to be the last one to go, and on this final tragic note, *From the Choirgirl Hotel* is done.

In the time leading up to the release of *Choirgirl*, Amos had one other important thing she wanted to do. She was going to marry Mark Hawley. The wedding was a private affair for 170 guests that was held at the Church of St. Lawrence in the lovely area of West Wycombe. Amos had chosen the area on the suggestion of friends who knew Edward Dashwood, the owner of the estate. Reverend Amos gave away the bride at the ceremony. (An Australian news weekly reported mistakenly that this was surprising because Amos and her parents were estranged.) Amos wore an ice-blue gown together with a purple cape. Waiters wore the traditional garb of monks. The bride and groom were driven away in a carriage, which was drawn by two black horses.

It all had something of a storybook quality, a mythical Arthurian feel. "It wasn't medieval in as much as…it's not like I ransacked the set of *Camelot* doing dinner theater up in Sheffield," Amos told *Q*. "We got married in West Wycombe and I just wanted something that…we wanted it really private but there is a side to me that believes in magic."[17]

Amos was mostly successful in keeping the marriage quiet from the press, but a photographer from *Hello!* magazine did catch wind of the ceremony and snap off some shots of the wedding. Even after the marriage, she tried to keep her marriage on the down low. "I've hardly told anyone, but with the Internet you can't keep anything secret. He's really, really private and I try to respect that. It's very precious and very fragile too," she told the *Times*. "I didn't get married because I didn't have anything to do. I really looked at this man and thought, 'This person is incredibly unique and I don't want to be with anybody else.' I'm trying not to say his name. I know you know it but it feels more private, you know, if I don't say it. I wanted the wedding to be real private, just our friends."[18]

One big surprise was the fact that with her stormy relationship with the church, Amos and Hawley decided to have a local reverend named Martin Gillham do the ceremony rather than having a nonreligious wedding with a judge.

"I thought about it, and if I'd got married in front of a judge, well, that wouldn't have meant anything to me. And, sure, I could have got married in the middle of the mountains and all the other nature spirits could have been there, but…in the end I tried to find a place that was very sacred. This place was an ancient site since the Bronze Age, and a pagan one before it was a church, and the vicar honored that."[19] She also says that they changed the vows a bit: they were going to love and honor, but they dropped the word *obey*.

Soon after the wedding, Amos appeared on the cover of the British music magazine *Q*. She wore a gold plastic breastplate that made it appear that she had been just doused with gold paint, nipples straining through their slight cover. Next to this in huge letters was the headline " 'How can I be a sacred being and a hot pussy?' You tell us, Tori Amos."[20] It wasn't a huge deal when she did it. Amos was used to selling somewhat provocative images of herself to help get the music noticed. Most of her family and friends knew it was part of the circus, just another way of selling herself. However, suddenly, as the magazine was hitting news-stands all over London and the world, Amos realized that she had a whole new series of responsibilities. She was getting along well with her new mother-in-law, but they still didn't know each other all that well. Amos suddenly realized that she didn't want this to be one of the woman's early impressions of her. She called Mark, panicked, and told him that he had to keep his mother away from the news dealers for the next month or so. He laughed and told her that his mother had already purchased the magazine and that she had loved the cover.[21]

Amos and Hawley had barely gotten back from the honeymoon when the process of getting *From the Choirgirl Hotel* out to the public started to rear its head. Amos created the album's distinctive artwork with photographer Katerina Jebb by literally having herself Xeroxed. "Picture this," she told *Q*. "There's a photocopy office, the fluorescent light is still buzzing and there I am snogging the massive machine in the corner."[22] It certainly wasn't the easiest way of going about it; each shot took about seven minutes. However, it gave the album artwork a distinctive, otherworldly look.

Atlantic Records was excited by the prospects of the album, although even they had to admit at this point that they were never sure what would work for Amos and what wouldn't. They'd just come to trust that she would be able to connect with her swelling following. *Boys for Pele* had been her best-selling album yet, and on the heels of the reissue of "Silent All These Years," the momentum was looking good. Even though the album was on a sad subject, it was more accessible than *Pele*. As her new husband, Mark Hawley, told *Sound on Sound* magazine, "The last album was quite a classical-sounding thing and a very personal project for Tori. It did extremely well in the States and it will always be one of my favorites, but the record company was rather unsure about it. I guess it was not too great on radio because it was so dynamic, and so this time we decided to make a bit of a pop album."[23]

Not that everyone respected her suffering for her art. In a syndicated article previewing albums due in the spring of 1998, writer Jim Farber gave her the very backhanded compliment, "After three platinum LPs, the world's most self-involved modern singer-songwriter, Tori Amos, is releasing her fourth full-length album. The buzz on Amos has been increasing and so has her audience. Expect another hit."[24] Other writers looked forward to the album more enthusiastically. *Alternative Press* called *From the Choirgirl Hotel* one of the "25 Most Anticipated Albums of 1998."[25]

The anticipation was well founded. *From the Choirgirl Hotel* sold 153,000 copies in its first week alone…higher than even *Pele*, although it debuted lower on the charts (*Hotel* debuted at number five to *Pele*'s two.) "Spark" and "Jackie's Strength" became Amos's two highest-charting singles ever in the U.S. (numbers forty-nine and fifty-four, respectively). Amos was yet again making the talk-show circuit, hitting *Letterman* and *Leno*. It seemed like she was on the cover of every music magazine on the racks. Beyond the infamous *Q* cover, she also graced the front of *Rolling Stone*, *Musician*, and others.

Things were going so well that it was decided for the first time for Amos to tour with a whole band. In the past she had mostly done concerts solo on piano, or took Steve Caton on the road on guitar. They decided to call the new trek the "Plugged" tour. The name was a play on a joke she had made on the popular series *MTV Unplugged* that since she was always unplugged, this episode of the show should be called "Plugged." Joining Amos and Caton on the road were drummer Matt Chamberlain and bassist Jon Evans. "There's something about the first time for anything," she told CNN.com. "The newness of being with the band—now is the time to put it out there."[26]

Amos's 1998 "Plugged" U.S. tour began with a set of twelve band shows played at much smaller clubs than Amos would normally play. She headlined in places like the Irving Plaza in New York, the Fillmore in San Francisco, the Electric Factory in Philadelphia, the Chili Pepper in Fort Lauderdale, and the Park West in Chicago. The club shows were planned as a way for the group to get the kinks out before they started playing their normal stadiums. Amos wanted the tour to be a gift for the longtime fans, a way for them to see the show in a more personal setting. She severely limited the number of press tickets given out. Usually, if Atlantic would give them out at all, it was one ticket maximum to members of the press, which was against the tradition of the "plus one." Amos didn't want a bunch of glad-handing journalists at these special shows. This was for the hard-core fans.

"More than anything, the sneak preview is just what it is: It's like the audience is watching us sort it all out," she told the *Detroit Free Press*. "That's why I wanted to do it in really small clubs, where it's more intimate. People are a little more not-so-mean-and-nasty. I wanted them to feel like we were in their living room, like some local band that's trying to figure it out. You know, friends playing in front of friends."[27]

Atlantic once again used the Internet as a way to promote the new Amos album. They put together a promotion with Tower Records so that if someone preordered *From the Choirgirl Hotel*, they would receive a free music download of an unreleased Amos track called "Merman." It was a new type of download, an antipiracy technology called A2B music, which made the song playable only on the computer it was downloaded onto. The problem with this, of course, is that the song was only good for as long as the computer was good, and way too much time and money has been spent by the computer industry to make computers obsolete immediately after they are purchased. So if you downloaded the song, you could not play it if you traded up. The song was never released on any other Amos album or maxi-single, but the next year it was used on the various-artist charity album *No Boundaries: A Benefit for the Kosovar Refugees*.

While the Internet was being used to promote her, Amos herself had become rather wary of it. She had always refused to go on the fan sites that were dedicated to her. She felt this would be an invasion; that the people should be able to say what they wanted without worrying about her reaction. However, as a celebrity and a woman in the public view, she was finding that many personal fights or conversations she had in public would get posted online—or often a distorted view of the occurrence. The final straw happened when she was touring and had forgotten some underwear in her hotel room, only to find out that they were being shopped around the Internet. It all seemed like a huge invasion of her privacy, and for someone who had been in the spotlight for years, she cherished her privacy. If this important source of world communication and information was being squandered to tell what color panties she wore during a concert sound check, well, that was the kind of brave new world that she had no interest in being a part of.[28] There had to be boundaries. She needed some privacy in her world, too. "I talk to a lot of strangers through my music," she told CNN.com. "But it's not like I sit down with everybody and have spaghetti afterwards."[29]

Looking to the future.

Amos throwing herself into a live performance. PHOTO BY JIM RINALDI

"Excuse me, but can I be you awhile?"
PHOTO COURTESY OF PHOTOFEST

Publicity still, circa *Little Earthquakes*.

Posing for *Under the Pink*.

Photo promoting *From the Choirgirl Hotel*.

Getting dirty for *Boys for Pele*.

Getting back to the land for *Scarlet's Walk*.

Relaxing in her garden in *The Beekeeper*.

Straddling her beloved Bösendorfer. PHOTO BY JIM RINALDI

The passion of
performance.
PHOTO BY JIM RINALDI

Turning on the rock star lighting. PHOTO BY JIM RINALDI

Marquee from Tower Theater, Philadelphia, May 1–3, 1996.
PHOTO BY JIM RINALDI

Looking playful in concert. PHOTO BY JIM RINALDI

Amos's unique piano style. PHOTO BY JIM RINALDI

"Never was a cornflake girl..." PHOTO BY JIM RINALDI

"I relate more to the fire." PHOTOS BY JIM RINALDI

chapter 7

Glory of the Nineties

After the deep emotional strain of putting together *From the Choirgirl Hotel*, Amos decided she wanted to take it easy a bit. On the "Plugged" tour she let several reporters know that she had decided her next album would be a live album. There were a couple of reasons for this. First of all, she really didn't feel up to throwing herself into another series of songs. Not only that, she realized that she had become one of the most bootlegged artists in music. She was tired of inferior recordings of her live music and rare nonalbum tracks being out there, making money for criminals and cheating her core fans with questionable sound quality. Maybe it was just as simple as the fact that Tori Amos is hugely territorial about her work, and she wanted to make sure that at least one live recording lived up to her high standards. Either way, the plan was clear. The next album was going to be a concert recording.

Plans have a way of not turning out the way you expect, though, and the album *To Venus and Back* is just further proof of this. By the time she was off the tour, she was thinking that maybe she'd prefer to add a second disc of what the Who once so memorably called "odds and sods," some B-Sides, rarities, and oddities to make the album more special for the fans. In an America Online chat in January 1999, she told her Internet fans, "We go into the studio the end of February and start putting the live part of the double box set together.... It includes B-sides and some others you can't get anymore. There'll be songs that I kept, that I wasn't ready to finish. It's got a lot of different things on it. It'll be out Christmas '99. I haven't decided what to call it yet."[1] Amos went into the studio to record a new track as a bonus for the fans. One song became two, two became four, four became eight, and soon she had enough new songs to make an entire new studio recording. Which put her in a bit of a bind. She was already committed to the idea of a B-sides collection and a live album, but the new tunes just wouldn't stop coming to her.

She decided that you just couldn't ignore it when the songs start flowing. "When the muse stalks me, I start hunting her," she told *Us* magazine.[2] Amos was never one to think inside the box, so she decided to make this embarrassment of riches work to her favor. *To Venus and Back* would be an all-new studio album *and* a live one. One disc would comprise fresh recordings; a second disc would have a concert overview of her career. The B-sides would have to wait. "It became quite exciting because we had no idea we were cutting a new record," she told *Billboard*. "It just grabbed me by the throat, really. We ended up working around the clock and putting it together pretty quickly."[3]

It came together so much more rapidly than she expected that the complete project was ready to be released in the summer of 1999, not around the holidays, as she had earlier speculated in the online chat. The songs were all special to her in their own way. When asked on Los Angeles radio station KROQ's *Kevin and Bean* show if she had a favorite new tune, Amos demurred, "I know this sounds really masked but it's hard to choose. They're sort of like children to me....Well, I like the freckly fat one."

It is left up to the imagination which song is the freckly fat one. They all tend to sound rather lean and in fighting shape to me. However, *To Venus and Back* is the continuation, perhaps the culmination, of Amos's musical transformation. The wistful piano musings of *Little Earthquakes* have been left far behind. The experiments with new sounds and textures that Amos has been moving toward on the last few albums have nearly taken over. This is made all the more obvious by the inclusion of the live disc. It is an immediate reminder of the length of the journey that Amos has taken, the technical and stylistic changes that have taken root in less than a decade. In that amount of time, she had almost completely shed the Kate Bush comparisons that followed her around early in her career and was recognized as an innovator herself. A month before *To Venus and Back* would release, VH1 named Amos to its list in a special counting down the *100 Greatest Women of Rock and Roll*. Amos was number seventy-one.

To Venus and Back was most certainly an artistic step forward, although, honestly, it was not one of her more accessible albums. On the album, Amos had more fully embraced the beat-driven techno style that she had previously tested in "Raspberry Swirl." This made the music on many of the tracks a dense, churning wash of sound. It was quite obvious that Amos had been keeping track of the musical developments on the British radios and dance floors. At the time, many more established artists were toying with techno, Madonna had done the *Ray of Light* album, David Bowie did *Earthling*, and U2 had recorded *Pop*. However, Amos was more impressed by the underground movers and shakers who were founding the style, like Fatboy Slim, Armand Van Helden (who had remixed her "Professional Widow"), and Moby. In fact, at about this time, Moby asked her to perform on his latest album and Amos would have loved to do so, but could not work it into her schedule.

This stylistic twist made the studio recordings of *To Venus and Back* stand out from most everything that she had previously recorded. It also made *To Venus and Back* an album that was a little bit easier to respect for its edgy artistry than it was to actually enjoy listening to. Perhaps the review on Spin.com nailed it best when it said that the album "exchanges Amos's classic sound for a more modern, packaged one guaranteed to both titillate and annoy her legions of loyal elves."[4]

The creation was more of a fever pitch than an actual enjoyment thing, too. Amos had committed to doing a U.S. tour in July 1999, which meant that she had to have her album ready to go before that. "In doing two albums in that amount of time, I was taking on more than I had any idea I was taking on," she told the *Baltimore Sun*. "I mean, I knew it was going to be [a] constant [grind], but there were no days off. There were no breaks. There was nothing."[5] However, she was looking forward to finishing the album and to hitting the road. She and the band hadn't been able to just play together in quite some time. Sure, there was the recording, but that wasn't playing for fun. That was more of a patchwork process of combining sounds and instruments to make a whole. She considered studio time "being in the trenches."[6]

While hunkered down in those trenches, Amos and her band (which on this album included longtime collaborator Steve Caton on guitars, Matt Chamberlain on percussion, and Jon Evans on bass) were able to put a distinctive sheen on the musical tales that the songwriter was spinning. The studio album, which Amos dubbed *Venus Orbiting*, full of spinning beats and swooshing noise was definitely a departure for Amos. And, to continue her own analogy, she had certainly spent enough time in the bunkers of the music industry to have earned the right to light off in a different direction. No one had better try and tell her otherwise. Atlantic Records had long since learned that it shouldn't even bother. "I've been known to get Tourette's syndrome [a neurological disorder whose victims display uncontrollable twitching, swearing, etc.] when I meet people in the music business. I'm intolerant of rudeness," she told *Jane* magazine.[7]

Amos's newfound fascination with "what knobs do"[8] shows up on the first track and never really goes away through the eleven songs on the studio album. The first song, "Bliss," was also the first single on the album, and it showcases the better aspects of Amos's sonic makeover. It is an atmospheric, driving, and touching song that features a strong Amos vocal and swooshing musical accompaniment from the band that does not overwhelm the melody. The song is held to earth on the bedrock of Matt Chamberlain's solid drum backbeat. (Amos nicknamed Chamberlain "The Human Loop" for his extraordinary talent at staying in perfect time.)

The song's poetry is a beautiful and yet sad assessment of family ties, how you become what you are through your influences. "I guess my parents are in there," Amos acknowledged to *Mojo*, "but to me it's not just about the biological father, but also the authority figure, whoever it is that I put in that position. 'Bliss' is really about control, and about certain things in our DNA that you can't use a strainer to get rid of. You can't separate completely from whoever made you, because they're a part of you."[8]

While some of her songs came from a personal place, others were inspired by the daily news. "Juarez" tells the violent story based on a series of women's rapes and murders that were going on in the town of Juarez, Mexico. This is of course a horrific subject for a pop song. However, as Amos has demonstrated going back to "Me and a Gun," she is not afraid to prod raw nerves in her lyrics. But as touching as the story may be, the sterile modern techno beats sap the song of much of the passion that Amos has come to be known for and that the heartrending subject matter deserves. The song is a little too cluttered and the lyrics are buried a little too far down in the mix. Granted, it has a very disorienting, ghostly, eerie vibe—musically, however, it almost seems a bit cold, which is a description that could rarely, if ever, be used to describe Amos's work in the past.

Much closer to home is the lovely "Concertina." After the aggressive instrumentation of "Juarez," here is a little island of shyness and quiet civility. Here is a song that would feel as comfortable on *Little Earthquakes* as on this album. It is a calliope swirl of sound and motion with a heartfelt vocal. It is also the first song on the album where the keyboards do not feel overwhelmed by the sonic fireworks exploding around them.

"You always have to be listening to the song itself and to the soul of the song," she told Australian magazine *Time Off*. "Because sometimes there were different directions I could have taken the songs into and it's not where the song itself wanted to go." In the recording studio, Tori's band thought that the song should be played as a piano-and-voice ballad as Amos had previewed it to them earlier that day. However, the song was insisting that she look at it another way. "I wanted those electronic drums that Matt was playing with because particle by particle, she slowly changes, and I wanted the sense of the acoustic piano with the electronic drums. That also reoccurs in 'Lust.' So there was this dichotomy going on and I'm really drawn to that."[9]

When asked on an online chat on mp3.com what her tune "Glory of the 80's" was about, Amos answered, "Decadence of the eighties, which I miss, actually."[10] Indeed, on an album that is mostly looking towards the future, this song was a nostalgic tribute to her days in Los Angeles. Musically it skips along on a retro beat that makes the song one of the catchiest on the new disc. Lyrically it was a memory of Tori hanging out on the Sunset Strip and starting out in the music business putting together the band Y Kant Tori Read while trying to make it with too much hair spray and wearing tights. She even refers in the lyrics to the Crystal Light commercial she was judged wrong for because actress Raquel Welch felt she was too vibrant and stole her spotlight.

She went into more detail in an interview with VH1.com. "The decadence of the eighties in L.A. brings out a smile. I wasn't into the L.A. [hard] rock scene even though I had big hair and I had thigh-high plastic boots. I think I was more into the gothic witch thing. Pirates. It was that whole dressing-up moment, Adam Ant with tits, but not really—his were much cuter than mine or my friends'. We used to wake up and go to Retail Slut and pick up a few pieces for the week. There was a balance of thigh-high plastic boots and going to see your shaman. I liked that. It was all happening at the same time. Everything was so much on the outside, pleasing things on the outside, but there was a lot of camaraderie that I really adored. A lot of us were friends, going to see different bands. It wasn't competitive in the way it became in the nineties."[11]

She examined her married life in the song "Lust"—or rather, what was expected from married life and the prejudices that she had brought to the institution.

She was so used to imagining married people as these very adult, bunny-slipper-wearing, unadventurous people that when she found herself in the position of being a wife, she wasn't sure how she was supposed to act. Is it okay to give in to temptations, or are you supposed to settle into a more comfortable life? Is it that wrong to sometimes prefer a good night's sleep to a steamy rendezvous? Can you continue to feel the same passion for someone after you've seen him or her first thing in the morning, every morning? Amos found that she could. Just because the passion had changed did not mean that it was less valid. In fact the intimacy made things better. The song overdubs ghostly backing vocals to Amos's old-fashioned piano fill and Amos's plaintive lead, giving the track a strange power. "I really got that what lust meant to me in my twenties was very different. I've loved people and not lusted [after] them. But I found that I hadn't experienced lust until I had some kind of trust for someone."[12]

The metronome precision of the click track and atmospheric swirl of sound also do not feel out of place in "Suede," which seems to be a rather traditional Amos piano ballad overlaid by a wash of unnatural instrumentation. She explained what she was trying to get across with the song on an online chat with mp3.com. "When the other person thinks you are the evil one. They have no idea why they are part of the seduction. Of course, it's all your fault. Meaning me."[13] While working on the album, Amos had invited old friend Neil Gaiman to visit her in England, and while he was there, she had played him the unmixed versions of the songs, and this one stood out to him. When Amos asked him what he thought of the new songs, Gaiman told the *Minnesota Daily* that he told her that it seemed to be "a greatest-hits album from an alternate universe.... 'Suede' and 'Bliss' and '1000 Oceans' seem to come from three completely different worlds, taking three tracks at random. It's wonderful stuff. I think 'Suede' is my favorite. I like the creepiness of it."[14]

An almost military-sounding drum lead by Matt Chamberlain drives the next song, "Josephine." In the song, Amos returns to the royal families of Europe for inspiration (they also were the spirit behind "Yes, Anastasia" on *Under the Pink*). This time Amos is singing of Empress Josephine, living alone in Paris while her husband, Napoleon, was fighting the Russians. "Josephine" is the closest thing to a traditional Tori Amos song on *Venus: Orbiting*, with the song driven just by piano, percussion, and Amos's impassioned singing. It is just a short, sweet, look backwards and the fact that it works so well without the intrusion of a complicated bed of instruments accents the fact that sometimes, for Amos, simplicity is a virtue.

I hate to mention Kate Bush again after all the work Amos has done to ward off the comparisons throughout her career, but "Riot Poof" is somewhat reminiscent of some of the more experimental soundscapes that crop up on the second side of Bush's *Hounds of Love* album. It is also oddly reminiscent of Amos's own "Raspberry Swirl." Amos found the inspiration for the song when she was on tour. Her chef for the trek was famous British chef Darren Staats, who had become a private chef for many touring musicians, including Madonna, Erasure, and Sporty

Spice. Staats was a thirty-two-year-old closeted homosexual who finally decided to acknowledge that he was gay. "Because I was cooking for Tori Amos when I came out, she wrote a song about me," Staats told the Web site UK.Gay.com. "It was called 'Drama Queen,' which, when translated into Dutch and back into English becomes 'Riot Poof,' so that's what she called it."[15]

"Datura" is a collage of sound that is more impressive as a technical exercise than it is as a song. It has a weird, hallucinatory sensation, eight minutes of otherworldly recitations of herb names and altered lyrics. This druggy impression makes perfect sense, as the title refers to a plant that can be used as a drug, but it must be done very carefully or the person taking it can die. Amos was growing it in her garden at her Florida home when Hurricane Irene hit in 1999. The entire garden was destroyed, except for the datura. Actually, as her futuristic experiments on the album go, this is probably one of the better ones simply as far as bizarre catchiness, although the words seem almost like a long, disjointed haiku.

Actually, in the song she is cataloging an oddly sexual list of different kinds of plants in her garden, followed by a few minutes of Amos repeating "Dividing Canaan" over and over again. Honestly, the song goes on probably three minutes longer than it should. Strangely, the song is also meant as a look at the differences between the sexes, although one has to do a little spelunking to find this connection. In writing the song Amos started to compare the plant to men. It could be wonderful or it could be poisonous. "Men can be dangerous," Amos told *Attitude*, "like in the song 'Datura' about how sometimes they can bring you gold and sometimes they can be the bearer of poison. The plant datura is a hallucinogen and it's like men. If you get the right amount, you'll walk into the garden and become a woman, but if too much seeps in the wrong way and at the wrong time, it'll kill you."[16]

After the trippy excesses of the two previous songs, the relatively simple, vaguely reggae-tinged "Spring Haze" is a bit of a shock. This song is more of a curio, a delicate gossamer confection that starts off nearly a capella with just an unobtrusive piano in deep background. As the song moves from verse to chorus, a tasteful swash of instrumentation serves as a spice to the song—it adds flavor without ever coming close to overwhelming the taste of the original melody.

The studio disc closes out on another delicate meditation on life and death, with the gorgeous "1000 Oceans." Amos has said that the song came to her in a dream, when an older African woman visited her. Amos could not understand her language, but the woman suggested the melody in her speech. The tune ended up having particularly deep meaning to Amos. Mark Hawley's father died of cancer in February 1999, while they were working on the album. Hawley was an only child and very close with his father. He had believed that his father was recovering, and then suddenly the man was just gone, leaving her husband distraught. Amos admitted that she was having trouble getting through to Hawley because he was so upset. Then he kept asking her to play the ocean song, and Amos came to realize that the tune was having a very different meaning for her husband than she had originally intended. The song "1000 Oceans" became the light in the darkness for Hawley, a salve for his sorrow. The two of them turned the song into an anthem for the people who were gone from their lives.

These last two songs returned the fans to the style of music that they had been more accustomed to from Tori Amos. However, the first disc as a whole was a departure for Tori Amos. One that was sometimes successful and sometimes not so lucrative, but at least Amos was not just repeating herself. She was stretching her art and delving into corners that were new to her. The best part of the collection was that those homesick for the old Tori Amos sound just have to switch discs to the live half of the package, called *Venus Live: Still Orbiting*. Unlike most live recordings, this could not exactly be called a concert recording of Amos's greatest hits. Significantly absent were favorites like "Silent All These Years," "God," "Caught a Lite Sneeze," "Crucify," "Raspberry Swirl," "Winter," "Pretty Good Year," "Cruel," "Professional Widow," "China," and more. In fact, on the live recording, only "Cornflake Girl" was a significant hit.

Instead the disc was made up of favorite album tracks and lesser-known songs. These were the best performances from her 1998 "Plugged" tour. Some were faithful to their source material. For example, "Precious Things" stays pretty close to the studio recording. "Mr. Zebra" is a similarly jaunty experience live, as is "Spacedog." Others were more deconstructed. "Cornflake Girl" has an entire intro added before settling into the recognizable beats. "Cruel" has a much sharper buzz-saw guitar attack. "Waitress" is nearly unrecognizable. The song, which was always rather deliberate anyway, is slowed down to a dirge pace, dripping more menace and vengeance than the more unhinged studio version. All in all, though, the live disc was as good a live album as you could hope for from Tori Amos.

Atlantic kept up with its campaign to use Amos's music as a vessel to experiment with marketing on the Internet. The new single, "Bliss," became the first song released on a major label to be sold via download through multiple Web music retailers. (Earlier singles like Duran Duran's "Electric Barbarella" had been sold on the Web, but only through their record company's Web site.) Atlantic Group co-chairman and co-CEO Val Azzoli explained the decision in a press release: "The time has clearly arrived for online downloads to become another readily available retail format, alongside the familiar CD, cassette, and vinyl. Tori Amos, who has long enjoyed a tremendous Web following and has been a powerful advocate of new media, is the ideal artist to initiate the widespread commercial launch of the download format."[17]

It didn't seem to work as well as her label would have hoped, though. With peer-to-peer services like Napster and KaZaA offering music for download for free (although, granted, doing it illegally), it was hard to talk Web-savvy consumers into pay for the download. They seemed to believe why pay the $0.99 to $1.99

that the official sites were charging when they could get it for nothing. Amos and Atlantic saw this as just another technically up-to-date way of bootlegging. Eventually some of the sites offered "Bliss" up for free if the user prepurchased *To Venus and Back* from the site. Still, five months after Atlantic launched the ambitious campaign, *Sound and Vision* magazine said that only 1,200 downloads were done.

This apathy did not bode well for the album, and while it did fairly well, it was considered something of a disappointment. Sales were pretty much stalled at her base of fans, and even some of them balked a bit in regard to her new sound. Also, for the first time in her career, the singles from the album did worse than the previous albums'. "Bliss" just barely dented the U.S. charts and later singles "1000 Oceans" and "Glory of the 80's" did not reach at all.

The pop music world was evolving yet again, and the intelligent female singer-songwriters who were the rage just a year before were being replaced by pop tarts—attractive, created-by-committee singers who were willing to do any song the record labels would send their way. In a new atmosphere where teenyboppers like Britney Spears, Christina Aguilera, Jessica Simpson, and Mandy Moore held sway, inventive singer-songwriters suddenly seemed quaintly old-fashioned. But Amos was out there, pushing for her newest creation. She once again hit *The Late Show with David Letterman* and *The Tonight Show.* She did many radio interviews to keep the buzz going. She was in almost every magazine imaginable. However, perhaps the best-selling point for the album was the interesting new tour she used to preview the CD.

In the months leading up to the release of *To Venus and Back,* she decided to hit the road with singer Alanis Morissette, who had released one of the biggest albums of 1996 with *Jagged Little Pill.* The so-called 5½ Weeks Tour (although it ended up lasting nine weeks) was a bit of a surprise pairing. Amos had insisted when discussing Lilith Fair that she felt it was important to have a little testosterone on a tour lineup. However, somehow the matchup with Morissette seemed to make sense. Morissette was promoting the long-awaited follow-up album, *Supposed Former Infatuation Junkie,* which had come out late the previous year. As with Amos, Morissette's latest had met with a bit of resistance in a new radio world that valued beats over tunes. However, both had a strong audience base.

Agreeing to this tour was a change in ideas for Amos in several ways. Beyond the concept of sharing her audience with a fellow female star, Amos had earlier been rather dismissive of Morissette's breakthrough album. In *Q* magazine a year before the tour was conceived, Amos had said that while she liked Morissette as a person, she just couldn't handle the CD. It was not even because of the songwriting or Morissette's singing, but on account of the album's production. "I have a hard time listening to that record, just on a sonic level. It would make a dog's ears hurt. I hate records that have so much high end and no bottom."[18]

Morissette took the criticism in good spirit, though, when asked about Amos's "dog's ears" reference in her own article in *Q,* Morissette was philosophical. "I was very inspired by her," Morissette said. "Inspired by her empowerment through her vulnerability. I'll always be a fan. Everyone has their opinion. Whether they love it or hate it, I just think being in the public eye and sharing music is an amazing way for people to define themselves....People loving it or hating it, I just take it in the same way. Other people's relationship to what I do doesn't really affect me that much."[19]

She took it in such good spirit, in fact, that her people contacted Amos about the idea of doing a series of concerts together. By the time the tour came about, though, Amos and Morissette had come to an agreement. "Alanis put me in charge of food and wine. I'm hoping she handles hair, because I'm not known for having any knowledge on that end."[20] (For the record, Amos has said that she handles her own hair regimen to keep her distinctive red with peroxide 30, Clairol Torrid Torch Crimson, and Beautiful Reds Rosewood Brown. The cost of the treatment was approximately $3.70 every five weeks.)[21] However, to keep her part of the deal, Amos brought along her own personal chef who specialized in Greek cuisine and some nice wines from Tuscany.[22]

Touring with Morissette opened Amos's eyes to the other singer's work, too. What had not moved her on CD was suddenly connecting, with Amos saying that she was particularly fond of Morissette's single "Hand in My Pocket." During a dual chat with Morissette on America Online to promote the tour, Amos said, "I'm excited about the tour because when [I] hear another person's work live....I start having a relationship with it. Once I hear someone's work on a CD, because I'm in my own little world when I listen and I don't have those visuals. You know we don't have those huge artwork things that we can take around anymore. To get the real person's essence when they're singing that I feel like songs shift when they start coming out live. Having done a few shows now, I still really get excited about how the songs change with each tour and they're always showing me different sides that I missed. So I'm sure when I'm standing from the stage watching your show that there are certain songs that I will see in ways that I haven't before and that always excites me, being able to be near the essence of the person who wrote it. And I really enjoy it. I like that."[23]

The whole tour became a study in cooperation. It was billed as a dual tour and each artist had the same time onstage, about seventy-five minutes. Amos was always the opening act. Morissette always closed things out. Morissette had actually suggested that they flip-flop the positions for the different shows, sometimes Amos would open and sometimes she would. However, Amos was secure enough in her career that she felt that would be an unnecessary ego stroke. She knew she wasn't being looked at as Alanis Morissette's opening act. It didn't really matter who went on first—the tour was for both of them. Of course, there was also the added dynamic of what each artist's fans would think of the other. "I said to her, 'Are we both confident enough that your audience will come early and stay, and that mine won't leave early?' We knew we had to have the courage to do this, and it's working," she told the *Boston Globe*.[24]

Most importantly, Amos just enjoyed hanging out with her fellow headliner before the show, catching up on the day's events, talking about music, and, even better, not talking about music. They became good friends as the tour crisscrossed America. Not that they were hanging around all of the time when not onstage, but they made sure to leave time to have a spot of tea and just relax whenever possible.

On November 11, 1999, soon after the London show of her concert tour, misfortune occurred yet again for Amos. For the third time in as many years, she had a miscarriage. She and Mark were distraught. They had been in Paris when Tori started hemorrhaging. They went to England by train. She didn't realize it was the fetus. She was afraid that she had become ill. But as she lay in the hospital, the nurse looked at her and told her that there was no heartbeat. Amos and Hawley decided to go to Florida to try and keep their minds off of their sorrow. They lived in their beach house and spent a lot of time on the powerboat, taking it out on the water every day.

Even though she had not lived in the U.S. full-time for years, she kept up with the comings and goings of her homeland and she had kept her citizenship. Amos decided to vote for third-party candidate Ralph Nader in the infamous Florida election where both Republican George W. Bush and Democrat Al Gore claimed they had won the state, and thus the country. Eventually the votes were not even counted, due to a ruling by the U.S. Supreme Court, which depending on whom you ask may or may not have been a partisan decision. Amos did not regret her vote for the very unlikely candidate; she felt he had some very good ideas and policies, and she had come to feel that she could not trust professional politicians. However, in the years since, Amos has been quietly vocal in her distrust of the man handed the election, George W. Bush, who reminded her way too much of the people who had made her start to question the church in the first place.

Amos was also asked several times in interviews when *To Venus and Back* was coming out about the plane crash that killed John F. Kennedy Jr. and his wife. Since Amos's song "Jackie's Strength" was based on the young man's mother, it seemed a natural question. Since she was in England when the crash happened, she observed the occurrence on two different levels. As an American whose mother had worshipped his president-father (who was assassinated when Amos was just three months old), it was a jolt; she knew that the Kennedys were as close to royalty as Americans got. Europeans didn't have the history with the family, so they tended to look at it more as a conspiracy. In the long run, Amos decided, the young man seemed to have a good head on his shoulders and believed in trying to help the world. "Integrity's a hard thing to find these days," she told KROQ-FM, "and I don't know if any of our leaders…in that position really have it, and that's the sad thing."[25]

For Christmas, Amos and Hawley returned to Cornwall. Tori gave away all of the presents that she had bought for the coming baby. In January she was pregnant again. At first she thought that she had contracted the stomach flu. Food and wine all tasted funny. Amos called her sister, Marie, who told her that had she better go out and buy a home pregnancy test. Four positive tests later, Amos and Hawley were finally convinced. They were thrilled, and yet they were worried at the same time. After three miscarriages, they wondered if they could possibly see this fetus to full term.

Amos and Hawley returned to her home area of Washington, D.C., to see a specialist in April 2000. The ultrasound was successful, and Amos and Hawley were able to see the baby moving, alive inside her. At this point Amos decided to not drive herself into a frenzy worrying about the baby, just to relax as much as she could and do whatever was necessary to facilitate a safe childbirth. She was not going to obsess about the little things; she was just going to enjoy the work of becoming a mother.[26]

During this time, Amos kept a little active in music, contributing a track called "Carnival" to the soundtrack of the Tom Cruise film *Mission: Impossible II*. However, as the pregnancy went on, she did not want to get involved with anything that would cause her too much stress. The filmmakers actually asked Amos to fly to L.A. to do some more work on the song slightly before its release in May, but Amos politely refused, saying that right now she was conserving her energy toward childbirth. Amos hoped that the producers could use the song as is, but told them if they couldn't, she understood. The song was released as she had originally done it on the soundtrack.[27]

She also continued whenever possible to help her charity. One opportunity was a particular stroll down memory lane. As a fund-raiser for RAINN, the white baby grand piano that Amos used to play in the Georgetown club Mr. Smith's was auctioned off. In the years since she had worked at the bar, the bartender Bill Reckert (part of the family that owned the place) had taken the piano for himself. He taught his daughters on the piano, and also had kept it because of the novelty that one of its users had become a famous musician. The piano ended up bringing in slightly more than $5,000, half of which went to RAINN.[28]

As the childbirth drew near, a specialist found a condition that had been missed by the doctors who had been caring for Amos during her previous pregnancies. A protein deficiency made her likely to get blood clots, a condition that might explain the previous miscarriages. The specialist prescribed Heparin to the pregnant singer. She took shots of the drug in her legs twice daily to control the condition.[29]

In July 2000, Tori did a photo spread for Sam Jones of *Vanity Fair*, lying across a bed, looking very pregnant and happy. It would not be released until the magazine's November issue. By the time it hit the racks, Tori Amos would no longer be pregnant. Finally, after so much heartbreak in trying, Tori Amos had given birth to a little girl. Natashya Lórien Hawley was born on September 5, 2000. She was seven pounds and one ounce and measured twenty-one inches. Amos's management shared the good news, sending out a press release that exclaimed, "Tori Amos announces long-awaited new release: a baby girl!" In the press release, the giddy mother showed her joy in the way that only she could, telling people that after feeding Natashya she realized the breast milk was even more intoxicating than the best tequila.[29] Her daughter had been born safely. Tori Amos was finally a mother.

chapter 8
Covers Girl

Throughout her entire career, Tori Amos has made a specialty of rethinking other artists' songs and making them her own. She had a long history of doing adventurous cover versions in concert and had also released several as bonus tracks on EPs and CD maxi-singles. So, even though she was known and respected as a songwriter, it was only a matter of time before she recorded an album completely made up of other musicians' tunes. Tori Amos was not going to go into a project like this haphazardly, though, and just throw out a bunch of songs she liked. She wanted to come up with an interesting angle for the collection. She decided that the ideal choice would be to pick a group of songs that were decidedly masculine and sing them from a woman's perspective. "I've always found it fascinating how men say things," she explained to *Mojo* while still in the recording process, "and how women hear them."[1]

An article that she read in the *Guardian* (Manchester) inspired the idea, at least partially. It was written in March 2001, an inside look at the pornography industry written by Martin Amis. In the article, one adult actress said that she found the vagina to be "bullshit." The ass, on the other hand, was quite nice, she said. Amos was touched by this woman's deception (and possibly self-hatred). But it got her thinking of the way that sex was sold as a commodity, and usually it was mixed in with violence and debasing the very people who were being put on the market. This type of idea was prevalent because sometimes men and women both bought into antiquated stereotypes and ideals of what was a woman's worth.[2]

As a new mother, Amos was even more fascinated by the place of a woman in the world. It not only affected her, now it was a condition that would be a vital part of Natashya's life as well. Perhaps she could come to understand it better by looking at women as men looked at them, and then filtering it back through her personal experiences and her system of beliefs. Maybe, for example, she could help make sense of how rapper Eminem could write a song like " '97 Bonnie and Clyde," which was a fever-dream fantasy about the Real Slim Shady violently murdering his wife, Kim, as their daughter watched. Maybe if she tilted the perspective and she sang it in the character of the victim, it would take on a different meaning, a different dynamic.

"I believe in freedom of speech, but you cannot separate yourself from your creation," she told the *Los Angeles Times*. "We go back to the power of words, and words are like guns....Whether you choose the graciousness of Tom Waits or the brutality of 'Bonnie and Clyde,' they're equally powerful, and that's what drove me."[3] Another thing that drove Amos was that the other people's songs were like playing dress-up. In honor of this, Amos created thirteen distinct characters, one for each of the songs (except for Neil Young's "Heart of Gold," which got twins). She dressed in costumes to play the different personalities of the songs. Inside the CD booklet of the package, Amos poses in a series of retro-looking glamour shots in which she is playing a totally different person. We get Tori as glamour-puss, librarian, gun moll, lady cop, club girl, mom, angel of death, party girl, goth, cosmopolitan, spy twins, debutante, roller girl, and butch lesbian. The obvious conceit of the packaging is that we are going to see all sorts of conflicting and surprising views of who and what Amos is.

Or rather, who she isn't. Because, though Amos did understand and sympathize with each of her heroines, they are all still fictional to her. They are all roles. *Strange Little Girls* is music as an acting exercise. Which is not to say that Amos did not feel strongly about what she was doing, it is just that she was exploring herself and the gender gap through the work of others. As always with her cover versions, Amos takes some serious liberties with the structures of the original models. In this way, she imposes herself upon the artistry of others. Here she is placing her own positions and beliefs into the mix. Here she compels some femininity and feeling upon a series of songs that are very masculine in their viewpoint. Amos even collaborated with friend Neil Gaiman on a series of short stories about the characters of the songs. "Well, they are all powerful songs written by male artists," Amos told Virgin.net. "Each one has its own unique story and voice, and I wanted to try and inject a female voice and expression to them. It does not come from an interest in the particular artists, it is the message, passion, and power of the songs."[4]

Many of the songs she did not choose herself—she instead had a "laboratory of men," male friends who made suggestions of songs that moved them. These included her band for the album, drummer Matt Chamberlain, former King Crimson guitarist Adrian Belew, bassists Justin Meldal-Johnsen (from Beck's band), and Jon Evans. (This was the first album that Amos recorded in which guitarist Steve Caton did not appear since she was signed by Atlantic fifteen years earlier.) "Straight men, gay men, all sorts of men contributed ideas," says Amos. "It was tricky to assemble this material because a lot of the songs just didn't work. But the men were my control group. They brought the songs to me that meant something to them as men."[5] They suggested songs that soothed them and songs that made them uncomfortable.

"I kept my interpretations under my hat until the eleventh hour because I was not seeking approval," she said on the Web site RedDirect.com. "I'm not having a relationship with the song mothers—the male writers—I'm having a relationship with their song children. My loyalty was to the integrity of the work, not to the composers."[6] Some of the song children are misogynistic; some of them are just a little thoughtless, and most of them don't have happy endings. However, by shifting perspective on them, by looking at the songs through a different window, many of them find a fragile, sad beauty and a ring of truth. Other costumes, sadly, are kind of a bad fit for Amos. But it took bravery to try them on and model them for the entire world to see.

It also brings to mind a basic flaw with the concept of the CD. Boiled down to the meat of the matter, the songs are all about the hurtful things that men can say and do to women. It is a valid point and certainly worthy of scrutinization. However, it's not exactly a Eureka-stop-the-presses moment of insight. This same idea has made Oprah Winfrey and Dr. Phil rich. The *Lifetime* network has created a twenty-four-hour-a-day oasis to this belief (with occasional reruns of *The Nanny* and *The Golden Girls* sprinkled in). However, when Amos was in Florida nursing new baby Natashya, she noticed that a lot of the songs she was hearing on the alternative stations seemed to be angry men who truly seemed to be fuming at women. Songs like "Nookie" by Limp Bizkit, "A.D.I.D.A.S." by KoRn, and even more jokey ditties like "Song for the Dumped" by the Ben Folds Five seemed to be spewing venom across the lines of the battle of the sexes. And don't even get started with rap, where it was "bitch" this and "ho" that.... It is something that Amos felt strongly enough about to devote the time and the effort to explore, and for the most part, she does it well. The review by *Entertainment Weekly* may have nailed the album, calling it "part off-the-rails feminist art project, part sheer genius."[7]

The songs start off with the Velvet Underground's "New Age." When recorded for the Underground's 1970 *Loaded* album, it was a somewhat decadent look at lustful urges and zipless sex in seventies New York. The song was literally about an aging actress giving in to her dark side. However, the group had played the composition on a live album the year before that, with different lyrics and a different thrust. Amos went back to this original recording for her version, which punctuates the stately Wurlitzer organ line with stabbing guitar lines by Belew. Amos rethinks the song so that it becomes a more desperate look at desire and the craving for another person, and how sometimes this leads people to do things that aren't in their best interest.

"It's just about passion," Amos told the *Orange County Register*. "I love the idea that when this song came out (in 1970) it was part of a new freedom movement. Freedom from this yoke that had been around mankind, womankind—the Martin Luther Kings and Gloria Steinems of the world having cut holes in walls built up in suppression. Yet now we're in a place thirty years later...[and] you're seeing hostility take hold again, this malice against women—women agreeing to be demeaned."[8] This of course fit Amos's thesis perfectly, and she ran with it. It helps that it was a terrific song to begin with, and Amos's changes in the structure and texture of the song feel very organic to it. The Velvet Underground has been covered hundreds of times over the years by everyone from Nirvana to David Bowie to New Order, and Amos's cover stands among the best of them.

The most effective moment on *Strange Little Girls* is all the more impressive because it could have easily been the showiest and emptiest gesture if left in less talented hands. Rap superstar Eminem had a huge dance-floor hit with " '97 Bonnie and Clyde," a song where he imagines killing his wife and sticking her in the trunk, and then driving to a lake with his daughter to dump the body. Marshall Mathers (Eminem's real name) was able to keep his song somewhat cartoonish, piling on the beats, boasts, and a sample from Grover Washington Jr.'s classic ballad "Just the Two of Us." Therefore, all the people getting jiggy with it all around the world probably weren't even comprehending the true horror and disturbing nature of the song. Or if they did, they didn't really care; it was just a goofy gangsta fantasy. One person who did care, who cared deeply, was Tori Amos. "I was attracted to the wife, who was faceless and nameless," she told *Blender*. "Everyone's grooving to this tune, and nobody seemed to care about her."[9]

So she did the subtlest and most powerful switch-up on the disc. Instead of singing the song from the point of view of the rampaging daddy, as Eminem did, Amos instead took the viewpoint of the murdered woman in the trunk. Even after death, she is trying to comfort her child, trying to soothe her and make what has happened all right. The comforting is not just implied in Amos's vocals, which are gentle, understanding, and selfless, but it is also put forth by the stately, quiet, almost classical musical tone of the backing music. It stays unobtrusively in the background so that the listener and the child can hear every single word, every mad moment, and every violent gesture of the murder. Amos has often said that artists have to take responsibility for what they put out, so she was going to make sure that each one of Eminem's bloody images was out there for everyone to see. "Half the world is dancing to this, oblivious, with blood on its sneakers," she told the *Daily Telegraph*. "To me, certain thoughts kicked into place really fast. It was like her hand was reaching out of the trunk and pulling me towards her and saying: 'I see this kind of differently.'"[10]

Amos was sure that there was no way that little girl could grow up normal after this horrific experience, so she pointedly followed the song with a cover of "Strange Little Girl" by longtime British faves the Stranglers. "I started to really see the influence that [the Stranglers] had on a lot of people. These were two British men, not jock-y kind of guys, not football hooligans. They're not really like that, and yet they thought that they were sexy songwriters. You know, 'Girls on the beaches / Looking at the peaches,' the whole thing. And I think they are, in a way. I was just drawn to them….What a catalog they've written."[11]

You can tell how much Amos likes them by just listening to her version of the song. It is probably the most upbeat and catchy song on the album, and she sings it with a lightness and sense of fun that is often missing on this project. Belew plays a pointed guitar line over Amos's swirling keyboards and the song skips along at a giddy pace. It is no surprise that the song was chosen to be the first single from the project. What *is* a surprise is, if you listen to the lyrics, this happy little tune is about the daughter of a murderer coming to terms with her father and her past.

The next New Wave cover doesn't quite work as well, although she does come up with an interesting rethink of Depeche Mode's synth-popper "Enjoy the Silence." It is just not a completely successful one. Silence has always been an idea that intrigued Amos, going back to her first solo single, "Silent All These Years," so she thought it would make for an interesting fit. Amos took the basic musical line of the original, but played it on piano and voice, instead of the electric beats of the original. Sadly this does no favors to the composition. It was never meant to be anything more than a vaguely cooler-than-thou single. By laying it bare, Amos just points out the fact that it was never much more than a trifle. The song also strains to fit into the theme of the disc. What does this really have to do with the way men treat women?

"Enjoy the Silence" was not the only one of the songs that became a study in minimization for her. Amos also stripped the old 10cc single "I'm Not in Love" to the bone. The original recording of the lovely song of denial and rationalization from the mid-seventies was known for its lush production, dense instrumental thrust, and a heavenly backing choir. "It's just a silly phase I'm going through," explained the singer to a woman who thought they were becoming a couple. We all know that the singer is indeed in love, and no matter how many times he keeps trying to tell himself differently, it doesn't change anything. On some level, he may not want to be in the middle of this relationship, but his weak protestations like "I keep your picture upon the wall, / It hides a nasty stain that is lying there" all ring hollow. The more he disputed it, the more obvious his passion was.

Amos decided that she wanted to come at the song from a very different viewpoint. She overlooked any irony or humor in the lyrics and the vocal performance, instead playing it completely straight. "She's a little fetish girl—she's into BDSM," Amos told *Alternative Press*. "It's all about power with her. And she's not really in love; she really isn't. She was at one time and she's having a different adventure in life. She will walk down many roads."[12] This is certainly a legitimate interpretation of what songwriters Graham Gouldman and Eric Stewart were trying to say, but truthfully it doesn't seem to be a very imaginative one. Amos scoffed at the idea that it is about a man's inability to express his love in the *Independent*. "Yeah, but the damage is done! He says, 'Don't forget it.' He says, 'It's just a silly phase I'm going through.' It's manipulation."[13] However, her take on the words is not the real problem here. It is the musical bed that Amos made to set them in.

Honestly, Amos may have cut the song's atmosphere and instrumentation back a bit too much. The overwrought melodrama of the sound was as much a part of the original tune's success as its words and music. Instead the new version is notable for its sparse instrumentation. It is simply made up of a martial drumbeat and some odd guitar noodlings by Adrian Belew. This brings Amos's voice front and center, and strangely enough, for as good of an interpretive singer as Amos can be, this doesn't work at all. Her vocal sounds affected, like she is playing a role that she really does not believe in. "I'm Not in Love" is not a disastrous miscalculation (only her version of Neil Young's "Heart of Gold" seems that far off the mark), but it is not really a triumphant experiment, either.

Much better was one song that came very close to not making it on the album before sneaking up on Amos. She didn't expect Lloyd Cole and the Commotions' "Rattlesnakes" had much chance of making it onto the final album. However, as time went by and she listened to the songs over and over, it became her favorite.

(It was also voted to be the Toriphiles' favorite song on the album by a land-slide on the Web site TheDent.com.)[14] She had known of Lloyd Cole and the Commotions from when she was living in L.A. and listened to famed radio DJ Rodney on KROQ. However, she hadn't given the song much thought in some time when her laboratory of men suggested it. She resisted for a while, until she finally just suddenly understood the song.[15] "In 'Rattlesnakes,' I loved the way that he [Lloyd Cole] was so aware of the pain that she was in, for her never-born child. And he was able to, I think, feel her in a way that sometimes that I haven't been able to feel her."[16]

The song has a gothic-folk rocking beat that and a throbbing bass line giv-ing beautiful counterpoint to the touching lyrics of the song. Amos reserved her highest praise for Cole, telling the *Washington Post*, "He's able to go inside the mind of a woman like I haven't been able to go inside the mind of a woman."[17] Cole himself said in the "Ask Lloyd" section on his Web site, LloydCole.com, that he was always flattered when someone recorded one of his songs. He did admit that he was happy that Amos was none too faithful to his vision. "I only heard it once but I didn't mind it at all. I was glad she made no attempt to stick to the original tune or beat."[18]

The one song on the album that Amos was relatively faithful to the source material was a sparse, beautiful take of Tom Waits's "Time" from his album *Rain-dogs*, which also spawned the classic song "Downtown Train." The piano-based version of the song was actually a more natural fit than even Waits's original; the song had always sounded like a natural for piano, but in a fit of instrumental ex-perimentation, Waits had performed the song on bass and accordion. "I thought about taking [it] to the organ, but I stripped it back," Amos explained to *ICE* mag-azine. "It's from the point of view of Death, so I felt you need to feel like you are sitting on the piano stool. No masks, no effects, it's right here, dry, with a little compression on the vocals."[19]

As stated before, the only true misstep here was Amos's puzzling decision to take Neil Young's country-folk lament "Heart of Gold" and turn it into a nearly unrecognizable swirl of sound. Strangely, Amos herself acknowledges that the song was far from her favorite by the Canadian icon. She greatly preferred "The Needle and the Damage Done" and "Cinnamon Girl." She has performed several other Young songs in concert over the years, such as "Old Man" and "Philadelphia." So why did she decide to take on a song she wasn't particularly close to and try to deconstruct it? Even Young has been known to disparage the original recording, saying that after it became his biggest hit ever, he was suddenly looked at as a middle-of-the-road balladeer. He never felt comfortable with that tag, so he has spent most of the rest of his career trying to prove he could not be pigeonholed, delving into all sorts of styles like rock, soul, synth-pop, rockabilly, country, and grunge. Therefore, the song was ripe for a complete reinvention.

Certainly Amos has the right to add air-raid guitars to the song and just pay lip service to some of the lyrics, which are changed from the original and mixed so low and multitracked so much that they are nearly impossible to understand. But why did she want to change a plaintive (okay, maybe just a little sappy) ballad about trying to find true love into a throbbing exploration of corporate espionage? Why did she think that it would be interesting to perform "Heart of Gold" as if she was Iggy and the Stooges banging through "I Wanna Be Your Dog"? Beats me. It didn't really work, though.

This may just be chalked up to the fact that men and women tend to see different things in the song. Amos decided to deconstruct the music because she did not appreciate what the song represented. It was nothing personal; she just didn't like the idea of a heart of gold as it was painted in the lyrics. "I adore Neil Young's music, and adore what he is as an essence," Amos told *Slamm* magazine. "However, how this song affected a lot of guys in my group was pretty consistent. And I was going, 'No, a definition of a heart of gold is not a doormat, guys, somebody who is just going to take you back every time you hurt her because she loves you.' A heart of gold is somebody who's going to say, 'Love you. Go fuck yourself!'"[20]

Strangely, the story behind the Boomtown Rats'"I Don't Like Mondays" was much more a product of the times when Amos recorded it than it was when it was originally written by punk singer and future Live Aid philanthropist Bob Geldof. It was based upon a shocking, true story of a Brenda Spencer, a tortured schoolgirl who brought a gun to school and starting to take potshots at the students who had made her life hell. Back in 1979, this kind of thing was unheard of, practically unthinkable. In the years since, Columbine High School and the Trenchcoat Mafia and many other similar occurrences have made it, if no less horrifying, at least more expected. In the original version of the song, Geldof acted as an impartial observer to the carnage; neither approving nor disapproving of what was going on, just reporting on it.

Of course, Amos could not remove herself so simply from the act. She knew the aftershocks of violence and made her version of the song much more sparse, much more immediate. The violence at the heart of the lyrics had truly become something that could happen to anyone. Amos also decided to not do the song from the point of view of the female sniper, nor from the vantage point of a fly on the wall, as Geldof had tried. Instead, Amos sang the song from the stance of a policewoman who was on the scene, who was charged with killing this girl before she took more lives. While this was not factually accurate (Spencer surrendered to the police later at her home and ended up being sentenced to twenty-five years to life in prison), it was a powerful slant on the story.

Amos decided to record the song after hearing about a school shooting in San Diego in 2001. With the spate of school shootings in the few years leading up to this, it only seemed natural. However, more importantly, she saw the violence growing all over, even in the most innocuous places. "That line about being 'switched to overload'; I've seen that happen in my own family," she told *Spin*. "My niece chased her mother with a knife the other evening—seriously. She calls me afterward and says, 'Auntie, sometimes I just get really mad.' And I'm like,

'Whew.' But that's the thing. You can't say that only the bad seeds do this. And some strange little girl has access to a certain type of weapon on that day the chip slips…. I know we have a gun culture in America. But it shouldn't be easier to get a gun than it is to get a driver's license."[21]

This problem is made even more specific on the next song, a cover of the Beatles' "Happiness Is a Warm Gun." Amos imagined it as a musical montage, with John Lennon's words playing very much a background role in the process. Instead, Amos samples from sound bites on guns and their control (or lack thereof) by George W. Bush, and his father, former President George H. W. Bush. Amos figured if she had a couple of Bushes in her song, it was only fair to have a pair of Amoses as well, and she invited her father to put on his best preaching voice and weigh in with his own view on the Second Amendment. Reverend Amos had only one proviso, that his daughter could not edit what he said to make her point. Tori agreed, saying that what he said unedited was what would most strongly make her point. Then, in case you still question what that view would be, as the song comes to a close, Amos samples news reports of the murder of the music's author, former Beatle John Lennon.

" 'Happiness Is a Warm Gun' is very much this Frank Zappa–inspired, nine-minute sort of a backdrop for the Second Amendment argument," Amos told RollingStone.com, "a song written by a man who was later killed by a gun. It was just something that I thought needed to be talked about especially after the San Diego shooting happened earlier this spring. And there's a thread between 'I Don't Like Mondays' and 'Happiness is a Warm Gun.' "[22] Amos is correct in this assessment of her own accomplishment, but this also points out the problem with this recording: it works better as a political statement than as a piece of music. Not many people are going to listen to this version over and over. At nine minutes and fifty-three seconds long, and with its heavy message, it would be too much hard work for the average listener. Instead they will take a listen, appreciate the artistry and viewpoint that went into it, and then move on to something with a bit more of a pulse.

Bassist Justin Meldal-Johnsen was the one who suggested Slayer's speed metal "Raining Blood" for the album. He told Amos that she had tried pretty much every other genre of music, from rap to New Wave to punk to country to pop, why not some metal? She asked him to play her something. He chose the album *Raining Blood* by Slayer. She listened to it and said, Okay, let's do it.

Instead of the pounding-guitar attack of the source, Amos turns the song into a cacophony on piano, a sullen wall of sound that lurks ominously over Amos's siren's call-wail. However, as always, she finds it most important to concentrate on each word and what it was saying. How when a woman sings a man's words, the emphasis and inflections will be different. She also took a bit of perverse pleasure in playing "Raining Blood" in a church. *Q* magazine said in its review of *Strange Little Girls* that the track was the editors' favorite, just because it tickled them to imagine how Slayer fans would react to the remake.[23] Their fans may not have liked it, but the band itself thought it was cool. Slayer was the only artist who contacted Amos to thank her for the recording; they sent her a batch of "God Hates Everyone" T-shirts.

The album closes out with a charming piano-and-voice rendition of Joe Jackson's "Real Men." In this song, she shook her theme up a bit again. Instead of the song being about how men treat women, she decided it would be interesting to explore how some women want to be submissive to men. As she told the *Dallas Morning News*, "I was surprised to find women who were turned on by the thought of being subservient, women who said, 'I think being dominated can be really sexy.' "[24] Though obviously Amos did not agree with them, she was fascinated by the mentality of it, and so she performs the song with suitable longing.

Jackson acknowledged Amos's version of his song at a concert in Cologne, Germany, in 2003. "My songs don't get covered too often," Jackson told the audience. "And when they are, the versions are usually crap. I always feel very humbled nevertheless. It's nice when your songs get attention. But one of my very old songs recently got covered by Tori Amos, and this version was not crap at all. But she changed some of the lyrics. I believe she did it on purpose, don't you think? Or do you think she just messed up? No, I think she did it on purpose. Anyway, I will now play my version of Tori Amos's version of my song."[25]

This kind of interaction with other songwriters made the recording of *Strange Little Girls* rather fascinating. As was the accepted procedure in the recording process with covers, Amos did not contact the copyright holders for the songs until the very last minute. While she was interested in how they would react, she did not allow that to change her approach to the songs. "Some of the messages and conversations were very personal. Yoko Ono had to approve 'Happiness Is a Warm Gun,' and she was absolutely divine."[26] Neil Young signed off on the song, allowing her to alter some of the words to his track. She was able to get the all clear from Eminem because they had the same attorney.

Of course there were quite a few songs that Amos and the band tried that did not make the final CD. Two of those, covers of Alice Cooper's "Only Women" (for which Amos used the better-known but incorrect title "Only Women Bleed") and David Bowie's "After All," did make it onto the limited-edition CD single for "Strange Little Girl" in Europe. Several others, like Elvis Costello's "Hoover Factory," Iggy and the Stooges's "I'm Sick of You," and Peter Murphy's "Marlene Dietrich's Favourite Poem," never quite made the cut. The song that Amos was most disappointed that she couldn't bring to life was possibly her most surprising choice, "Fear of a Black Planet" by rap collective Public Enemy. "I thought, a white woman singing 'Fear of a Black Planet' was something that could work and needed to be done, especially when you consider what the song is about. But by the time I thought I had knew how to achieve it, I was in the mix room and I was running out of steam and I needed an anti-inflammatory. My head hurt. This project took a lot of investigating."[27]

Even with the songs that she could not include, Amos was very proud of what she had achieved with *Strange Little Girls*. For the first time in her career, she thought about what her legacy would be, not just to her listeners and fans, but also to her daughter. As she told *Elle*, "I don't know what my daughter's choices will be in twenty years—any of our daughters could be these strange little girls," she says. "I didn't know that these words from men would take hold of me. I thought I'd find out something about them. Instead, I found something out about myself."[28]

Amos previewed the songs from *Strange Little Girls* at a special show at the Union Chapel in London, England. Soon after that, she was on her way across the sea to help as the promotion cycle shifted into high gear. However, fate would take a hand in making the selling of a new album suddenly seem very unimportant. Two weeks to the day before *Strange Little Girls* was being released, the whole world came to a halt. Amos was in New York City on September 11, 2001, when catastrophe struck in the form of two hijacked planes pointed directly at the World Trade Center. "I was about to do a television appearance," Amos recalled to the *Record*. "I was getting ready when my tour manager came in and flicked on the television and we watched the tragedy, transfixed just like everybody else."[29]

Later she ventured out into the streets and saw the dazed-looking Manhattanites trying to come to terms with the destruction of the office towers and the billowing cloud of smoke wafting up from downtown. "I remember in a weird way being in New York City…the smell of her [America], and her being attacked…being in the same city where she was attacked…I started to question, as did everybody else, is she being represented right? Because how does the world see her? I began to see that the world as I traveled sees her as a bully. And that's not who she is to me. And that really ripped my heart out."[30] She was moved to write a message of solidarity and hope on her Web site, in which she said, "Those of you who are strong need to be there for those who have lost someone, we have to be here for each other right now."[31]

Soon after the disaster, Amos started a tour with singer Rufus Wainwright, who was the son of folksinger Loudon Wainwright III and a native New Yorker. The younger Wainwright had fostered quite a following for his own self-titled album and the follow-up, *Poses*, as well as a hit remake of the Beatles'"Across the Universe"from the soundtrack to the Sean Penn and Michelle Pfeiffer drama *I Am Sam*. Wainwright said that it was good that he got right on the road soon after. "I was here for September 11," he told Outsmart.com. "I actually started my tour, with Tori Amos, right after September 11. I was out there for two months. That actually ended up being a therapeutic good thing. Tori was good music to listen to and perform with after that."[32]

The U.S. Strange Little Tour started in West Palm Beach, Florida, on September 28, 2001. From the beginning it was planned to be a short tour. This was not because of the World Trade Center disaster, although that may have contributed to the decision not to extend it. It was for a much more basic reason. For the first time in her touring life, Tori Amos was a mother. She and Mark did bring Natashya on the road with them; they wanted to see how the little girl would react to life on the road, going from town to town and living in hotels. Amos found that having her little baby on tour changed the whole dynamic of being on the road in a very simple way. Natashya wanted to play. She wanted attention. Amos and Hawley were more than happy to provide it; Amos quickly found that spending time with her family was the best time that she was having in her life. She loved reading the baby books and playing with toys and marveling at the look of astonishment that crossed the girl's face at the simplest of things.

It was a change, because Amos was a perfectionist. Now the time that she used to spend obsessing about the sound and the show was spent singing "The Wheels on the Bus." Go round and round. Round and round. Round and round. Natashya helped her put it all in perspective. Of course, the music was hugely important, and she always still wanted to do the best job that she possibly could. However, if you couldn't take the time to enjoy the little things, to bask in the laugh of a child or take pleasure in a quiet night with your husband and daughter, what was the point? For over thirty years, music had been the most important thing in Tori Amos's life. Now it was number two.

The relationships between mother and child became even more vital to Amos in November 2001, when her mother, Mary, had major surgery. Amos was on tour at the time, so she couldn't be with her mother through the ordeal. She did often play the song "Mother" in concert as a tribute to Mary Amos and her own little way of trying to help her with her recovery. Luckily Amos's worst fears turned out to be avoided—Mary Amos recovered nicely from the procedure.

The changes in the world were brought into even sharper focus when her van was pulled over at the border on the trip from the Seattle date on the Strange Little Tour to Vancouver. Armed border patrolmen who had insisted on doing a thorough search surrounded the vehicle. Amos was less concerned with the fact that she was considered a terrorist threat than the fact that she had a sleeping baby in the back. If these guys woke her, there was going to be hell to pay.

Another major change was going to take place in Amos's life, though certainly not as significant as some that had happened in the past year. But on a personal and business level, it was a time for decisions. *Strange Little Girls* was the last album that Amos owed to Atlantic Records on her contract, a contract whose roots reached back to the days in Los Angeles when she was putting together Y Kant Tori Read. Many things had changed in Amos's life, and also in the corporate structure of WEA, the umbrella company that included Warner Brothers, Elektra, Asylum, and Atlantic records. The company had been merged into America Online in 1999. A new business model was being embraced. Suddenly, with the reduction of sales and the rampant expansion of peer-to-peer music trading on the Internet with companies like Napster and KaZaA, the labels were cutting back significantly. Longtime staples of the WEA artist stable, such as Rod Stewart and Bette Midler, were given their walking papers, as well as newer but still popular groups like Collective Soul and Poe. Tori Amos had only known one home, as far as labels go, in her entire career. With the change in the air at Atlantic, was it time for Tori Amos to change as well?

After all, she had become very well off working for the label. She and her new family owned three homes—the houses in Cornwall and Florida, and she was restoring a home in Ireland. She was able to build her own dream studio. Her life had become rather quiet and low-key. She wasn't the local celebrity in any of her homes. She was just another neighbor. A wife and mother who fit in completely and the only time that she seemed at all different was when record company execs would helicopter in and they would have to land at the local rugby club. But the people surrounding her knew that Amos was not all about that kind of Los Angeles conspicuous consumption. Amos had lived that lifestyle and now found she preferred the simple life.

In the long run, it was a mutual decision between Amos and Atlantic that perhaps it was time that she moved on. It was a tough decision to make. Her manager, Arthur Spivak, admitted to *Billboard* that it was a sad but necessary change to make. They had been with Atlantic for a long time, but the label had come to the point where it had developed tunnel vision about what Amos had to offer—it saw her as a niche artist who could only do one thing. "It was time to find a new energy with a new point of view," Spivak concluded. Atlantic co-chairman and co-CEO Val Azolli concurred, saying, "Both Tori and I thought it was better to try something new. It was a very happy divorce; we had a nice long run."[33] Amos agreed to release a greatest hits album (or, since she never had many big hits, maybe "best of" is a better term) on Atlantic, and suddenly for the first time since she was an unknown, Tori Amos was a free agent.

Not that it was a big surprise or that Amos or Spivak did not have a plan in place. They were being wooed by Epic Records, which was part of the Sony dynasty. However, that left *Strange Little Girls* in a strange state of limbo. After a strong debut on the album charts, it sank like a stone. It had been released in the shadow of one of the world's most horrific acts of terrorism. The reviews for the album were rather mixed. Many people felt that the album was just a bit too serious—little of Amos's sense of humor or levity were really shining through. The planned single, "Strange Little Girl," had been met with reluctance from radio and music television, so it was never officially released in the States and only given a halfhearted release in Europe. Perhaps Amos's realization that music was being overrun by male anger was more prophetic than she realized. The rock-rap merge espoused by Limp Bizkit, Linkin Park, KoRn, and other groups who couldn't spell was the prevailing wind on alternative radio, which had always been Tori Amos's home ground. The female singer-songwriter movement was sputtering, looked at as "Oh, so three years ago." Suddenly Tori Amos was back on the outside looking in.

Even the hardcore Toriphiles didn't seem to embrace *Strange Little Girls* with their normal fervor. Most seemed to respect it more than like it, but saw it as a bit of a holding pattern until Amos was ready to record her own music. And, now, barely two months after the album's release, Amos had left the record label. Atlantic exec Azolli promised that the imprint would continue to push and promote *Strange Little Girls*, but no one really believed that, and the album sort of fell between the cracks. Its sales were the worst for an Amos album since *Y Kant Tori Read*, although, in fairness, it sold significantly more copies than that debut album. However, for only the second time in her solo career, a Tori Amos release did not even become a gold album (which marks sales of 500,000 copies) in the United States. (*To Venus and Back* had also narrowly missed the mark.) *Strange Little Girls* was the closing of a door in Amos's career, but she was determined it would not be the closing of *the* door.

chapter 9
A Sorta Fairy Tale

The year 2002 opened up with Tori Amos finding a new musical home. The talks with Epic Records had gone extremely well, and she signed up with the label. The contract gave her even more artistic freedom than her Atlantic contract, and more control over her work and song rights. However, the big selling point was that she would have the opportunity to work with one of the few women in a true seat of power in the business—Epic president Polly Anthony. "I went to my mother, and I went to other people that are part of that belief system, and that's where I am today," she told *Women That Rock*. "Polly Anthony, president of Epic, came to visit me while I was pregnant, and she wanted to take me with her."[1]

In Anthony, Amos saw a kindred spirit. When Anthony heard that Amos might be looking to move on to a new label, she jumped at the opportunity to collaborate with Amos. Amos felt that they had arrived at the same place for the same reason; they were both strong women who believed in artistic freedom. Amos was so impressed by the exec that she was the major reason Amos decided to make Epic her label choice. "The philosophy has changed [at Atlantic]," Amos told the *Rocky Mountain News*. "The focus was more on stock shares. It became so huge that the music wasn't even secondary." It was all a big change, yet at the same time Tori Amos felt that it was business as usual. "[The term] 'Fresh start' is not something I use," Amos continued. "It's a cliché. I don't want anything to do with it. Everything in my past is part of who I am. There are calluses on your hands."[2]

Not only were there calluses on her hands, but also there were black rings under her eyes. Tori Amos was experiencing one of the great joys of parenthood—with daughter Natashya being on the road, sleep had become a distant, wistful memory. "Motherhood affects you in ways you don't even realize," Amos said. "Being a mother means that you can't be the one that is in the center—the needy one all the time. You become this sort of nurturing protective force."[3] One way in which she has changed is that she has calmed down somewhat. Suddenly in interviews she is less likely to make sexual references and more likely to tell cute baby stories. It is just part of the process of becoming a mother, she felt the need to put some of her wild ways behind her. When you have a small child, she realized, you can't have datura growing in your garden.

So this meant planning her days around little Natashya's needs. And it meant that she wasn't going to get close to a full eight-hours slumber. (When an interviewer mentioned that when she was young she used to fantasize about

Jesus and asked what she imagined now, Amos quickly answered being able to sleep through the night.)[4] She had spent many wakeful nights during the Strange Little Tour, sitting up in the bus, writing new songs. This was a new experience for Amos, who had never written on the road before. However, since sleep was rare and fleeting, it only seemed right to spend the time usefully. Amos was crafting songs for a post-terrorist-attack world. They came to her and she found an odd thing, the compositions were coming together as something of a whole. The lyrics for the new album seemed to all be telling one grand, epic story. It was shaping up to be a sonic novel.

On the back cover of the six-song preview disc for the press, there was a rather cryptic description of the storyline of the upcoming set, which was going to be a concept album. "The CD's about America—it's a story that's also a journey, that begins in L.A. and crosses the country, slowly heading east. America's in there, and specific places and things, Native American history and pornography and a girl on a plane who'll never get to New York, and Oliver Stone and Andrew Jackson and madness and a lot more. Not to mention a girl called Scarlet who may be the land and may be a person and may be a trail of blood."[5]

So *Scarlet's Walk* was going to be a heroic road trip through the highways and byways of a country touched by war. In it we would see the United States, politics, man's inhumanity to man and struggle through the eyes of Scarlet, who was an alter ego for Amos. ("Scarlet is walking in my shoes. You could say she is based on me. Or perhaps I'm based on her.")[6] Each song touches down at a different place on the map and experiences the culture, has a little adventure, and moves on to her next destination. Amos said the sagas of the great Native American warriors and ancestors that were told to her as a child by her mother inspired the grand adventure. "She's any woman," Amos told the Associated Press. "Scarlet is a thread. She's weaving her way through this country. She's running into different people who are changing her view of how she sees the country and her relationship with it."[7]

Scarlet's quest was also an exploration of an America that Amos saw spinning far astray. The September 11 terrorist attacks had for a short time succeeded in bringing the world together. However, she saw a trend in the opposite direction—Americans were starting to be viewed with suspicion. Many people were starting to feel betrayed by their government, by the American dream. Amos saw the journey as a way to explore the needs of the people of the country and return to the land. "Some of our leaders were suggesting that if you were questioning anything about what we were doing as a country, then you didn't love America," Amos told the *St. Petersburg Times*. "I found that offensive. And I found that incredibly manipulative. So that kind of emotional blackmail started to stir up: 'Hang on a minute, if we are the land of the free and if we really love this creature we call America, her soul, then we must begin to ask the questions.' "[8]

If the album was very different lyrically and thematically, after the sonic experiments that Amos had been making on her last few albums, musically *Scarlet's Walk* is a bit of a return to basics for her. This album is probably Amos's most accessible in years (quite possibly since *Under the Pink.*) The techno experiments were pretty much left in the past; instead Amos's deft piano lines again anchored the album. Her now-regular band of drummer Matt Chamberlain and bassist Jon Evans was augmented with the guitar of Robbie McIntosh (formerly of the Pretenders and Paul McCartney's band), as well as the return of the skills of string arranger John Philip Shenale. There is also credited as guitarist on *Scarlet's Walk* the mysterious Mac Aladdin. There is no record of a guitarist by that name working on any other album by any other artist. However, Mac Aladdin is the name of a computer program, leading many people to believe that it is either a pseudonym for Mark Hawley or Marcel von Limbeck, or perhaps some guitar work was just done with an Apple computer.

Like *Strange Little Girls*, the new album was mastered by late-eighties one-hit wonder Jon Astley (he hit the charts on his own with the 1987 New Wave single "Jane's Getting Serious," as well as a couple of lesser-known follow-ups, "Been There, Done That" and "Put This Love to the Test"). Astley had since become an in-demand studio force, best known for mastering the entire catalogue of the Who, as well as all of that band's lead guitarist Pete Townshend's solo work.

Scarlet's journey starts off in Los Angeles with the song "Amber Waves." It was named not only for the grain from the song "America the Beautiful," but also for the character name of actress Julianne Moore's bruised lost-soul porn actress in the popular 1997 film *Boogie Nights.* In the film, Amber was trying to keep her children while fighting addiction and debilitating self-doubts. Like the movie character, *Scarlet's Walk*'s Amber Waves was a young girl who went to L.A. seeking stardom, but instead found herself stuck in a seedy underworld of strip bars and porn videos. Now in her late twenties, Amber is no longer the hot new thing and is being left behind even in the world she never expected to join. Therefore, she hops into a bus with friend Scarlet to see the country, though she will not end up seeing nearly as much as Scarlet.[9]

Musically the intro and verses of "Amber Waves" are somewhat reminiscent of Neil Young's plaintive lament "After the Goldrush" (which Amos has performed in concert), before the chorus perks up out of the introspective mood. However, Amos respects and admires the character of Amber in her story. "She's America personified into our sweet porn star," Amos said on National Public Radio, "who has made some choices that she's got to pay for now. She's chosen to maybe turn her back on some information. She's chosen to align herself with certain characters and there are consequences to that."[10]

In the second song (and the album's first single), "A Sorta Fairytale," Scarlet leaves Amber and returns to L.A. to see a man she believes may be the man for her. The two hop into a huge old car and speed on up the Pacific Coast Highway searching for an illusive sense of togetherness, but the farther they make it up the road, the more they realize that it was all a mistake. They weren't destined to be together, in fact it turns out that they really had little in common. Everything they had believed about the other person turned out to be just an act. So back to the

City of Angels Scarlet heads, this time determined to set out on her own. "Well, in the story, *Scarlet's Walk*, it's the second song and she thinks she's met her soul mate," Amos explained on *The Isaac Mizrahi Show*. "And maybe she has, but you don't always stay together with a soul mate. You can't always live with them."[11]

"A Sorta Fairytale" was Amos's catchiest single in years. It was couched in a lovely piano fill; however, Amos's keyboards do not dominate the track, rather add spice to the bedrock percussion beat of Chamberlain and a dreamy guitar line. It was a song that excited radio and video programmers and got more airplay than any single she'd done since "Jackie's Strength" four years earlier. It has a mysterious gothic depth that does make it an ideal introduction to Amos's return. *USA Today* ended up calling the song the fourth-best single released in 2002, saying the song was "so flat-out pretty a melody and arrangement that it wouldn't matter if the words were gibberish—which the part about almost smacking Oliver Stone comes perilously close to."[12]

The next song, "Wednesday," finds Scarlet involved with a new lover, but again the relationship is not what she imagines. Scarlet is worried that he was not open with her, withholding his emotions and beliefs. It is making her jealous and possessive, and finally she realizes that it is not what she wants to be. She realizes she is lost in the middle of America. The song has a fun, retro, almost-skiffle beat before slowing to a delicate piano chorus. (Actually, the verses of the song sound eerily like the work of the late British singer Kirsty MacColl, who had died in a boating accident a couple of years before.)

Therefore, in "Strange," Scarlet goes back on the road, in search of the memories of tragedies of Native Americans (places like the Trail of Tears and Battle of Little Big Horn) and through the Badlands. This trip is accompanied by a haunting, gorgeous melody, which is augmented by the continued return of Amos's love affair with her piano. The exquisite keyboard bleeds into the next tune, the charmingly downbeat "Carbon." It has a lovely tune that vaguely recalls Amos's own long-ago Y Kant Tori Read ballad "Fire on the Side." In the story, Scarlet meets a person named Carbon who suffers from despair and the two continue the voyage, ending up at Wounded Knee, site of the massacre of the Lakota Indians in 1890. Then later, after they reach a ski resort, Scarlet has to find Carbon and stop her from taking her own life. It seems it would be a depressing subject for a song, but the track has a divine spiraling piano motif that soothes the pain of the story.

The next character to enter Scarlet's life is the title character of the song "Crazy." (I assume that is a nickname, not a given name.) Crazy is a charmer; a confident and fun-loving man who convinces Scarlet that he knows the way. Scarlet knows that she'll never be able to hold on to him—eventually he will be in the wind—however she can't help herself. So she straps herself in for the ride and enjoys it while it lasts, until he leaves her in Phoenix. "Crazy, he makes a lot of sense to me and to Scarlet in the middle of our journey," Amos said on French TV, "after the guy that was supposed to be our soul mate wasn't really. So, Crazy comes along and makes a lot of sense at the time."[13]

Next, Amos and Scarlet channel an elderly Indian woman in "Wampum Prayer." After the earthly pleasure that she indulged with Crazy, in this song Scarlet returns to trying to find something a little more spiritual. While visiting the land where the Apaches were slaughtered, Scarlet dreams of this woman who sings her a traditional-sounding native hymn of the wampum. The woman's vocals lead Scarlet to the Cherokee country of her ancestors. The song is a short (forty-four seconds long) a capella lament that genuinely sounds like it could be an ancient Cherokee prayer.

"Don't Make Me Come to Vegas" was an opportunity for Amos to put her distinctive stamp on several genres of music, with an idiosyncratic box-step structure that straddles country and western, jungle drums, subtle tango rhythms, and bossa nova jazz. In the storyline, Scarlet finds that her eighteen-year-old niece is in trouble and needs to be saved from a letch in Sin City. However, Scarlet would have to confront her past in order to rescue the girl. An ex-lover who is called the Prince of Black Jacks is in charge of the city, and Scarlet knows that if she goes to Las Vegas, she will have to deal with him.

She avoids that dilemma, instead winding up in Austin, Texas, to the tune of "Sweet Sangria." In this song, Scarlet hooks up with a Hispanic revolutionary who believes the end always justify the means, so Scarlet must come to terms with her beliefs and decide whether anything is worth hurting innocent civilians. Musically the song was a tasty mix of exotic rhythms, snare drums and a fluid piano line. "I was working with rhythms and tones that came intrinsically with the land," Amos said on the Web site GalleryofSound.com. "So in 'Virginia,' for instance, I would pull in certain instruments and rhythms and voicings. The song 'Don't Make Me Come to Vegas,' it's like *Blazing Saddles* or something, and 'Sweet Sangria' has this whole Mexican revolutionary moment. So a lot of the musical influences are coming from the land itself, and the history."[14]

The next song is the extraordinarily beautiful and delicate "Your Cloud." In the song, Scarlet drives through Memphis, visits another area where Cherokees were massacred and ends up in Philadelphia ruminating on the crack in the Liberty Bell. "At a certain point in 'Your Cloud' you have this couple—or one of them anyway—decides that 'we need to break apart, we need to divide this up,'" Amos told *Hot Press*. "But then you're thinking, parts of me are now you. I'm a different person because of you. I carry you in me. It's like the land, you can't keep cutting it up and dividing it up. There is a thread that ties all of us together, and you can't segregate that. The massacres, the brutality, the births and the sacrifices are all a part of her. The same is true of governments."[15]

A snaky charm seethes from the catchy "Pancake" which finds Scarlet down in Delaware and then heading up to Boston looking to find knowledge. Instead she meets a prophet who speaks a good game but is unable to follow up his beliefs with any action or changes. He claims to be there for the people, but he puts his own needs before others. He claims to be pure, but he is instead becoming power hungry. "'Pancake' is really about the abuse of power, whether by presidents or rock stars. There seems to be a right wing ideology held by some young hipsters—Jesse Helms in tattoos. This thinking has to find something to hate, whether it's a gay person, a woman, a different race or a different religion. It's so boring! But people get drawn in by it."[16]

The longest song on the album is "I Can't See New York," which starts with a quiet melancholy piano line and Amos's bereft vocal. The other instruments slowly, subtly join in until it reaches a crescendo of sound on the second verse before scaling back to the piano and vocal for the chorus. It is only natural that the song has a quiet urgency because it is a mirror image of the September 11 terrorist attacks, while Scarlet is in New York she sees an airplane crash. The song is a strange and horrible piece of foresight—Amos wrote the song before the World Trade Center disaster. However, the way that current events followed the storyline gives the song an exceptional emotional wallop.

It caught on to a sense of confusion and fear that many people were feeling after that fateful day. Amos certainly felt it even though she was a part-time citizen. It was a hurt that Amos tried to personalize with her song. "I think that my relationship with the country, especially I guess being in New York on the eleventh [of September] of last year, I began to see people relating to America as an alive being," Amos told the radio show *Morning Becomes Eclectic* after the album was released. "I crossed the country touring at that time, and a lot of people would speak about it. Speak in ways that they don't normally speak. So that was different, the way that people started to talk about her. Whether it was a mother or a friend or a creature that was alive. She wasn't an object anymore."[17]

After the horror of the crash, Scarlet finally leaves Manhattan. "She hitches a ride with Mrs. Jesus, which I figured was a good way to get out," Amos explains to the *Melbourne Herald-Sun*.[18] The song is a pretty Amos piano ballad, lushly orchestrated and enjoyable but not exactly revolutionary musically. The story is also a bit of a continuation, as Scarlet leaves New York with the title character of the song (in the Epic publicity department's description of the album's backstory, Mrs. Jesus is referred to with the pronoun "him," which I assume is a typo, unless I'm missing a much deeper layer to the song). Together, they head back out westward-bound, trying to figure out what happened to them and the world in the city. Scarlet enjoys Mrs. Jesus's company because she is basically an optimistic person, and the brightness of her personality helps her find hope.

In Chicago, Scarlet looks up some old acquaintances and finds that one of her friends—a homosexual—has died. He lived in Baton Rouge, Louisiana, so Scarlet heads south to visit his home in "Taxi Ride." The song is a mix of acoustic guitar, a sweet bass backbeat, and slightly hushed, distorted vocals. The music is pretty but not sad, it is much more a celebration of a life than a dirge that so many songs about dead associates tend toward. Amos plays with the audience's expectations, referring to the friend as "just another dead fag to you"; however, there is an obvious fondness and love there.

The song "Taxi Ride" ended up touching Amos even more than she originally intended. The song suddenly became extremely personal to Amos when her longtime friend and celebrated makeup artist Kevyn Aucoin succumbed to a pituitary brain tumor at age forty. Beyond working together, which they often did (Aucoin put together all the looks that Amos had used in the *Strange Little Girls* project), they were also extremely close. Aucoin and his partner had been at Amos's wedding and she had asked him to be Natashya's godfather. Although Amos knew that he was sick, Aucoin was gravely hurting for a while before his death and became dependent on painkillers, but his death was still shattering to Amos. "Yes, he was a master painter, but it was what he did in the conversation that made your inside glow, and helped you find the part of you that had grace or humor," she told the *New York Times*. "This was a man who loved women, even the ones who weren't good—the nice-seeming people who were closet Cruella DeVils."[19]

Amos had been working on the song for a while before his death made it more poignant to her. In fact, Aucoin had heard the song, never knowing that it would eventually become a tribute to him. "For those of you who knew him, this is really for Kevyn Aucoin," Amos told *Windy City Times*. "I think his death brought up a lot in a lot of people. He would hear me working on it and he would come up to me and say, 'Who's the fag who's dying?' I would look at him and I would say, 'Well, today [I] don't know.' I did not know that it would embody him."[20]

The quietly lovely "Another Girl's Paradise" finds Scarlet in New Orleans. She is trying to come to grips with the way that women sometimes envy what other women have. "In 'Another Girl's Paradise,' it really tries to go into that, even with women," she tells *Pulse*. "Why does one woman feel that, if she doesn't get the guy, she's lost? These are just core questions we have to ask ourselves."[21] The road beckons as she goes to Florida, flies to Hawaii, and ends up back in Miami.

On the album's title track, Amos takes a tour of her grandfather's life and the hardships of the Native Americans who became outsiders in their own land. It is an acknowledgment of an America that no longer exists, a mixture of the gothic South and the Cherokee empire that was long ago destroyed by the encroachment of foreigners. "She's propelled to find this being that we call America—what her soul is—not how she's been pimped out by her leaders over the last several years," Amos told the *San Francisco Examiner*.[22] In this real America, Scarlet finds pain and suffering but also great beauty and strength.

Scarlet then makes her way north near Amos's former home of the Washington, D.C. area, in the lushly provocative "Virginia." In Jamestown, Virginia, one of the earliest settler colonies of the Europeans in the New World, she ponders how people crossing the ocean to find freedom and equality could not extend those same basic rights to the natives of the land they settled upon. The earth provided plenty for all, so why did some feel that they had to deny others to get what it was that they needed? Why was one culture able to trump the history and beliefs of another?

Scarlet's journey comes to an end in the ethereal "Gold Dust," when she gives birth to a child. "Scarlet has a daughter; I had a daughter," she told the BBC. "The difference is I know who the father is. Scarlet doesn't really, because it could be between four, which…keeps us guessing. Maybe the end of the record is that

Scarlet realizes that it's time for her to give back. And not just to her daughter. But as she becomes a mother, she starts thinking about her mother. And her mother… as in the Earth. Instead of taking from it, what does she need to do to be more of a caretaker than a taker."[23]

And so Scarlet's voyage comes to a halt, but do these voyages ever really finish? The whole idea of the concept album can be a scary one for people, keeping track of the threads of a story over seventy-four minutes can be a chore. So we have discussed how the chapters of the sonic novel worked, but it overlooks a larger question. How does it work in the big picture? Can you glean the intricacies of Amos's plot just from listening to the album? Well, the clues are all there, but it is certainly helpful to have a map of the story included; otherwise, a good deal of detective work is required on the part of the listener.

On the other hand, there is another problem with concept albums. Does the story overwhelm the songs? In this case, *Scarlet's Walk* is a definite artistic success. You do not have to pay the least bit of attention to the storyline to still enjoy the CD. Likewise, often in this type of album, songs taken out of context seem the lesser for being a little piece of a big puzzle that can't survive on their own. This is quite definitely not the case with the songs from *Scarlet's Walk*, which do not need the context of the voyage to be enjoyed.

With her huge masterwork finally finished, Amos settled into the spin zone once again. The job of the artist was done for now. The question was, could *Scarlet's Walk* find her rabid audience—an audience that had taken hits from the passing of time and changing musical tastes? It was all the same and yet it was all very different. She was on a new record label. There was a new musical landscape. And, of course, a new set of priorities, as *Scarlet's Walk* was the first album of original material she had released since the birth of her daughter. Tori Amos's last two albums had been considered somewhat to be letdowns, sales-wise. Was there still a following for her idiosyncratic style?

It turns out the answer was yes. *Scarlet's Walk* was the first album Amos had released since *Boys for Pele* to spend its first ten weeks on the charts in the Top Ten albums chart. By January 2003 it was certified a gold record. The single "A Sorta Fairytale" got Amos back into heavy rotation on VH1 and on radio.

That song was helped out by a very distinctive music video. The clip for the song "A Sorta Fairytale" was most certainly different. (If you get technical, there were two videos, one was specially made for the bonus DVD on the limited-edition version of the CD, but I am speaking of the one that received airplay on VH1, MTV, and MTV2.) It costarred actor Adrien Brody, who had just won an Academy Award for Best Actor for his powerful role in Roman Polanski's Holocaust drama *The Pianist*. Essentially, he is a disembodied head at the end of a hand that falls in love with Amos, who is a head at the end of a leg. He falls in love with her, but then offends her by laughing at her toes. She jumps onto a passing skateboard and ends up on a beach, where Brody reappears. They finally kiss and grow entire bodies.

It is certainly a visually arresting idea, though most viewers did acknowledge it was really rather odd. However, in the "Making of 'A Sorta Fairytale'" documentary on the DVD of the video, Amos acknowledges that she had been bombarded by ideas based around the idea of the fairy tale. Many of them seemed to be things she found uninteresting, like making the video with puppets as an homage to British children's TV producer Gerry Anderson (*The Thunderbirds*). Then music video director Sanji approached her with this idea. He had the idea of looking at the false allure of the fairy tale…how everything doesn't always become happy ever after. "When I was making the video, I knew we were doing something special," she explained in the documentary.[24]

Amos also used the Internet and new marketing strategies to excite the faithful. By sticking the CD into your CD-ROM drive you could go to an area of her official Web site called Scarlet's Web. The World Wide Web was devised to help track the path of the story. It included little pieces of information and unreleased songs as bonus features. "The CD, when you put it into your computer, it becomes a key and it takes you to Scarlet's Web. There, the maps come alive so you can follow where she went," Amos told radio station Mix 94.7 in Austin. "You get a map with your CD booklet…but they come alive on the computer and there are layers of the maps."[25] She also released a special limited-edition version of *Scarlet's Walk*, which included a map of the trip, stickers, Polaroid snapshots of Amos in different locales as Scarlet, a DVD of three music videos, and little trinkets, all of which could unlock different sections of the Web.

Amos was back in the musical spotlight, but she was able to put it into better perspective now. The music was vital to who she was, but mother and wife was her true job. It was lucky for her that she was able to work with her husband, and since they owned the studios, their daughter could always be with them. Little Natashya was slightly demoted on this album's liner notes. In the previous album, *Strange Little Girls*, she had been given a credit as executive producer. On *Scarlet's Walk* her credit was as entertainment coordinator. However, more importantly she was Amos's entertainment and her muse. Life was finally coming together as it should be. "I think motherhood is a place that you live in," Amos told CNN.com. "I think it's something that's changed every cell in my body. I'm much more comfortable being in a place of nurturing than I was [when I was being] warrior woman out there! Sometimes it's a very lonely place to be. And it can be very competitive."[26]

Amos still loved motherhood, but she realized her limitations. In fact, she told *Rolling Stone* that she had a whole new respect for the famous Disney nanny Mary Poppins, played by Julie Andrews. "I'm a mother and I'm so out of my depths on this one. My daughter just runs circles around me, and I'm just learning how to say no without her completely laughing at me. So Mary Poppins is on my altar right now. Do you know what she says? 'I am kind but extremely firm.'"[27] Natashya is also following her mother's passionate love of music and piano. "She said, 'I want to learn to play the piano, Mommy,'" Amos said on *The Ryan Seacrest Show*. "I try to find her a piano teacher. I am not teaching because that is not good.

So I couldn't find one that would teach a three-year-old, so I put on this hat and became Mrs. Paris. And so, she goes to lessons with Mrs. Paris."[28]

With Amos back on the charts, she returned to the place she had been so many times before—the concert trail. Unlike the abbreviated Strange Little Tour only a year before, Amos was not going to make this a short little trip. Amos would end up spending months on the road—over six months from November to May on the *Scarlet's Walk* tour. Then she took a break for about a month and a half before she was off on her next tour. Amos called upon hip pianist Ben Folds to open for her tour, which they called the Lottapianos tour.

Folds had made his name a few years before as the head of the Ben Folds Five. The Five was remarkable for two reasons. First, there were only three players in the band. (Folds just thought the name Ben Folds Five sounded cool, like an old jazz combo.) Second, there was no guitarist. In fact, on the group's albums like *Whatever and Ever Amen* and *The Autobiography of Reinhold Messner*, no guitars were used. The band had some hits, like the lovely ballad "Brick" and the venomous rocker "Song for the Dumped." Before the Amos tour, Folds had broken up the band and released his first solo album, *Rocking the Suburbs*.

Folds felt the lack of a guitar made him better as a songwriter. Too many bands relied on the guitar to get noticed. Folds was not going to use that safety net. "You try to find what freedom you do have because we're locked in to much fewer textures," Folds explained. "A guitar player has a lot more textures than a piano does, and can sustain. There are a lot of things you can do with a guitar that you can't do with a piano. So, having that limitation, I think it makes you pull more from, you know, you have to be more creative about it."

It made prefect sense for him to play with Amos, who was also a piano-based artist. Like Folds, she had always tried to keep the piano front and center. It was a good fit. "I kind of always heard my songs that way," Folds told me. "Piano-based and drums. So it was really no real decision. It was just a decision I guess on when to start the band because it seemed like something like this would be something that I could actually do, people would listen to it, I would make money doing it. It seemed like it was time for it. So I never really thought about a guitar part. I'm not really the kind of person who would have thought this is the age of guitars, so I'm just going to add a guitar. It was more like this age of guitars just doesn't really feel right. It seemed like that shit was dying."

The tour by the two singers was for the most part a success, although it did cause a legal headache for Amos and her manager, Arthur Spivak, when a planned show at the Interlochen Centre for the Arts in Michigan ended up not happening. The concert promoters at the facility sued Amos for breach of an agreement and the return of a $40,000 deposit when final arrangements could not be hashed out. The venue claimed that they could not reach a deal due to Amos's camp's insistence on money spent on catering, complimentary tickets, and Amos's demand that three "awareness groups" be allowed to put up booths at the show.[29] The tour also started a relationship between Folds and drummer Matt Chamberlain. In 2004, when Folds was producing the album *Has Been* by *Star Trek* actor William Shatner, Folds contacted many well-known artists to contribute to the project, including Joe Jackson, Henry Rollins, Aimee Mann, Brad Paisley, Adrian Belew, and Chamberlain.

After the tours were completed, Amos remained busy. In a move to help celebrate new artists, Amos was added to an eclectic group of music industry judges to decide the winner of the third annual Shortlist Music Prize. Based on the Mercury Music Prize in England, the Shortlist Prize is formed to find the most daring and original new album of the year, spanning every genre and style. The star-studded list of judges for the 2003 prize included Amos, Dave Matthews, Tom Waits, Chris Martin of Coldplay, Erykah Badu, Flea of the Red Hot Chili Peppers, the Chemical Brothers, ?uestlove of the Roots, Josh Homme of the Queens of the Stone Age, Musiq, Mos Def, Perry Ferrell, and the Neptunes, as well as music-oriented filmmakers Cameron Crowe and Spike Jonze. The judges had to pick from a pool of nominees that included eclectic musical talents such as the Yeah Yeah Yeahs, Cody Chestnutt, Sigur Ros, Floetry, the Streets, Bright Eyes, Cat Power, Interpol, and the Black Keys. The award was given to singer-songwriter Damien Rice for his acclaimed debut solo album, *O.*[30] Amos would end up working with Rice when he contributed vocals to the song "The Power of Orange Knickers" on her 2005 album, *The Beekeeper.*

Amos was also able to take it in good humor when she fell victim to Ashton Kutcher's popular MTV series *Punk'd.* The show sort of updates the old *Candid Camera* format with celebrities as the victims of extreme practical jokes. Amos was gotten on the very first episode, but it was just a harmless gag. She was on a red carpet when a child actor started asking her questions about *Beverly Hills 90210,* as if he thought that she was Tori Spelling, not Tori Amos. She just good-naturedly tried to explain who she was to the little boy, but he kept asking questions about Shannon Doherty. "There was this little guy at the end of this long line," Amos later told the *Las Vegas Sun,* "and I just thought he was some guy doing a school project who didn't get to talk to the person he wanted. I kind of felt bad for him. Then I heard he's got his own TV show, and I went, 'Oh heavens.' You never know."[31]

Kutcher nearly made pop star Justin Timberlake cry when he "punk'd" him by making him believe that the Internal Revenue Service was repossessing his house, so, all in all, Amos got off pretty light. But Amos acknowledged that she would not be happy to be part of one of the bigger gags on the show. "I do feel sorry for [celebrities] when people they trust are in on it," she told the *Sun.* "That would really throw me. I don't know how I would react. But it does make you wonder, doesn't it? Because if my friends did that, they wouldn't be coming to my tea party that week."[32]

Amos took a small role in the 2003 Julia Roberts/Kirsten Dunst film *Mona Lisa Smile* as a fifties big-band singer. She plays at a wedding and sings two standards from the day, Doris Day's "Murder, He Says" and Jo Stafford's "Tonight You Belong to Me." "It's cool," she told Los Angeles morning-radio personalities Kevin and Bean. "[Julia Roberts] is lovely and I loved doing the music. Trevor Horn [Yes, Frankie Goes to Hollywood] produced, [and] is one of the greats in the music industry....He pulled in the orchestra and I sang to full orchestra these songs from the forties. Two songs, 'You Belong to Me' and 'Murder, He Says.' And it was just a hoot."[33]

Amos also appeared briefly in the 2004 documentary *Mayor of the Sunset Strip*, which was about the life of legendary California radio disc jockey Rodney Bingenheimer from Los Angeles station KROQ. Rodney on the 'ROQ (as he is known) was famous for discovering and championing such acts as David Bowie, Alice Cooper, the Ramones, Blondie, Coldplay, and No Doubt. Those artists and many more discuss the enigmatic deejay in the film. Amos shows up towards the end of the film, when Rodney goes backstage after one of her Los Angeles shows. The camera records their conversation, but they were out of range of the microphone, so what they said to each other was unfortunately lost to posterity.

In September 2003, Amos was shocked when Polly Anthony, the exec who had convinced her to sign with Epic Records, stepped down from her position as president of the label. This put her into a rather precarious position: She was newly signed to Epic Records and suddenly it was being run by a whole different set of executives than the ones she had connected with. Amos felt it was important that she and the people she trusted most reevaluate her position as an artist. It was decided that Amos would create a new company called the Bridge Entertainment Group. "Polly was one of the main reasons why I signed with the label," Amos said in the press release announcing the new company. "After she left, it became clear I had to pull together my own creative team that wouldn't miss a beat in the development of my various projects."[34]

The Bridge Group was not unlike United Musicians, the company created by husband-and-wife singers Michael Penn ("No Myth") and Aimee Mann ("Voices Carry"), together with singers Pete Droge ("If You Don't Love Me I'll Kill Myself") and Bob Mould (former leader of the bands Hüsker Dü and Sugar). All of the artists had been through serious problems with the major labels that they had been signed with, so they created the cooperative to help artists with legal and financial problems, as well as promotion of self-released albums. Likewise the Bridge Entertainment Group would offer management services, marketing, help in preparing tours, and artist development. Amos noted in the press release that the music world was shifting and that artists had to be ready to help themselves and each other.

Amos signed on as the first artist for the new business entity. The first two projects that it would be involved with were likewise ones that centered on Amos. In November 2003, she would be releasing the career compilation that she promised Atlantic Records when she left the label. The soundtrack to *Mona Lisa Smile*, which included the two songs Amos recorded for the film, as well as other standards by contemporary artists like Seal, Celine Dion, Mandy Moore, Macy Gray, Chris Isaak, Kelly Rowland (of Destiny's Child), Alison Krauss, and Barbra Streisand. The soundtrack also featured an original recording by Elton John and was to be released on Epic two weeks after the anthology.

Amos called her compilation CD *Tales of a Librarian*. It was a chance for her to revisit and totally remaster some old songs, pull out a couple of old B-sides, and even record two new ones. The album was made up of songs from all of Amos's albums except *Strange Little Girls* (she decided to do all originals on the set, no covers) and *Scarlet's Walk* (because that album was not on Atlantic). If *Scarlet's Walk* was a sonic novel, Amos said that *Tales of a Librarian* was her autobiography. "My whole life with songs has been about chronicling time," Amos told the *Independent*. "I would write a piece of music so that, six months later, when everybody had forgotten about, say, our glossing over of that embarrassing incident at church, I could remember what actually happened."[35]

Amos was determined to make sure that it was a valid representation of her work, not just some profit-driven hits platter. Of course there was more than one reason for that. Amos explained her feelings about the anthology succinctly on RollingStone.com, where she said, "I'm referring to it more as a 'best-of' because I think to have a 'greatest hits' you need like ten Top 10 hits."[36] The title *Tales of a Librarian* also had great meaning for her, as she had come to realize that in many ways, that was exactly what she was. "People project their relationships with the songs in a certain manner," Amos told the *Cleveland Free Times*. "By the end of the day I'm a librarian."[37]

The remixing opportunity allowed her to redo some things that she was uncomfortable with when they were first released. For example, in the original recording of "Winter" she had a string section. A record exec had suggested it may dilute the commercial potential, so she removed it. For the compilation, she was able to return the strings to the recording. Other songs felt a little uncomfortable because of time constraints or availability of time or money or simple technical problems. "When you're a new drink that nobody's tasted, everybody wants to taste it, devour it, and once they've had it they want to taste something else," she told *Attitude*. "Some wine does not age well, but some wine ages very well, which goes back to the vines, how it was harvested, the weather, how it's stored."[38]

Amos also redid the older outtakes "Mary" and "Sweet Dreams," both of which were originally recorded for *Little Earthquakes*. Both had gotten limited release previously: "Mary" was on a limited-edition European single for "Crucify" and "Sweet Dreams" showed up on the "Winter" CD single. The two new compositions were "Snow Cherries from France," a song that she had been trying to get written over several years and a brand-new track called "Angels." That final track continues Amos's political discourse—it was about the votes for Al Gore that disappeared during the 2000 U.S. presidential elections. Amos doesn't think that it is so strange that her lyrical focus has changed somewhat from her personally to the world at large. "Look," she told the *Times*, "if you as a listener need people to be tortured to write, in your mind, 'good' stuff, then I think you're part of the problem."[39] The revamp of "Mary" was tapped to be the first single from the package, although of course since Amos was not still signed to Atlantic Records it was not pushed exceptionally hard. A video was released for the song made up of quick little cuts from Amos's earlier clips. However, Amos was glad that the song got a renewed life with its inclusion on the project. In fact, it was nice to be able to revisit many of these old friends and lovers. Amos had come a long way since some of these songs were written and had to be worried that they would bring up some a lot of memories—some good and some bad. She made herself a little scarce when they were working on "Me and a Gun," for example. For the most part, though, it was okay. It was part of her life, part of her history. These songs were all a part of her and she was comfortable revisiting places that she had been when writing them. "I like where I am now," she told the Press Association. "I wouldn't want to be twenty-six for anything. Of course, there are things I wish I had physically that I had when I was twenty-six, but I'm talking about here inside. That's where I'm happy."[40]

Hot on the heels of the compilation (well, about six months later), Amos took a step into another format, releasing her first live concert on DVD. The final show of the Lottapianos Tour had been filmed live in West Palm Beach, Florida (not far from her summer homestead), to be released as a concert DVD called *Welcome to Sunny Florida*. The early press release for the video said that it was her first concert video. What they meant was in the DVD format, because obviously *The RAINN Concert* was released on videotape, and the *Little Earthquakes* video also had much live performance footage. The press releases were quickly fixed to add that it was the first time she'd released a live show on DVD.

The new format gave Amos the opportunity to give her fans much more for their time and money, including a two-hour-long concert featuring eighteen favorites from throughout her career. Amos and mother Mary also did extensive interviews (father Edison Amos crashed his wife's interview as well). The ironic title (it was pouring rain through the whole show) does fit the hot performance that went on in that soaked shed, starting off with an extended version of "A Sorta Fairytale" and climaxing with a lovely "Hey Jupiter." It is as close as you can get to experiencing an Amos performance without actually being there. "Before I take the stage I guess I do go into a place of…prayer," she told the TV show *Faith and Music*. "But it's not quote-unquote a religious prayer, its about allowing myself to be a key so that the songs can invade me, but it's an agreed invasion."[41]

The video also gave Amos and her people a chance to celebrate the fans who had been so rabidly behind her for years. In the beginning of the concert, there were interviews with some of Amos's passionate fans, who said they had seen her multiple times—eighty-seven, twenty-two, fifty-seven, ninety-five, seventy-five, and one hundred twenty-five were some of the figures thrown out by the concertgoers.[42] In fact, Amos has compared her fans to the notoriously fervent fans of the Grateful Dead, adding that her fans don't smell of patchouli oil and have much superior taste in footwear.[43]

These fans are not the only ones that Amos has inspired. A whole series of singers who grew up listening to her music have come of age. Early on in Amos's career, when she was asked whether the Kate Bush comparisons bothered her, Amos once said no, if she was lucky, maybe someday there would be singers who were compared to her. It was only natural, really. With the circular motion of fame, many new artists who grew up listening to Tori Amos are now releasing their own albums and acknowledging the influence that Amos was on them. Singers like Anna Nalick, Vanessa Carlton, Amy Lee of Evanescence, Charlotte Martin, Toby Lightman, Jill Cohn, and Sarah Hudson are hearing the same kind of comparisons to Amos as she used to hear to other artists when she was establishing herself. Like the young Amos, the singers are both flattered and slightly ambivalent to the association. Most of them respect and love Amos's work, but want to be appreciated for their own talents.

Critically acclaimed singer Charlotte Martin, whose album *On Your Shore* was released in 2004, is in a similar position to Amos when she started out and was constantly getting compared to Kate Bush. Hardly a review of Martin's work does not compare her to Tori Amos and Fiona Apple. While Martin does love the two singers' work, she doesn't totally see the resemblance (actually, she concedes that Kate Bush was a bigger influence). "People assume that because I have blonde hair that I should be on *The O.C.* or something," Martin says. "Which is the reason I keep my hair blonde, because I don't like to feed into anybody's stereotype.... If you get the Cure, you're goth. If you have blonde hair, you should be on *Beverly Hills 90210*. If you have long hair, you're female and play the piano, you're Tori Amos. It's easy to pigeonhole people."

Martin does say right out that she is a fan of Amos's work and that she did influence her performing style in ways. She also realizes that Amos blazed a trail that singers like her can now follow. She continues:

> I'm a huge Tori Amos fan. I'm more influenced by her piano playing and production than I am her voice....I think she's an extremely important artist....There are a lot of amazing female artists, but she had an opportunity and worked very hard and was able to get successful on that level, [that is incredible] being that I think she's a classical musician. Which is really exciting. I just wish there were more people that had the opportunity that she had. That a female could do that kind of theatrical [performance]...you know, Kate Bush didn't get quite as big. I wish she would have. I just wish there were more women, but I'm so thankful there is a Tori Amos out there, because if not there probably wouldn't be a Charlotte Martin.

Another young singer who says Amos has inspired her is Sarah Hudson, who released her first album, *Naked Truth*, in 2004. Hudson has been very vocal about her respect for Amos. Musically Hudson, who is the cousin of movie star Kate Hudson, is not too similar to Amos, but she does share the ability to be starkly and startlingly open in her lyrics. When she was a young teen living in Hollywood, her eyes were opened one day when she was watching MTV. "I remember seeing 'Silent All These Years.' I remember seeing that video," recalls Hudson. "I was floored. I can't even remember how old I was. She is so eccentric and she's so passionate and beautiful. Her music is like…you can interpret it almost any way that you want to. That's what I love about her. I went to go see her in L.A., one of her first shows, when she wasn't big at all. I remember just being blown away. From that moment, I've just been the biggest fan. She's amazing."

Young singer Anna Nalick was able to take it a step farther. Nalick was only twenty-one years old when her acclaimed 2005 album, *Wreck of the Day*, was released. The disc included the hit single "Breathe (2 a.m.)" She had grown up a huge fan of Amos's so it was a thrill when her album was coproduced by Tori's ex-boyfriend and ex-coproducer Eric Rosse. Rosse had formed a production partnership with Brad Smith and Christopher Thorn, surviving members of popular early-nineties rock group Blind Melon, who had a huge hit in 1993 with "No Rain" before lead vocalist Shannon Hoon died of an overdose while on tour in 1995. Nalick was thrilled to work with musicians who had been such an influence.

"I really like the way that he produces records," Nalick says. "Of course, I knew a little bit of what his style is based on the things he did with Tori. He's just got a really great feel for music and the direction that a song should go in. Of course, when I wrote all my songs on guitar and piano, they were very simply done. But I knew what I wanted from the bass, the drums, the cello, whatever we were using. He gave me a lot of creative control, along with his ideas for what the song should sound like fully produced." To further the Amos connection, drummer Matt Chamberlain played on several tracks on *Wreck of the Day* as well.

Amos spent much of 2004 working on her next album, *The Beekeeper*, and penning her memoirs. While recording the album, during the hurricane season of 2004, a boat was blown up on the lawn of Amos's Florida vacation home. This caused a bit of a legal problem when she tried to get it removed. Also, in Florida in November, she tried to do her part to get George W. Bush, of whom she has been critical, out of office. Along with many musicians and artists, Amos felt that the country needed a change. However, in a surprise decision, the somewhat unpopular American president was voted in for four more years.

Also in November, she announced the release of her next CD, *The Beekeeper*. However, soon after the joy of announcing a new project, tragedy returned to Amos's life. On Thanksgiving week 2004, Amos lost her first collaborator and one of her staunchest fans. Her older brother, Edison Michael Amos, was killed in a car crash at fifty years old in the rain near his home in North Carolina. Michael Amos's Porsche slid off the road when taking a turn at an intersection at sixty miles per hour. He was able to make his way back onto the road, however he overcompensated and lost complete control of the auto, which spun out. The car hit a street sign, went airborne, and slammed into a tree. Michael was taken to Duke Hospital, but they were unable to save him.[44] Their father, the Reverend Amos, officiated at the funeral, which was held in Aberdeen, Maryland, on November 26, 2004.

It was a tough blow to take, but Amos had to keep a strong resolve and continue on with her life and her work. She had a new album on the way, as well as a new tour. *The Beekeeper* was released in February 2005. The nineteen-track disc was again recorded at her Martian Engineering studio, with Matt Chamberlain and Jon Evans again working as Amos's band. Much like *Scarlet's Walk*, the new album was something of a concept disc; although the concept was a little more vague. It was basically a hugely autobiographical piece with the core idea of life as a garden. It's an idea that Amos has mined before ("Datura" comes immediately to mind), but it was a fertile ground for her new musical ideas, so to speak. The songs are divided into six "gardens," where they fit in, Amos felt, stylistically and lyrically. On the album, Amos was again trying to experiment with sounds, playing off her Bosendorfer piano with vintage Hammond organs. She also looked to try out world beat music and gospel choirs to shake up her sound. Like *Scarlet's Walk*, the CD was also released in a special bonus packaging, featuring an interview DVD, an additional song, photos, and a specially prepared container of flower seeds.

Listening to the finished product, it is hard not to notice that it is Amos's most musically diverse disc yet. Much like the last album, it is also one of her more commercial albums. Tori Amos is a respected singer and songwriter. However, in the thirteen years since her solo debut, she has become a little pigeonholed by her own distinctive style. It may seem unfair to take the fact that Amos is extraordinarily talented in creating ethereal piano ballads as a negative; however a certain section of the listening public has taken sort of a been-there, done-that attitude to some of her more recent albums. Not that Amos was not aware of that and trying to branch out in different directions—from the electronica of *To Venus and Back* to the faux-rock of some of the covers on *Strange Little Girls*, like "Heart of Gold." *Scarlet's Walk* flittered upon different styles but was couched in the familiar songcraft that has been her stock in trade.

So it is nice to report that while *The Beekeeper* keeps its eyes on Amos's strengths, it may be her most varied recording so far, and yet her musical side trips seem organic. It is stuffed to bursting (seventy-nine and a half minutes long!) with interesting musical ideas. "This is more of a global record," she explained to the *Cleveland Plain Dealer*.[45] It is also her most accessible album ever—and one of her best. The first single, "Sleeps with Butterflies," signals the musical changes. It is a simply gorgeous pop tune that is spiced with her otherworldly vocals. It was one of the most commercial tunes that she has recorded yet, and looked like it may help her finally get that elusive smash hit. Unfortunately radio was resistant and the song didn't even get the level of airplay as "A Sorta Fairytale" from the last studio album.

The disc actually starts off with "Parasol," a lovely piano-driven confessional that nonetheless does tread ground that Amos has mined before. It is gorgeous, but it is deceptively simple and a bit predictable. It is the second song where Amos starts to really shake things up. "Sweet the Sting" has a charmingly elastic bossa-nova vibe, which suits Amos's sultry vocals surprisingly well. The lyrics, with lots of references to injections, playing, loaded guns and cocked hats, are also more blunt than Amos tends to get, not relying on the audience to mine so deeply into the symbolic wordplay she has always specialized in.

"The Power of Orange Knickers" starts off with a surprisingly simple sing-song nature before the instrumentation, vocals and production become more and more complex. In the song, she works with guest vocalist Damien Rice, who won the Plymouth Prize that Amos helped judge. "I heard his voice, and I thought there needed to be a male voice on 'The Power of Orange Knickers,'" Amos told *Rag*. "It was really, really important. Because he was Irish—I did like that other subtext—the idea of [the Irish] as a people [who] know about terrorism." The song also got some notice for Amos's admittedly straightforward lyrics. (She did take perverse pride in being able to rhyme the word *terrorists* with the word *kiss*.)

" 'The Power of Orange Knickers' is, at its root, about invasion," she continued. "Whether the invasion is a terrorist—and if you kind of undress that idea for a minute, this whole context of a terrorist being a guy with a turban, or the terrorist being a guy in a uniform, depending on what part of the country you live in and what side. I wanted to really go further into the idea of a terrorist because I felt like you have to reclaim the word. In order to emancipate a word, sometimes you must undress it."[46]

"Ribbons Undone" is a quiet and extremely private tribute to daughter Natashya. Amos recognizes that her little girl is not having a typical childhood and she does somewhat regret it. "[Natashya] just knows that when I go onstage that Tori Amos takes Mommy away from Tash," Amos told the *Sunday Mail*. "So Tori Amos is not very popular with Tash right now. But she also knows that Tori Amos buys her cool presents."[47] The dramatic structure of "Ribbons Undone" gives it the feeling of an abnormally savvy Broadway show tune. Unfortunately, the musical adventurousness doesn't always work. "Cars and Guitars" has a sweet country swoon that is frankly sabotaged by Amos's sometimes affected vocal, which distracts from the tune. However, in "Witness," Amos sounds—dare I say it?—funky, which is not an adjective that often is trotted out for her. And you know what? It works great. She should mine this style some more.

The traditional, sweet, gothic tinklings for which Amos is known for are represented in songs like the lovely "Jamaica Inn" and "General Joy." This old-school Tori also flies high in "Original Sinuality," which Amos has said is the essential idea behind the concept album. "As you know, the honeybee represents sacred sexuality and ancient feminine mysteries," she told the *Montreal Gazette*. "In a time of not covert, but overt right-wing government, I felt it was essential to talk about sin and try and emancipate the idea of sexuality as being a sin. Therefore, I decided the word *sinsuality* needed to be planted in this garden."[48] Amos honors some of her more experimental tendencies on the longer track "Baron of Suburbia," the retro-sounding "Ireland," and the sassy, jazzy, man-done-wrong valedictory "Hoochie Woman." The album closes out with a last-minute tribute to her late brother, where she lifts her glass in "Toast" to Michael.

All in all, the sweet sweep of styles on *The Beekeeper* is a nice little reminder that Tori Amos can still surprise us. The disc became a moderate hit—it made it to number five on the *Billboard* albums chart but fell down and off the charts rather quickly. Perhaps it had something to do with radio and VH1's reluctance to give any airtime to "Sleeps with Butterflies." Whatever the reason, Amos had little time to worry about it—she had a worldwide tour to do.

In an ironic counterpoint to the *Strange Little Girls* CD, in the summer of 2005, British mag *Q* asked Tori to come up with a group of women's songs that male singers should record. It is a wide-ranging and interesting group of eighteen songs. Included were Suzanne Vega's introspective folk song "Small Blue Thing," Janis Joplin's female-empowerment blues "Get It While You Can," Gloria Gaynor's disco staple "I Will Survive," Joan Baez's "Diamonds and Rust," Heart's arena-rock favorite "Magic Man," Alicia Keys's nu-soul anthem "A Woman's Worth," Rickie Lee Jones's boho-jazz lament "Last Chance Texaco," Donna Summer's classic worker's tribute "She Works Hard for the Money," Carole King's girl-group classic "Will You Still Love Me Tomorrow?," and k. d. lang's countrypolitan hit "Constant Craving." Amos even helpfully suggested male artists who could pull off some of the songs; Bruce Springsteen for "Last Chance Texaco," Moby for "Magic Man," Metallica for Morcheeba's "The Sea," E of the Eels for "I Will Survive," Gavin Rossdale of Bush for "She Works Hard for the Money," and Prince for Sinéad O'Connor's "Three Babies."

One of the other songs she chose was Cyndi Lauper's "Girls Just Want to Have Fun." (Amos suggested that Nick Cave could make it "dangerous and cute.")[49] Perhaps Amos wasn't familiar with the original 1979 demo recording of the song by early-eighties Philadelphia rockers Robert Hazard and the Heroes, in which Hazard (who wrote the song) sang it from a very different point of view than Lauper would eventually espouse, that of a Casanova who spent all of his life chasing skirts. After all, "That's all they really want / some fun / When the working day is done / Girls just wanna have fun," as told from a male perspective takes on a whole new dimension.

Then again, knowing her offbeat sense of humor, maybe Amos was fully aware of the original thrust of the lyrics. After all, she grew up only a couple of hours' drive south of Hazard's base of popularity. While the song was never on either of Hazard's nationally released albums, the demo was definitely known and played in the Philadelphia music scene for years before it was introduced to Lauper by New York–born-but-Philly-based producer Rick Chertoff. Hazard's 1981 EP sold like hotcakes locally and spawned the minor national hits "Escalator of Life" and "Change Reaction" when remixed and re-released nationally in 1983 on RCA Records. Hazard reigned supreme in the Philly area and his popularity stretched up and down the Eastern Seaboard in the years that Amos was toiling in the bar scene.

In fact, a few other of these songs have also been recorded by men over the years. "I Will Survive" has been done several times. In 1996, it even became a bit of a radio hit as recorded as a tongue-in-cheek rocker by alt-band Cake. "Diamonds and Rust" has been reinterpreted into heavy metal by both Judas Priest and Ritchie Blackmore. Billie Holiday's "God Bless the Child" has been recorded by many men over the years. However, Amos's point is as valid as her earlier point with her covers CD—certain songs have a male or female sensibility that can be totally turned on its head by members of the opposite sex recording them.

As almost always happens, a new album for Amos means a new worldwide concert trek. As the tour continued to wind around the world into the summer of 2005, Amos and her Bridge Group came up with another way to use the World Wide Web to get her music out to the hardcore fans. She decided to release a limited-edition series of "official bootlegs" of her live concerts. Amos was perhaps inspired by former label mates Pearl Jam's bootleg series in 2001. The Seattle grunge superstars made every show of their 2000 tour available as limited-edition two-disc sets on Epic as a response to the rampant bootlegging of their shows. Much like the Pearl Jam discs, Amos's live sets are no frills affairs, with light cardboard covers and simple artwork. Because of this frugality, they are able to sell a two-disc set at the price of a single disc. Amos parted company with Pearl Jam in a couple of important ways, too. First of all, she realized that it was excessive to expect people to buy all of her shows, she decided to make six discs available, releasing them in groups of two packages at a time. The distribution was also different; Pearl Jam released the recordings to stores while Amos's were only made available through a special Web site set up for the collection, www.toriamosbootlegs.com.[50]

At the time of this writing, only the first two bootlegs had been released or even announced. These were two shows from the end of the first U.S. leg of the 2005 tour, *Auditorium Theater: Chicago, IL 4/15/05* and *Royce Hall Auditorium: Los Angeles, CA 4/25/05*. Of course, being complete shows from a single tour, there is a certain amount of repetition; songs like "Original Sinsuality," "Yes, Anastasia," "Parasol," and "Cloud on My Tongue" show up on each set. One intriguing selection is a gorgeous rethink of the old Y Kant Tori Read song "Cool on Your Island," which strips away the mid-tempo beat and tropical touches to make the song one of Amos's patented mournful covers—even though she was essentially covering herself.

Each CD also includes two actual covers—as always, Amos is adventurous with her remake choices. In fact, for the tour, Amos let the fans help her decide. On her tour, she set aside a section that she referred to as Tori's Piano Bar, in which people could go to her official Web site and request songs to be played live at local shows. She'd pick two of the suggested songs for each show. Amos listened to thousands of songs to decide. Amos's choices for these shows were Jim Croce's plaintive ballad "Operator (That's Not the Way It Feels)" and Joni Mitchell's "Circle Game" in Chicago and Bon Jovi's hair metal classic "Living on a Prayer" and Cyndi Lauper's "All Through the Night" in Los Angeles.

In announcing Croce's brokenhearted "Operator," Amos told the crowd the song was special to her because when she was a little girl, her brother, Michael, used to sing it for her on the guitar ("Poor thing, he was tone deaf, but he was a fantastic guitar player," she reminisced to the crowd.)[51] She sounds particularly vulnerable and moved on the line about thinking of the love that she thought would save her, leading the listener to think Michael was with her in some way as she let the song loose. Mitchell's "Circle Game" also took her back to her childhood, remembering the school concerts that she used to do as a girl.

Los Angeles ("the land of hair spray"[52]) seemed to her the perfect place to play Bon Jovi's voice-boxed New Jersey passion play "Living on a Prayer," because the song was such an integral part of her L.A. experience—it was at its most popular as she was in her metal-chick period leading up to the *Y Kant Tori Read* album. In her beautiful cover of Jules Shear's "All Through the Night" (which was popularized by Lauper), Amos is in the middle of the song and singing away beautifully when she loses the tune during a particularly complicated lyrical section. She stops briefly and exclaims, "Well, fucking how? That's a tricky one. That was weird."[53] Then she takes a deep breath and pushes on.

As Amos's career gets longer and she approaches two decades of recording, it has become a little fashionable for writers to take potshots at her and her fans. In a review of an August 2005 show, *Philadelphia Daily News* writer Stu Bykofsky (who, by the way, is a columnist who specializes in snarky local gossip, not a music journalist) claims that he is not a typical Amos concertgoer because, "I am neither unhappy and / or overweight and / or lesbian female, nor a gay male."[54] (Looking at Bykofsky's picture, it seems he's more likely a fan of Al Martino and Bobby Vinton.)

In an interview with writer Jude Rogers in *Word* magazine, the writer was passive-aggressively antagonistic toward the singer. (At least he hides it to her face; in the article itself, Rogers makes his disdain abundantly clear.) Finally, Amos gets a little fed up at the guy's mental eye-rolling and has to try to explain herself, "I'm not here to give you the Jackie Collins story, God bless her, that's not what I do.... I go after some uncomfortable subjects. I go after being empowered with force and not feeling that I need to justify myself to a male authority....But, hey, I like a giggle, too. I like baby-making music. I'm Mrs. Hawley sometimes. I can let things go. I've learned to say, 'Tori Amos has left the building.'"[55]

However, for every negative story, there are many more that are positive. The *Daily Telegraph* (London) compared her strength in concert to "a splay-legged minotaur with the head of Venus."[56] Of her most recent tour, *Keyboard* magazine said, "Tori Amos conjures musical and literary wonders."[57] The *Miami Herald* called her music a "contradiction of lovely and angry, of sweet and tart."[58] But perhaps *All Music Guide* summed up the change in Amos' career and music best: "If *Little Earthquakes*…could only have made in her twenties, *The Beekeeper* is…perfectly suited for…her forties."[59] It all comes down to growth. Like the plants in the garden of her album, Tori Amos continues reaching for the sun. And Amos's fans continue to flourish as well, if not necessarily quite as large a menagerie as they were five years ago; but they are still just as fertile.

   The Beekeeper was not exactly a huge hit for Amos, although it did fairly well. However, it seems clear that once again Amos is writing an album to explore her life, her world, and the demons that reside in both places. It is all a mechanism of survival for Amos. Life is full of hardship and discontent, but she has been able to channel those hurt feelings and distraught moments into her art. It is not only the stuff of a fascinating body of work, but it has also been somewhat therapeutic as she has followed her faeries and her bliss. In a recent interview, Amos acknowledged that her husband was like Paul McCartney, but she really related to John Lennon. Not that there was anything wrong with filling the world with silly love songs, but she was just more interested in the twist, in the dark side, in the regret. After all, it is something that all humans must learn to face. "We've all been let down by somebody," Amos told *Word*. "If you can't deal with disappointment, it terrorizes you. So that's how I deal with it, by writing songs."[60]

   Luckily for us, we've been allowed to go along for the ride.

Endnotes

Introduction

1. Maureen Callahan, "The Enchanted Forest," *Spin*, November 1999, 108–114.
2. Steven Daly, "Tori Amos: Her Secret Garden," *Rolling Stone*, June 25, 1998, 38–44, 102–103.
3. Ken Sharp, "When Tori Amos Talks, People Listen," *Concert News*, November 1992, 13.

chapter 1. Baltimore

1. About North Georgia by Golden Ink, "The Trail of Tears," http://ngeorgia.com/history/nghisttt.html.
2. Nigel Williamson, "Relative Values," *The Sunday Times Magazine* (London), May 24, 1998.
3. Dorian Lynskey, "33 Things You Should Know About Tori Amos," *Blender*, November 2002.
4. Justine Picardie, "Kooky or What?," *The Independent* (London), January 16, 1994, 13.
5. Joe Jackson, "Tori's Story," *Hot Press*, 1992.
6. Steven Daly, "Tori Amos: Her Secret Garden," *Rolling Stone*, June 25, 1998, 38–44, 102–103.
7. Ken Sharp, "When Tori Amos Talks, People Listen," *Concert News*, November 1992, 13.
8. Christopher John Farley, "Tori, Tori, Tori!," *Time*, May 11, 1998.
9. Charles Aaron, "Sex, God and Rock and Roll," *Spin*, October 1994, 50.
10. Daly, "Tori Amos: Her Secret Garden," 38–44, 102–103.
11. Ibid.
12. Greg Rule, "Tori! Tori! Tori!," *Keyboard*, September 1992, 40–51, 147.
13. Ibid.
14. "The Tori Party," *Deluxe*, May 1998.
15. Tom Doyle, "Single to Damascus Please…," *Q*, June 1995, 74–104.
16. Sharp, "When Tori Amos Talks, People Listen," 13.
17. The Peabody Institute, http://www.peabody.jhu.edu.
18. Tom Hibbert, "Tori Amos: From Rock Chick to Twisted Mystic," *Details*, November 1992, 153–154.
19. Michael Whitehead, "Tori and Drugs," *TheDent.com*, December 28, 2000.
20. Jonathan Takiff, "Amos' Piano Pop More Than Music," *Philadelphia Daily News*, March 24, 1994.
21. Ibid.

22.   Tori Amos, *Little Earthquakes*, (A-Vision, 1992), video.
23.   "Top Teens in Talent Test," *Montgomery Journal*, March 31, 1977, A9.
24.   Sharp, "When Tori Amos Talks, People Listen," 13.
25.   Lynskey, "33 Things You Should Know About Tori Amos."
26.   "The College Daze of Tori Amos," *Student Advantage Magazine*, winter 1998.
27.   Daly, "Tori Amos: Her Secret Garden," 38–44, 102–103.
28.   Richard Handal, *TheDent.com*, http://thedent.com/recordcoll99.html.
29.   Katherine Tolbert, "At 17, Student Sings a Song of Success," *The Washington Post*, December 18, 1980, MW2.
30.   Ibid.
31.   Tim Neely, *Goldmine Price Guide to Alternative Records* (Iola, WI: Krause Publications, 1996).
32.   James Blandford, "Tea with the Waitress," *Record Collector*, November 1999.
33.   Tom Doyle, "Ready, Steady, Kook!," *Q*, May 1998, 80–88.
34.   *The River Lounge*, WVRV-FM (St. Louis, MO), December 3, 2002.
35.   Laura Morgan, "Tori Amos Loved Leg Warmers!," *Seventeen.com*, November 2002.
36.   Tori Amos chat, *Prodigy.com.*, September 1994.
37.   Roger Piantadosi, "Ellen Amos: The Marbury Woman," *The Washington Post*, May 11, 1984, W13.

chapter 2. Y Kant Tori Read

1.   John Savage, "Tori Amos," *Interview*, May 1992, 86–87.
2.   "Kooky Singer Songstress Tori Amos' Latest Offering, *Strange Little Girls*, Is a Collection of Songs Written by Men Through Which She Wanted to Talk About Men. Hey, Who Were We Not to Oblige Her?," *Boyz*, September 17, 2001.
3.   Tom Hibbert, "Tori Amos: From Rock Chick to Twisted Mystic," *Details*, November 1992, 154.
4.   Joe Jackson, "The Hurt Inside," *Hot Press*, February 23, 1994, 32–34.
5.   *Prime Time Live*, ABC, August 21, 1996.
6.   Ken Sharp, "When Tori Amos Talks, People Listen," *Concert News*, November 1992, 13.
7.   Maureen Callahan, "The Enchanted Forest," *Spin*, November 1999, 108–114.
8.   "Y Kant Tori Read" press kit, Atlantic Records, 1988.
9.   James Blandford. "Tea with the Waitress," *Record Collector*, November 1999.
10.   Dorian Lynskey, "33 Things You Should Know About Tori Amos," *Blender*, November 2002.
11.   David Schwartz, "Local Rock 'n' Roller Shoots for Stardom," *The Gazette* (Montgomery County, MD), June 22, 1988, 30.

12.   Savage, "Tori Amos," 86–87.
13.   *Behind the Music 2: Tori Amos,* VH1, March 21, 2000.
14.   "Y Kant Tori Read" press kit.
15.   Christopher Smith, "Tori Amos: The Loudest Voice in the Choir," *Performing Songwriter*, September/October 1998.
16.   Ibid.
17.   "Album Reviews," *Billboard*, June 11, 1988.
18.   Tim Neely, *Goldmine Price Guide to Alternative Records* (Iola, WI: Krause Publications, 1996).
19.   Brian Griffith, "Tori! Tori! Tori!," *Hits*, April 6, 1992, 67.
20.   Al Stewart, concert, Royal Festival Hall (London, England), April 24, 1991.
21.   Tori Amos, concert, Royal Festival Hall (London, England), October 29, 1999.
22.   Tori Amos, "The Wisdom of the Wild: Singer—Actress Sandra Bernhard," *Interview*, August 1994.
23.   *Behind the Music 2*, VH1.

chapter 3. Excuse Me, but Can I Be You for a While?

1.   Ken Sharp, "When Tori Amos Talks, People Listen," *Concert News*, November 1992, 13.
2.   Mat Snow, "Can We Talk?," *Q*, February 1992, 20–21.
3.   Alec Foege, "Two New Feminist Voices, Tori Amos and Juliana Hatfield, Bring Women's Rock Beyond the Babe Factor," *Vogue*, June 1992, 64, 66.
4.   Tom Hibbert, "Tori Amos: From Rock Chick to Twisted Mystic," *Details*, November 1992, 154.
5.   Jesse Nash, "Sigerson Captures Amos' Emotional Tremors," *Billboard*, April 11, 1992, 50.
6.   "Little Earthquakes" tour program, 1992.
7.   Greg Rule, "Tori! Tori! Tori!," *Keyboard*, September 1992, 40–51, 147.
8.   Richard Harrington, "Finally, a Prodigy Finds Her Song," *The Washington Post*, March 22, 1992, G1.
9.   *World Café*, WXPN-FM (Philadelphia, PA), May 18, 1992.
10.   *VH1 Storytellers: Tori Amos.*, VHI, February 21, 1999.
11.   Tori Amos, concert, The Chili Pepper (Fort Lauderdale, FL), April 18, 1998.
12.   Robert L. Doerschuk, "Tori Amos: Dancing with the Vampire and the Nightingale," *Keyboard*, November 1994, 34–39, 92–95.
13.   Brook Hersey, "Listen to Tori Amos," *Glamour*, August 1992.
14.   John Everson, "Tori Amos: The Sacred and the Profane," *The Illinois Entertainer*, September 1998.
15.   Melinda Newman, "Tori Amos: Atlantic's Golden Girl," *Billboard*, February 20, 1993, 10, 86.
16.   John Savage, "Tori Amos," *Interview*, May 1992, 86–87.
17.   Westwood One Radio Network, February 27, 1992.
18.   "If You Don't Have a Stalker, You Don't Rate," *She*, May 1998.

19. "The 90 Greatest Albums of the 90s," *Spin*, September 1999, 113–164.

20. Larry Flick, "Tori Amos Shares Life Lessons," *Billboard*, March 28, 1992.

21. "Nirvana: Anarchy in the UK," *The Internet Nirvana Fan Club*, http://www. nirvanaclub.com/nfa/anarchy.html.

22. University Radio (Warwick-Coventry, England), February 25, 1994.

23. Tom Doyle, "Ready, Steady, Kook!," *Q*, May 1998, 80–88.

24. David Sinclair, "Dear Diary: The Secret World of Kate Bush," *Rolling Stone*, February 24, 1994.

25. Simon Reynolds, "Do Angels Want to Wear Her Red Shoes?" *Pulse*, December 1993, 58–64.

26. "Tori Amos" press kit, Atlantic Records, February 1992.

27. Interview with Noah Adams, National Public Radio, July 5, 1994.

28. Doerschuk, "Tori Amos: Dancing with the Vampire and the Nightingale," 34–39, 92–95.

29. Bill Dunn, "A Date with Tori Amos," *Esquire*, October 1999.

30. Sharp, "When Tori Amos Talks, People Listen."

31. *MTV Video Music Awards Opening Act*, MTV, September 10, 1992.

32. Sam Rooti, "Famous Amos," *Spin*, January 1993.

33. Sharp, "When Tori Amos Talks, People Listen."

chapter 4. Past the Mission

1. Brad Balfour, "What Really Gets to You?" *New Review of Records*, December 1993/January 1994.

2. Dorian Lynskey, "33 Things You Should Know About Tori Amos," *Blender*, November 2002.

3. Elysa Gardner, "Tori Amos Keeps Her Head," *Musician*, January 1993, 46–48.

4. Balfour, "What Really Gets to You?"

5. Ibid.

6. "Stories," *Q*, November 1993, 13.

7. David Hinckley, "A Fire in the Wheat Fields," *New York Daily News*, March 28, 1993, 43.

8. Joe Jackson, "The Hurt Inside," *Hot Press*, February 23, 1994, 32–34.

9. "Talking About Nothing with Trent Reznor," *Axcess Magazine*, September 1994.

10. Sue Smallwood, "Amos Speaks Cryptically," *The Virginian-Pilot* (Norfolk, VA), July 27, 1994, E1.

11. Larry Flick, "Label Tickled 'Pink' Over New Tori Amos Set," *Billboard*, December 4, 1993, 3, 78.

12. Tori Amos, concert, Meany Hall (Seattle, WA), March 20, 1994.

13. Balfour, "What Really Gets to You?"

14. Wayne Robins, "Songs of Sex and the Spirit," *New York Newsday*, April 5, 1992, 15–16.

15. Balfour, "What Really Gets to You?"

16. Steven Daly, "Tori Amos: Her Secret Garden," *Rolling Stone*, June 25, 1998, 38–44, 102–103.

17. "Tori Amos: Under the Pink" press kit, Atlantic Records, January 1994.

18. Balfour, "What Really Gets to You?"

19. Tori Amos, concert, Palace Theater (Louisville, KY), April 19, 1996.

20. Balfour, "What Really Gets to You?"

21. Ibid.

22. Chris Willman, "Brazen. Precious. Poetic. Profane.," *Los Angeles Times*, January 30, 1994, 53.

23. John Everson, "Tight Socks and Feminist Freedom," *The Illinois Entertainer*, August 1994, 22–24.

24. Balfour, "What Really Gets to You?"

25. Tori Amos, concert, Hard Rock Hotel (Las Vegas, NV), September 24, 1998.

26. Sandra A. Garcia, "Tori Amos: In the Name of the Mother," *B–Side*, April/May 1994.

27. *Baltimore Sun* transcript, *YesSaid.com*, January 1994, http://www.yessaid.com/interviews/94NewReviewofRecords.html.

28. Kim Fowley, "So You Found a Girl Who Thinks Really Deep Thoughts," *BAM*, March 11, 1994.

29. Tori Amos, concert, MECC Conference Center (Maastricht, The Netherlands), May 7, 1994.

30. Garcia, "Tori Amos: In the Name of the Mother."

31. Ibid.

32. Balfour, "What Really Gets to You?"

33. Tori Amos, "Q Diary—This Ain't LA, Baby," *Q*, February 1994, 38–41.

34. Flick, "Label Tickled 'Pink' Over New Tori Amos Set."

35. Balfour, "What Really Gets to You?"

36. Everson, "Tight Socks and Feminist Freedom."

37. Adrian Deevoy, "Hips. Tits. Lips. Power.," *Q*, May 1994, 90–97.

38. Tori Amos, concert, Trinitatiskrine (Berlin, Germany), April 9, 1994.

39. Lynskey, "33 Things You Should Know About Tori Amos."

40. Courtney Love, online chat, *Hole.com*, March 16, 2000.

41. *Behind the Music 2: Tori Amos*, VH1, March 21, 2000.

42. KSCA-FM (Los Angeles, CA), August 24, 1994.

43. Charles Aaron, "Sex, God and Rock and Roll," *Spin*, October 1994, 50.

chapter 5. Putting the Damage On

1. Lindsay Planer, "It's Best to Catch Her Live," *Break*, August 14–20, 1996, 10.

2. "Tori Amos" press kit, Atlantic Records, January 1996.

3. Lucy O'Brien, "Pianosexual," *Diva*, February/March 1996.

4. Ibid.
5. *The Ultimate Tori Amos FAQ Web Page,* http://www.geocities.com/ultimatetrifaq.
6. "Stories," *Q,* January 1996, 15.
7. Jeanne Marie Laskas, "Tori Adored," *Entertainment Weekly,* July 12, 1996.
8. Tori Amos, speech, University of California in Los Angeles (UCLA), February 27, 1995.
9. Domenic Pride and Chuck Taylor, "Amos Bares Soul on Atlantic Set," *Billboard,* January 13, 1996, 1, 66.
10. Matt Ashare, "One-Woman Choir: Tori Amos Unravels a Bit of Her Mystery," *Rollingstone.com,* August 8, 1998.
11. Tori Amos, concert, Macky Auditorium (Boulder, CO), November 11, 1996.
12. Sandra A. Garcia, "A Bottle of Red: Tori Amos," *B-Side,* May/June 1996.
13. Robert L. Doerschuk, "Voices in the Air: Spirit Tripping with Tori Amos," *Musician,* May 1996.
14. "Donald Leslie; Creator of the Leslie Keyboard Speaker; 93," The Associated Press, September 9, 2004.
15. Tori Amos, concert, Palace Theater (Columbus, OH), August 1, 1996.
16. Francesca Lia Block, "The Volcano Lover," *Spin,* March 1996, 42–48, 125.
17. Poppy Z. Brite, *Courtney Love: The Real Story* (New York: Simon & Schuster, 1998).
18. *The Ultimate Tori Amos FAQ Web Page.*
19. *World Café,* WXPN-FM (Philadelphia, PA), March 1, 1996.
20. Tori Amos, concert, Aranoff Center (Cincinnati, OH), June 3, 1996.
21. Lydia Carole DeFretos, "Tori Amos: Finding Her Own Fire," *Aquarian Weekly,* February 21, 1996.
22. Tori Amos, concert, Royal Albert Hall (London, England), March 8, 1996.
23. Matt Weitz, "Desperately Seeking Tori," *Dallas Observer,* June 13, 1996.
24. Lisa Robinson, "Men No Longer God to Amos," *New York Post,* January 12, 1996.
25. Amy Talkington, "A Few of Tori Amos' Favorite Things," *Seventeen,* March 1996.
26. DeFretos, "Tori Amos: Finding Her Own Fire."
27. Tori Amos, concert, Tampa Bay Performing Arts Center (Tampa, FL), April 9, 1996.
28. Garcia, "A Bottle of Red: Tori Amos."
29. CFNY-FM (Toronto, Ontario, Canada), January 29, 1996.
30. "The Fifty Most Beautiful People in the World 1996," *People,* June 1996.
31. Dorian Lynskey, "33 Things You Should Know About Tori Amos," *Blender,* November 2002.
32. KSCA-FM (Los Angeles, CA), August 24, 1994.
33. "Kooky Singer Songstress Tori Amos' Latest Offering, *Strange Little Girls,* Is a Collection of Songs Written by Men Through Which She Wanted to

Talk About Men. Hey, Who Were We Not to Oblige Her?" *Boyz*, September 17, 2001.

34.   Lynskey, "33 Things You Should Know About Tori Amos."
35.   J. D. Considine, "Page and Plant Shake the Led Out in Their Latest Tour," *The Baltimore Sun*, March 19, 1995, 1J.
36.   "Any Queries? Tori Amos.," *Attitude*, September 2001.
37.   Justin Bergman, "Amos Challenges Self on Other Side of Microphone," *Gannett News Service*, November 22, 1996.
38.   Chris Smith, "Tori Amos," *Us*, July 1998.
39.   Steve Hochman, "An Anthem in the Waiting," *Los Angeles Times*, May 15, 1997, 22.

chapter 6: Tori's Strength

1.   Sylvie Simmons, "Nice!," *Mojo*, May 1998, 116.
2.   Martian Engineering, Ltd., http://www.martianengineering.com/.
3.   Bill DeYoung, "Next-Door Celebrities," *The Stuart News*, November 6, 2004.
4.   John Patrick Gatta, "It's a Free Will Planet: An Interview with Tori Amos," *Magical Blend*, winter 1998.
5.   Tori Amos, online chat, *America Online*, September 29, 1999.
6.   Molly Knight, "Matt Chamberlain Talks About Tori, Summer Touring, and Datura's Chances," *Mollyknight.com*, August 11, 2003.
7.   Paul Verna, "Tori Amos Isn't Alone in Her Hotel," *Billboard*, April 4, 1998.
8.   "Tori Amos," *Columbia House*, spring 1999.
9.   "Tori Amos" press kit, Atlantic Records, May 1998.
10.   "The Tori Party," *Deluxe*, May 1998.
11.   Tom Stone, "Arena-sized Venues, a Band—What's Next for Tori Amos?" *Dallas Morning News*, October 4, 1998.
12.   *Louisville Observer*, October 1998.
13.   Steven Daly, "Tori Amos: Her Secret Garden," *Rolling Stone*, June 25, 1998, 38–44, 102–103.
14.   David Daley, "Magic and Loss," *Alternative Press*, July 1998.
15.   *End Sessions*, KNDD (Seattle, WA), September 20, 1998.
16.   J. D. Considine, "A Choirgirl with Charisma," *The Baltimore Sun*, May 24, 1998, 3E.
17.   Tom Doyle, "Ready, Steady, Kook!," *Q*, May 1998, 80–88.
18.   James Bennett, "The Big Interview: No Pain, No Gain," *The Times* (London), April 11, 1998.
19.   Ibid.
20.   Doyle, "Ready, Steady, Kook!"
21.   Considine, "A Choirgirl with Charisma."
22.   "Incoming…," *Q*, April 1998, 26.

23.   Hugh Robjohns, "Checking in with the Choirgirl: Mark Hawley Recording and Touring with Tori Amos," *Sound on Sound*, July 1998.

24.   Jim Farber, "Early Bird Artists Have a Jump on '98," *New York Daily News*, January 1998.

25.   Randee Dawn, "The 25 Most Anticipated Albums of 1998," *Alternative Press*, January 1998.

26.   Donna Freydkin, "Tori Amos: Clearly in the Right Band," *CNN.com*, August 27, 1998.

27.   Brian McCollum, "This Time Tori Amos Is Bringing a Band to Detroit," *Detroit Free Press*, April 28, 1998.

28.   "If You Don't Have a Stalker, You Don't Rate," *She*, May 1998.

29.   Freydkin, "Tori Amos: Clearly in the Right Band."

chapter 7. Glory of the Nineties

1.   Tori Amos, online chat, *America Online*, January 20, 1999.

2.   James Ireland Baker, "Tori Amos," *Us*, October 1999, 38.

3.   Chuck Taylor, "Tori Amos Unveils 'Venus,'" *Billboard*, July 17, 1999, 1, 116.

4.   Julie Ann Pietrangelo, "To Venus and Back," *Spin.com*, September 1999.

5.   J. D. Considine, "Amos' Magic Shines Through," *The Baltimore Sun*, August 25, 1999, 1E.

6.   Ibid.

7.   Esther Haynes, "Music Q & A: Tori Amos," *Jane*, October 1999, 52.

8.   James McNair, "Her Indoors: Tori's Lesson in Marital Harmony," *Mojo*, November 1999.

9.   "Tori Amos: Interplanetary, Most Extraordinary," *Time-Off*, November 24–30, 1999.

10.   Tori Amos and Alanis Morissette, online chat, *MP3.com*, September 20, 1999.

11.   Michael Hill, "Tori Amos: Stars, Planets, Wine and Song," *The Wire, VH1. com*, September 1999.

12.   Natalie Nichols, "For Amos, Passion Fuels 'Venus' Voyage," *Los Angeles Times*, September 23, 1999, 22.

13.   Tori Amos and Alanis Morissette, online chat, *America Online*, August 17, 1999.

14.   Hannah Kuhlmann, "A Glimpse Into the Mind of Neil Gaiman," *The Minnesota Daily*, November 18, 1999.

15.   Julie Devine, "Riot Poof on the Road," *UK.Gay.com*, January 8, 2001.

16.   Matthew Tood, "Tori's Glory," *Attitude*, November 1999.

17.   "Online 'Bliss': Atlantic to Sell New Tori Amos Single via Web" press release, Atlantic Records, August 13, 1999.

18.   Tom Doyle, "Ready, Steady, Kook!," *Q*, May 1998, 80–88.

19.   Tom Doyle, "Cash for Questions: Alanis Morissette," *Q*, March 1999, 12–16.

20.   "Road Runners," *Rolling Stone*, July 8–22, 1999.
21.   Tori Amos, online chat, *Prodigy.com.*, September 1994.
22.   "Road Runners," *Rolling Stone.*
23.   Tori Amos and Alanis Morissette, online chat.
24.   Steve Morse, "Venus of the Road," *The Boston Globe*, August 27, 1999, E14.
25.   *The Kevin and Bean Morning Show*, KROQ-FM (Los Angeles, CA), September 19, 1999.
26.   Tori Amos, "Celebrity Real Life: Tori's Joy After Her Miscarriage Heartbreak," *She*, December 2003.
27.   Ibid.
28.   "The Reliable Source," *The Washington Post*, June 22, 2000.
29.   "Tori Amos Announces Long-Awaited New Release: A Baby Girl!" press release, September 6, 2000.

chapter 8. Covers Girl

1.   "In the Works," *Mojo*, September 2001, 10.
2.   Randee Dawn, "Motherhood, Murder and the Missus," *Alternative Press*, October 2001, 68–74.
3.   Steve Hochman, "Tori Amos Offers a Woman's-Eye View of Songs by Men," *Los Angeles Times*, July 1, 2001, Calendar–1.
4.   Justin Stoneman, "World of the Strange," *Virgin.net*, September 11, 2001.
5.   Steve Morse, "Tori Amos Play-acts Pop's Images of Women," *The Boston Globe*, September 16, 2001.
6.   Sarah Stone, "Tori Amos," *RedDirect.com*, September 2001.
7.   Laura Morgan, "Rock," *Entertainment Weekly*, September 21, 2001.
8.   Ben Wener, "She Seeks the Woman Within," *The Orange County Register*, November 13, 2001.
9.   David Quantick, "In the Piano Room with Tori Amos," *Blender*, August/September 2001.
10. Julia Llewellyn Smith, "I Needed a Child in My Life More Than I Knew," *The Daily Telegraph* (London), September 5, 2001.
11. Gregg Shapiro, "Cover Girl: An Interview with Tori Amos," *Next*, September 5, 2001.
12. Dawn, "Motherhood, Murder and the Missus."
13. Glyn Brown, "Tori Amos: In the Company of Men," *The Independent* (London), September 14, 2001.
14. Poll results, *The Dent.com*, http://www.thedent.com/pollresults.html.
15. *World Café*, WXPN-FM (Philadelphia, PA), November 9, 2001.
16. Tori Amos, speech, "New York Times' Critic's Choice," City University of New York (CUNY), January 12, 2002.
17. Richard Harrington, "Tori Amos Flips the Perspective," *The Washington Post*, October 22, 2001, WE06.
18. Lloyd Cole, posting, "Ask Lloyd," *LloydCole.com*, November 28, 2004.

19. "Tori Amos Covers All the Bases," *ICE*, September 2001, 6–7.
20. Troy Johnson, "People Are Strange…Tori Amos Rewrites Songs and Sex on Her New Album," *Slamm—The San Diego Music Magazine*, October 31–November 13, 2001.
21. Will Hermes, "Don't Mess with Mother Nature," *Spin*, October 2001.
22. "Strange Little Tori," *RollingStone.com*, October 4, 2001.
23. Clark Collis, "Tori Amos: Strange Little Girls," *Q*, October 2001, 116.
24. Thor Christenson, "Tori Amos Dresses Up to Personify the Women Men Sing About," *Dallas Morning News*, November 2, 2001, W1.
25. Joe Jackson, concert, Live Music Hall (Cologne, Germany), April 24, 2003.
26. Dorian Lynskey, "33 Things You Should Know About Tori Amos," *Blender*, November 2002.
27. Bill DeMain, "Mother of Invention Tori Amos," *Performing Songwriter*, January/February 2002.
28. Matt Diehl, "Almost Amos: Amos Bends Genders in *Strange Little Girls*," *Elle*, September 2001.
29. Ed Condran, "Her Stamp on Men's Words," *The Bergen County Record* (New Jersey), October 5, 2001.
30. Annie Zaleski, "Journey Woman," *Boston Phoenix*, November 14, 2002.
31. Tori Amos Official Web Site, http://www.toriamos.com.
32. Gregg Shapiro, "Whatever Rufus Wants," *Outsmart.com*, November 2003.
33. Melinda Newman, "The Beat," *Billboard*, November 24, 2001, 16.

chapter 9. A Sorta Fairy Tale

1. Bob Gulla, "Walk on the Wild Side," *Women Who Rock*, fall 2002.
2. Marc Brown, "America at Her Gait," *Rocky Mountain News*, December 4, 2002.
3. Christa Gable, "Amos Bleeds 'Scarlet' During Palace Performance," *The Lantern* (Ohio State University), November 25, 2002.
4. Esther Haynes, "Music Q & A: Tori Amos," *Jane*, October 1999, 52.
5. *Scarlet's Walk—Selections*, Epic Records, 2002.
6. "Scarlet's Walk—A Prologue" press kit, Epic Records, September 2002.
7. Kim Curtis, "Five Questions with Tori Amos," The Associated Press, December 31, 2002.
8. Brian Orloff, "Gathering 'Round with Music," *St. Petersburg Times*, November 3, 2002.
9. "Scarlet's Walk—A Prologue."
10. *Morning Edition*, National Public Radio, November 27, 2002.
11. *The Isaac Mizrahi Show*, Oxygen Cable Network, March 10, 2003.
12. "Top Ten Singles of 2002," *USA Today*, December 31, 2002.
13. *ARTE—Music Planet 2Nite*, November 26, 2002.
14. Gary Graff, "Songstress Tori Amos Takes a Walk Through America a Year After September 11," *Galleryofsound.com*, October 2002.

15. Steven Robinson, "Red Letter Day with Tori," *Hot Press*, November 20, 2002.
16. Brian Ives, "An American Journey Gooses the Singer-Songwriter's Imagination," *VH1.com*, October 28, 2002.
17. *Morning Becomes Eclectic*, KCRW-FM (Santa Monica, CA), December 17, 2002.
18. Cameron Adams, "Scarlet's Web," *The Herald Sun* (Melbourne, Australia), October 31, 2002.
19. Ellen Tien, "In the Eye of One Beholder, Only Beauty," *The New York Times*, May 12, 2002, I6.
20. Gregg Shapiro, "Walking and Talking with Tori Amos," *Windy City Times*, November 13, 2002.
21. Chris Chandar, "Tori Amos: The Idiosyncratic Singer-Songwriter Reclaims Her Roots in *Scarlet's Walk*," *Pulse*, November 2002.
22. Tom Lanham, "Going on 'Scarlet's Walk,'" *San Francisco Examiner*, October 30, 2002.
23. *Music Biz*, BBC World Service, October 31, 2002.
24. Tori Amos, *A Sorta Fairytale* (Epic Music Video, 2002).
25. Mix 94.7 (Austin, TX), November 1, 2002.
26. "Tori Amos' Musical Journey Across America," *CNN.com*, February 13, 2003.
27. Jancee Dunn, "Tori Amos," *Rolling Stone*, October 31, 2002, 64.
28. *The Ryan Seacrest Show*, April 15, 2004.
29. "Singer Tori Amos Sued," *AAP*, August 30, 2003.
30. Lyndsey Parker, "Damian Rice Wins Shortlist Music Prize," *Launch.com*, October 6, 2003.
31. Spencer Patterson, "Amos True," *The Las Vegas Sun*, July 27, 2003.
32. Ibid.
33. *The Kevin and Bean Morning Show* (KROQ-FM Los Angeles, CA), December 1, 2003.
34. "Tori Amos Announces New Business Venture" press release, The Bridge Entertainment Group, October 9, 2003.
35. James McNair, "Tori Amos: Fairytale Endings," *The Independent* (London) November 21, 2003.
36. Brian Orloff, "Tori Amos Bears New Fruit," *RollingStone.com*, September 5, 2003.
37. Ed Condran, "Soundcheck: Tori Amos—Singer/Songwriter," *Cleveland Free Times*, August 13–19, 2003.
38. Nick Taylor, "Toritelling," *Attitude*, November 2003.
39. Andrew Billen, "Tori the Librarian and Other Odd Tales," *The Times* (London), November 4, 2003.
40. Wil Marlow, "Tori Goes Back to the Future," The Press Association, November 10, 2003.
41. *Faith and Music*, ITV1 (U.K.), February 29, 2004.

42. Tori Amos, *Welcome to Sunny Florida* (Epic Music Video, 2004).

43. *Behind the Music 2: Tori Amos*, VH1, March 21, 2000.

44. Matthew Moriarty, "Man Dies from Wreck Injuries," *Pilot.com*, November 24, 2004.

45. Gary Graff, "Staying Creative," *The Cleveland Plain Dealer*, August 26, 2005.

46. Monica Cady, "Tori Amos," *Rag*, May 2005, 32–35.

47. Sally Browne, "Tori's Own Land of Oz," *The Sunday Mail* (U.K.), May 15, 2005.

48. T'cha Dunleavy, "Tori's Weird World," *The Montreal Gazette*, August 24, 2005.

49. Tori Amos, "The Mix Sessions," *Q*, June 2005, 128.

50. "Tori Amos to Release Live Bootleg Series" press release, Epic Records, August 8, 2005.

51. Tori Amos, concert, Auditorium Theatre (Chicago, IL), April 15, 2005.

52. Tori Amos, concert, Royce Hall Auditorium (Los Angeles, CA), April 25, 2005.

53. Ibid.

54. Stu Bykofsky, "Concert Advice," *Philadelphia Daily News*, August 26, 2005, 29.

55. Jude Rogers, "Will the Real Tori Amos Ever Shut Up?," *Word*, August 2005, 69–70.

56. Bernadette McNulty, "Goddesses on Parade," *The Daily Telegraph* (London) June 23, 2005.

57. Michael Gallani, "Tori Amos—Metaphysics and Music," *Keyboard*, July 2005.

58. Leslie Gray Streeter, "Tori Amos' Lyrical, Emotional Appeal," *The Miami Herald*, August 10, 2005.

59. Stephen Thomas Erlewine, "The Beekeeper," *AllMusic.com*, April 2005.

60. "Lyricists: The Sense Impressionist—Tori Amos," *Word*, February 2005.

Discography

Y Kant Tori Read
Atlantic 81845 (1988)

1. The Big Picture *(Tori Amos and Kim Bullard)*
2. Cool on Your Island *(Tori Amos and Kim Bullard)*
3. Fayth *(Tori Amos and Brad Cobb)*
4. Fire on the Side
5. Pirates *(Tori Amos and Kim Bullard)*
6. Floating City
7. Heart Attack at 23
8. On the Boundary
9. You Go to My Head
10. Etienne Trilogy
    The Highlands
    Etienne *(Tori Amos and Kim Bullard)*
    Skyeboat Song *(Traditional)*

All songs written by Tori Amos except for where noted.

Produced by Joe Chiccarelli. Co-produced by Kim Bullard.

Mixed by Ed Thacker.

Recorded at Hollywood Sound Recorders (Hollywood, CA), Southcombe Studios (Burbank, CA), Ground Control Studios (Santa Monica, CA), Sound Castle Studios (Los Angeles, CA), Capitol Studios (Hollywood, CA), and The Grey Room (North Hollywood, CA).

Art direction by Bob Defrin. Photography by Aaron Rapoport.

Notes: Amos's misguided art-rock metal-band effort was a wrong step for her creatively and a colossal disappointment sales-wise, but it does show little nuggets of the talent for which she will become known.

Little Earthquakes
Atlantic 82358 (1991)

1. Crucify *
2. Girl **
3. Silent All These Years *

147

4. Precious Things **
5. Winter *
6. Happy Phantom *
7. China ***
8. Leather *
9. Mother *
10. Tear in Your Hand **
11. Me and a Gun ***
12. Little Earthquakes **

All songs written by Tori Amos.

   * Produced by Davitt Sigerson.

  ** Produced by Tori Amos and Eric Rosse.

*** Produced by Ian Stanley.

Mixed by Paul McKenna, Jon Kelly, Ross Collum, and John Beverly Jones.

Art direction and photography by Cindy Palmano.

Notes: A gloriously personal and intimate album in which Amos stops trying to be everything for everyone and instead writes for herself. Though she has done some stunning work since, this is still her best album, and "Silent All These Years," "China," "Winter," and "Me and a Gun" rank among her greatest compositions.

Under the Pink
Atlantic 82567 (1994)

1. Pretty Good Year
2. God
3. Bells for Her
4. Past the Mission
5. Baker Baker
6. The Wrong Band
7. The Waitress
8. Cornflake Girl
9. Icicle
10. Cloud on My Tongue
11. Space Dog
12. Yes, Anastasia

All songs written by Tori Amos.

Produced by Eric Rosse and Tori Amos.

Mixed by Kevin Killen and Ross Collum.

Recorded at The Firehouse (Taos, NM) and Westlake Studios (Los Angeles, CA).

Photography and art direction by Cindy Palmano. Design by Alan Reinl.

Notes: Amos avoids the sophomore jinx with her second solo album, which takes the beautiful piano ballads of *Little Earthquakes* and expands into other styles, like the industrial thud of "God" and the pop buoyancy of "Cornflake Girl."

Boys for Pele
Atlantic 82862 (1996)

1. Beauty Queen
2. Horses
3. Blood Roses
4. Father Lucifer
5. Professional Widow
6. Mr. Zebra
7. Marianne
8. Caught a Lite Sneeze
9. Muhammad My Friend
10. Hey Jupiter
11. Way Down
12. Little Amsterdam
13. Talula
14. Not the Red Baron
15. Agent Orange
16. Doughnut Song
17. In the Springtime of His Voodoo
18. Putting the Damage On
19. Twinkle

All songs written by Tori Amos.

Produced by Tori Amos.

Mixed by Mark Hawley, Marcel von Limbeck, and Bob Clearmountain.

Recorded at a church (Delgany, County Wicklow, Ireland), a wonderfully damp Georgian house (County Cork, Ireland), The Egyptian Room (New Orleans, LA), and Dinosaur Studios (New Orleans, LA).

Cover art by Cindy Palmano. Design by Paddy Cramsie at Kono Design and Paul Chessell at East West.

Notes: One of Amos's biggest hits, this album was created in a time of personal trial for Amos, and the sense of quiet melancholy and anger are palpable.

From the Choirgirl Hotel
Atlantic 83095 (1998)

1. Spark
2. Cruel
3. Black-Dove (January)
4. Raspberry Swirl
5. Jackie's Strength
6. i i e e e
7. Liquid Diamonds
8. She's Your Cocaine
9. Northern Lad
10. Hotel
11. Playboy Mommy
12. Pandora's Aquarium

All songs written by Tori Amos.

Produced by Tori Amos.

Mixed by Mark Hawley and Marcel von Limbeck.

Recorded at Martian Engineering (Cornwall, England).

Artwork by Michael Nash Associates. Cover image by Katerina Jebb.

Notes: After the success of the dance remix of "Professional Widow," Amos toys more with modern dance beats in what she calls her first album written with her band in mind rather than a pure solo album.

To Venus and Back
Atlantic 83230 (1999)

Disc 1: Venus—Orbiting *(studio recordings)*

1. Bliss
2. Juarez
3. Concertina
4. Glory of the 80's
5. Lust
6. Suede
7. Josephine
8. Riot Poof
9. Datura
10. Spring Haze
11. 1000 Oceans

Disc 2: Venus—Live. Still Orbiting *(concert recordings)*

1. Precious Things
2. Cruel
3. Cornflake Girl
4. Bells for Her
5. Girl
6. Cooling
7. Mr. Zebra
8. Cloud on My Tongue
9. Sugar
10. Little Earthquakes
11. Space Dog
12. Waitress
13. Purple People

All songs written by Tori Amos.

Produced by Tori Amos.

Mixed by Mark Hawley and Marcel von Limbeck.

Studio tracks recorded at Martian Engineering (Cornwall, England).

Live tracks recorded during the "Plugged" Tour '98.

Cover art and all photographs by Loren Haynes.

Notes: A half-studio, half-live two-disc set shows Amos experimenting even more with electronica beats on the first CD, then taking a quirky traipse through her back catalog in concert.

Strange Little Girls
Atlantic 7567-83486 (2001)

1. New Age *(Lou Reed)*
2. '97 Bonnie & Clyde *(Jeff Bass, Mark Randy Bass, and Marshall Mathers III)*
3. Strange Little Girl *(Jean Bumel, Hugh Cornwell, Brian Duffy, David Greenfield, and Hans Warmling)*
4. Enjoy the Silence *(Martin Gore)*
5. I'm Not in Love *(Graham Gouldman)*
6. Rattlesnakes *(Neil Clark and Lloyd Cole)*
7. Time *(Tom Waits)*
8. Heart of Gold *(Neil Young)*
9. I Don't Like Mondays *(Robert Geldof)*
10. Happiness Is a Warm Gun *(John Lennon and Paul McCartney)*
11. Raining Blood *(Jeff Hanneman and Kerry King)*
12. Real Men *(Joe Jackson)*

Produced by Tori Amos.

Executive produced by Natashya.

Mixed by Mark Hawley and Marcel von Limbeck.

Recorded at Martian Engineering (Cornwall, England) and the Nut Ranch (Los Angeles, CA).

Photographed by Thomas Schenk.

Notes: After years of performing other artists' music in concert and as B-sides, Amos does an album where she takes on songs by some of the greatest male voices in songwriting and gives them a distinctly feminine twist.

Scarlet's Walk
Epic 86939 (2002)

1. Amber Waves
2. A Sorta Fairytale
3. Wednesday
4. Strange
5. Carbon
6. Crazy
7. Wampum Prayer
8. Don't Make Me Come to Vegas
9. Sweet Sangria
10. Your Cloud
11. Pancake
12. I Can't See New York
13. Mrs. Jesus
14. Taxi Ride
15. Another Girl's Paradise
16. Scarlet's Walk
17. Virginia
18. Gold Dust

Bonus DVD—Scarlet's DVD

1. Gold Dust *(video)*
2. A Sorta Fairytale *(alternate video)*
3. Taxi Ride *(video)*

All songs written by Tori Amos.

Produced by Tori Amos.

Mixed by Mark Hawley and Marcel von Limbeck.

Recorded at Martian Engineering (Cornwall, England).

Art direction by Sheri Lee and Dave Bett. Photography by Kurt Markus.

Notes: Amos's "sonic novel" takes the listener on a journey across the United States to ponder personal changes and the changes in the country after the terrorist attacks of 2001.

Tales of a Librarian: A Tori Amos Collection
Atlantic 83658 (2003)

1. Precious Things *
2. Angels ****
3. Silent All These Years **
4. Cornflake Girl *
5. Mary ****
6. God *
7. Winter **
8. Spark ****
9. Way Down ****
10. Professional Widow *(single dance remix)* ****
11. Mr. Zebra ****
12. Crucify **
13. Me and a Gun ***
14. Bliss ****
15. Playboy Mommy ****
16. Baker Baker *
17. Tear in Your Hand *
18. Sweet Dreams ****
19. Jackie's Strength ****
20. Snow Cherries from France ****

Bonus DVD

1. Pretty Good Year *(video)*
2. Honey *(video)*
3. Northern Lad *(video)*
4. Putting the Damage On *(video)*
5. Mr. Zebra *(video)*

All songs written by Tori Amos.

  * Produced by Tori Amos and Eric Rosse.

 ** Produced by Davitt Sigerson.

 *** Produced by Ian Stanley.

 **** Produced by Tori Amos.

Remixed by Mark Hawley and Marcel von Limbeck.

Reconditioned, recorded, and remixed at Martian Engineering (Cornwall, England).

Art direction by Richard Bates and Liz Barrett. Design by Allen Hori. Photography by Thierry le Goues.

Notes: Amos and husband Mark Hawley remixed and remastered some of their favorite tracks from the Atlantic Records years.

The Beekeeper
Epic/Sony EK 92800 (2005)

1. Parasol
2. Sweet the Sting
3. The Power of Orange Knickers *(with Damien Rice)*
4. Jamaica Inn
5. Barons of Suburbia
6. Sleeps with Butterflies
7. General Joy
8. Mother Revolution
9. Ribbons Undone
10. Cars and Guitars
11. Witness
12. Original Sinsuality
13. Ireland
14. The Beekeeper
15. Martha's Foolish Ginger
16. Hoochie Woman
17. Goodbye Pisces
18. Marys of the Sea
19. Toast

All songs written by Tori Amos.

Produced by Tori Amos.

Mixed by Mark Hawley and Marcel von Limbeck.

Recorded at Martian Engineering (Cornwall, England).

Mastered by Jon Astley.

Art direction by Sheri Lee and Dave Bett.

Notes: After the relatively somber song cycle of *Scarlet's Walk*, Amos experiments with styles and tones on this album, touching upon funk, reggae, and old-fashioned pop.

Auditorium Theatre: Chicago, IL, 4/15/05
Limited-edition concert disc available from www.toriamosbootlegs.com
E2L 96442(2005)

Disc 1

1. Original Sinsuality
2. Father Lucifer
3. Mother Revolution
4. Yes, Anastacia
5. Apollo's Frock
6. Parasol
7. Mother
8. Operator *(Jim Croce)*
9. Circle Game *(Joni Mitchell)*
10. Cars and Guitars

Disc 2

1. Space Dog
2. Marianne
3. Barons of Suburbia
4. Cool on Your Island *(Tori Amos and Kim Bullard)*
5. The Beekeeper
6. Honey
7. Sweet the Sting
8. Cloud on My Tongue
9. Ribbons Undone

All songs written by Tori Amos except where noted.

Produced by Tori Amos.

Mixed by Mark Hawley and Marcel von Limbeck.

Notes: One of the first two released of a planned six-title "official bootlegs" series, chronicling a Chicago show on Amos's 2005 tour.

Royce Hall Auditorium: Los Angeles, CA, 4/25/05
Limited-edition concert disc available from www.toriamosbootlegs.com
E2L 96443(2005)

Disc 1

1. Original Sinsuality
2. Silent All These Years
3. Parasol
4. Doughnut Song

5. Apollo's Frock
6. Yes, Anastacia
7. Jamaica Inn
8. Livin' on a Prayer *(Jon Bon Jovi, Desmond Child, and Richie Sambora)*
9. All Through the Night *(Jules Shear)*

Disc 2

1. Barons of Suburbia
2. Take to the Sky
3. Cloud on My Tongue
4. Ruby Through the Looking Glass
5. The Beekeeper
6. Tear in Your Hand
7. Toast
8. Sweet the Sting
9. Twinkle

All songs written by Tori Amos except where noted.

Produced by Tori Amos.

Mixed by Mark Hawley and Marcel von Limbeck.

Notes: One of the first two released of a planned six-title "official bootlegs" series, chronicling a Los Angeles show on Amos's 2005 tour.

Paramount Theater: Denver, CO, 4/15/05
Limited-edition concert disc available from www.toriamosbootlegs.com
E2L 97634 (2005)

Disc 1

1. Original Sinsuality
2. Little Amsterdam
3. Icicle
4. Your Cloud
5. Jamaica Inn
6. Father Lucifer
7. Cool On Your Island
8. I Ran (So Far Away) *(Frank Maudsley, Paul Reynolds, Ali Score, and Mike Score)*
9. Suzanne *(Leonard Cohen)*

Disc 2

1. The Power of Orange Knickers
2. Cloud on My Tongue
3. Spacedog
4. Parasol
5. Carbon

6. The Beekeeper
7. Leather
8. Putting the Damage On

All songs written by Tori Amos except where noted.

Produced by Tori Amos.

Mixed by Marc Hawley and Marcel von Limbeck.

Notes: Third of the "official bootlegs" chronicling a Denver show on Amos's 2005 Tour.

Manchester Apollo: Manchester, England, 6/5/05
Limited-edition concert disc available from www.toriamosbootlegs.com
E2L 97635 (2005)

Disc 1

1. Original Sinsuality
2. Little Amsterdam
3. Leather
4. Beauty Queen/Horses
5. Liquid Diamonds
6. Suede
7. Strange
8. Don't Look Back in Anger *(Noel Gallagher)*
9. My Favorite Things *(Richard Rodgers and Oscar Hammerstein II)*

Disc 2

1. Winter
2. Carbon
3. Ribbons Undone
4. Spring Haze
5. The Beekeeper
6. Not the Red Baron
7. Never Seen Blue
8. Sweet the Sting

All songs written by Tori Amos except where noted.

Produced by Tori Amos.

Mixed by Marc Hawley and Marcel von Limbeck.

Notes: Fourth of the "official bootlegs" chronicling a Manchester show on Amos's 2005 Tour.

Hammersmith Apollo: London, England, 6/4/05
Limited-edition concert disc available from www.toriamosbootlegs.com
E2L 97790 (2005)

Disc 1

1. Original Sinsuality
2. Father Lucifer
3. Icicle
4. Mother Revolution
5. Take to the Sky
6. Yes, Anastasia
7. Bells for Her
8. Father Figure *(George Michael)*
9. Like a Prayer *(Tom Patrick Leonard and Madonna Ciccone)*

Disc 2

1. Winter
2. Cooling
3. Jamaica Inn
4. Witness
5. The Beekeeper
6. Sweet the Sting
7. Rattlesnakes *(Neil Clark and Lloyd Cole)*
8. Hoochie Woman
9. Hey Jupiter

All songs written by Tori Amos except where noted.

Produced by Tori Amos.

Mixed by Marc Hawley and Marcel von Limbeck.

Notes: Fifth of the "official bootlegs" chronicling a London show on Amos's 2005
Tour.

B of A Pavilion: Boston, MA, 8/21/05
Limited-edition concert disc available from www.toriamosbootlegs.com
E2L 97791 (2005)

Disc 1

1. Original Sinsuality
2. Caught a Lite Sneeze
3. Amber Waves
4. Martha's Foolish Ginger
5. Winter

6. Pancake
7. Cool on Your Island *(Tori Amos and Kim Bullard)*
8. Total Eclipse of the Heart *(Jim Steinman)*
9. Angie *(Mick Jagger and Keith Richards)*

Disc 2

1. Barons of Suburbia
2. Garlands
3. Tear in Your Hand
4. The Beekeeper
5. Dream On *(Steven Tyler)*
6. Pretty Good Year
7. Playboy Mommy
8. 1000 Oceans

All songs written by Tori Amos except where noted.

Produced by Tori Amos.

Mixed by Marc Hawley and Marcel von Limbeck.

Notes: Sixth of the "official bootlegs" chronicling a Boston show on Amos's 2005 Tour.

Singles

"Baltimore" *(Myra Ellen [Tori] Amos and Michael Amos)* b/w "Walking with You" *(Myra Ellen Amos) (billed as Ellen Amos)* (MEA 5290) (7" single) (1980)

"The Big Picture" *(Tori Amos and Kim Bullard)* b/w "You Go to My Head" *(billed as Y Kant Tori Read)* (Atlantic 89086) (7" single) (1988)

"Cool on Your Island" *(Tori Amos and Kim Bullard)* b/w "Heart Attack at 23" *(billed as Y Kant Tori Read)* (Atlantic 89021) (7" single) (1988)

"Crucify" *(remix)* b/w "Me and a Gun" (Atlantic 87463) (cassette single) (1992)

"Don't Make Me Come to Vegas" *(Timo on Tori House Remix)*, "Don't Make Me Come to Vegas" *(Timo on Tori Alternate Version)* b/w "Don't Make Me Come to Vegas" *(Timo on Tori Breaks Remix)* (Sony 79888) (12" single) (2003)

"Silent All These Years" b/w "Upside Down" (Atlantic 87511) (cassette single) (1992)

"Silent All These Years" *(album version)* and "Silent All These Years" *(live version)* (Atlantic 83001) (CD single) (1997) *(reissue)*

"A Sorta Fairytale" b/w "A Sorta Fairytale" (Epic 76988) (7" single) (2002)

"Winter" b/w "The Pool" (Atlantic 87418) (cassette single) (1992)

All songs written by Tori Amos except where noted.

EPs and CD 5 Maxi-Singles

Caught a Lite Sneeze (CD 5 maxi-single)
Atlantic 85519 (1996)

1. Caught a Lite Sneeze
   Silly Songs
2. This Old Man *(Traditional)*
3. That's What I Like Mick (The Sandwich Song) *(Chas Hodges and Dave Peacock)*
3. Graveyard
4. Toodles Mr. Jim

All songs written by Tori Amos except where noted.

Produced by Tori Amos.

Cornflake Girl (CD 5 maxi-single)
Atlantic 85655 (1994)

1. Cornflake Girl *(edit)*
2. Sister Janet
3. Dead Daisy Petals
4. Honey

All songs written by Tori Amos.

Produced by Eric Rosse and Tori Amos.

Cornflake Girl (limited-edition U.K. 2–disc EP)
East West A7281 (1994)

Disc 1

1. Cornflake Girl
2. Sister Janet
3. Piano Suite:
   All the Girls Hate Her
   Over It

Disc 2

1. Cornflake Girl
2. A Case of You *(Joni Mitchell)*
3. If 6 Was 9 *(Jimi Hendrix)*
4. Strange Fruit *(Lewis Allan)*

All songs written by Tori Amos except where noted.

Produced by Eric Rosse and Tori Amos.

Crucify (EP)
Atlantic 82399 (1992)

1. Crucify *(remix)* *
2. Winter *
3. Angie *(Mick Jagger and Keith Richards)* **
4. Smells Like Teen Spirit *(Kurt Cobain, David Grohl, and Krist Novoselic)* **
5. Thank You *(Jimmy Page and Robert Plant)* **

Songs written by Tori Amos except where noted.

* Produced by Davitt Sigerson.

** Produced by Ian Stanley.

Cruel/Raspberry Swirl (CD 5 maxi-single)
Atlantic 84412 (1998)

1. Cruel (Shady Feline Mix)
2. Raspberry Swirl (Lip Gloss Version)
3. Ambient Raspberry Swirl—Scarlet Spectrum Feels
4. Mainline Cherry—Ambient Spark

All songs written by Tori Amos.

Produced by Tori Amos.

God (CD 5 maxi-single)
Atlantic 85687 (1994)

1. God (LP version)
2. Home on the Range—Cherokee Edition *(Traditional—Tori Amos)*
3. Piano Suite:
   All the Girls Hate Her
   Over It

All songs written by Tori Amos except where noted.

Produced by Eric Rosse and Tori Amos.

Hey Jupiter (EP)
Atlantic 82955 (1996)

1. Hey Jupiter (The Dakota Version) *
2. Sugar *(live)* **
3. Honey *(live)* **
4. Professional Widow *(Merry Widow Version—live)* **
5. Somewhere Over the Rainbow *(live) (Harold Arlen and E. Y. "Yip" Harburg)***

All songs written by Tori Amos except where noted.

* Produced by Ian Stanley.

** Produced by Tori Amos.

Jackie's Strength (CD 5 maxi-single)
Atlantic 84163 (1998)

1. Jackie's Strength
2. Never Seen Blue
3. Beulah Land

All songs written by Tori Amos.

Produced by Tori Amos.

Past the Mission (2–disc EP)
East West (U.K.) 85665

Disc 1

1. Upside Down *(Live in Boston, The Sanders Theatre, 3/31/94)*
2. Past the Mission *(Live in Chicago, Vic Theatre, 3/24/94)*
3. Icicle *(Live in L.A., Wadsworth Theatre, 3/22/94)*
4. Flying Dutchman *(Live in Chicago, Vic Theatre, 3/24/94)*

Disc 2

1. Past the Mission *(LP version)*
2. Winter *(Live in Manchester, Free Trade Hall, 3/1/94)*
3. Waitress *(Live in Boston, The Sanders Theatre, 3/31/94)*
4. Here in My Head *(Live in Bristol, Colstan Hall, 3/7/94)*

Two discs sold separately.

All songs written by Tori Amos.

Produced by Eric Rosse and Tori Amos.

Scarlet's Hidden Treasures (EP)

Bonus disc with the Greetings from Sunny Florida DVD
Epic Music Video EVD 55323 (2004)

1. Ruby Through the Looking Glass
2. Seaside
3. Bug a Martini
4. Apollo's Frock
5. Tombigbee
6. Indian Summer

All songs written by Tori Amos.

Produced by Tori Amos.

Scarlet's Walk (Selections) (EP)

Promo-only EP
Epic AEK-00700 (2002)

1. Amber Waves
2. A Sorta Fairytale
3. Pancake
4. Crazy
5. Taxi Ride
6. Gold Dust

All songs written by Tori Amos.

Produced by Tori Amos.

A Sorta Fairytale (CD 5 maxi-single)
Epic 673043 (2002)

1. A Sorta Fairytale *(The 101 Mix)*
2. Operation Peter Pan
3. A Sorta Fairytale *(original single version)*
4. The Scarlet Story

All songs written by Tori Amos.

Produced by Tori Amos.

Spark (CD 5 maxi-single)
Atlantic 84105 (1998)

1. Spark
Macthirsty's Lounge B-Sides
Last Stop on the Kufürstendam:
2 Purple People
3. Bachelorette

All songs written by Tori Amos.

Produced by Tori Amos.

Spark (U.K. 2-disc CD 5 maxi-single)
East West AT0031 (1998)

Disc 1
1. Spark

Macthirsty's Lounge B-Sides
Last Stop on the Kufürstendam:
  2. Purple People
  3. Have Yourself a Merry Little Christmas *(Ralph Blane and Hugh Martin)*
  4. Bachelorette

Disc 2

  1. Spark
  2. Do It Again *(Walter Becker and Donald Fagen)*
  3. Cooling

Songs written by Tori Amos except where noted.

Produced by Tori Amos.

Strange Little Girl (CD 5 maxi-single)

Atlantic Europe AT0111CD (2001)

  1. Strange Little Girl *(Jean Bumel, Hugh Cornwell, Brian Duffy, David Greenfield, and Hans Warmling)*
  2. After All *(David Bowie)*
  3. Only Women Bleed *(Alice Cooper)*

Produced by Tori Amos.

Winter (CD 5 maxi-single)
Atlantic 85799 (1992)

  1. Winter *
  2. Pool **
  3. Take to the Sky *
  4. Sweet Dreams *
  5. Upside Down *

All songs written by Tori Amos.

* Produced by Davitt Sigerson.

** Produced by Iain Stanley.

Music Videos

1000 Oceans (1999)

The Big Picture *(Y Kant Tori Read)* (1988)

Bliss (1999)

Caught a Lite Sneeze (1996)

China (1992)

Cornflake Girl *(U.S. version)* (1994)

Cornflake Girl *(European version)* (1994)

Crucify (1992)

Down by the Seaside *(with Robert Plant)* (1995)

Glory of the 80s (1999)

God (1994)

Gold Dust (2002)

Hey Jupiter (1996)

Jackie's Strength (1998)

Mary (2003)

Past the Mission (1994)

Pretty Good Year (1994)

Professional Widow (1996)

Raspberry Swirl (1998)

Silent All These Years (1991)

Sleeps with Butterflies (2005)

A Sorta Fairytale (2002)

A Sorta Fairytale *(alternate video—Scarlet's DVD)* (2002)

Spark (1998)

Strange Little Girl (2001)

Sweet the Sting (2005)

Talula (1996)

Taxi Ride (2002)

Winter (1992)

Music Video Albums

Little Earthquakes
A-Vision 50335 (1992)

1. Silent All These Years *(video)*
2. Leather *(live)*
3. Precious Things *(live)*
4. Crucify *(video)*
5. Me and a Gun *(live TV appearance)*
6. Little Earthquakes *(live)*
7. China *(video)*
8. Happy Phantom *(live)*
9. Here in My Head *(live)*
10. Winter *(video)*
11. Song for Eric *(live)*

Tori Amos: The Complete Videos 1991–1998
Atlantic 83154 (1998)

1. Silent All These Years
2. Cornflake Girl *(European version)*
3. Past the Mission
4. China
5. Raspberry Swirl
6. Hey Jupiter
7. Spark
8. Caught a Lite Sneeze
9. Winter
10. Talula
11. God
12. Crucify
13. Jackie's Strength
14. Cornflake Girl *(U.S. version)*
15. Pretty Good Year

Tori Amos: Live from New York
Warner Music Vision (1998)

1. Beauty Queen/Horses
2. Leather
3. Blood Roses
4. Little Amsterdam
5. Cornflake Girl

6. Waitress
7. Little Earthquakes
8. Upside Down
9. Winter
10. Precious Things
11. Caught a Lite Sneeze
12. Talula
13. Me and a Gun
14. Marianne
15. Silent All These Years
16. Muhammad My Friend *(with Maynard James Keenan of Tool)*
17. Pretty Good Year

Scarlet's DVD

(Bonus DVD with special version of the *Scarlet's Walk* CD)

Epic EK 86939 (2002)

1. Gold Dust
2. A Sorta Fairytale
3. Taxi Ride

A Sorta Fairytale: DVD Single

Epic 34D 29884 (2003)

1. A Sorta Fairytale *(video)*
2. A Sorta Fairytale *(making of the video)*
3. Biography
4. Interview with Tori Amos

Tales of a Librarian: A Tori Amos Collection

(Bonus DVD with the *Tales of a Librarian* CD)

Atlantic 83658 (2003)

1. Pretty Good Year
2. Honey
3. Northern Lad
4. Putting the Damage On
5. Mr. Zebra

Welcome to Sunny Florida

Sony EVD 55323 (2004)

1. A Sorta Fairytale
2. Sugar
3. Crucify

4. Cornflake Girl
5. Bells for Her
6. Concertina
7. Take to the Sky
8. Leather
9. Cloud on My Tongue
10. Cooling
11. Your Cloud
12. Father Lucifer
13. Professional Widow
14. I Can't See New York
15. Precious Things
16. Tombigbee
17. Amber Waves
18. Hey Jupiter

Also includes *Scarlet's Hidden Treasures* (Audio EP)

1. Ruby Through the Looking Glass
2. Seaside
3. Bug a Martini
4. Apollo's Frock
5. Tombigbee
6. Indian Summer

Fade to Red: Tori Amos Video Collection
Rhino/Atlantic R2 970295 (2006)

Disc 1
1. Past the Mission
2. Crucify
3. Jackie's Strength
4. A Sorta Fairytale
5. Winter
6. Spark
7. Sleeps with Butterflies
8. Cornflake Girl *(US Version)*
9. Hey Jupiter *(Dakota Version)*
10. Silent All These Years

Disc 2
1. Caught a Lite Sneeze
2. 1000 Oceans
3. God
4. Bliss

5. China
6. Raspberry Swirl
7. Talula *(The Tornado Mix)*
8. Sweet the Sting
9. Pretty Good Year

Guest Appearances on Various-Artists Albums or Soundtrack Albums

"Blue Skies" *(with B.T.) (Brian Transeau)*

On the album *Party of Five: TV Soundtrack* Warner Bros. 46431 (1996)

"Butterfly"

On the album *Higher Learning: Music from the Motion Picture* 550 Music/Epic Soundtrax BK 66944 (1994)

"Carnival" *(Luiz Bonfá)*

On the album *Music from and Inspired by Mission Impossible II* Hollywood 910501 (2001)

"Cornflake Girl"

On the album *The Brits Awards 1995* Alex 5029 (1995)

"Cornflake Girl"

On the album *Hits '94 Volume 1* Telstar 2710 (1994)

"Cornflake Girl"

On the album *Natural Woman* Alex 5482 (1995)

"Cornflake Girl"

On the album *Now, That's What I Call Music 27* Virgin/EMI/Polygram UK 7243 8 29344 (1994)

"Cornflake Girl"

On the album *Triple J Hottest 100 Volume 2* EMI 209562 (1994)

"Down by the Seaside" *(duet with Robert Plant) (Jimmy Page and Robert Plant)*

On the album *Enconium: A Tribute to Led Zeppelin* Atlantic 82731 (1995)

"Famous Blue Raincoat" *(Leonard Cohen)*

On the album *Tower of Song—The Songs of Leonard Cohen* A&M 31454 0259 (1995)

"Finn (Intro)" *(Patrick Doyle)*

On the album *Great Expectations: The Album* Atlantic 83058 (1997)

Also on the album *Great Expectations: The Score* Atlantic 83063 (1997)

"God"

On the seven–disc box set *Whatever: The '90s Pop and Culture Box* Rhino 79716 (2005)

Also on the promo-only album *A 12-Track Sampling from Whatever: The '90s Pop and Culture Box* Rhino PRCD 400150 (2005)

"The Happy Worker" *(Trevor Horn and Bruce Woolley)*

On the album *Toys: Music from the Original Motion Picture Soundtrack* Geffen 24505 (1992)

"Hey Jupiter" *(live)*

On the album *WLIR-KIVES Unplugged* Restaurant 1003 (1997)

"I'm on Fire" *(live) (Bruce Springsteen)*

On the album *VH1 Crossroads* Atlantic 82895 (1996)

"The Little Drummer Boy" *(Katherine Davis, Henry Onerati, and Harry Simeone)*

On the KROQ various-artists charity cassette *Kevin and Bean: We've Got Your Yule Logs Hanging* KROQ CS-4 (1992)

"The Little Drummer Boy" *(Katherine Davis, Henry Onerati, and Harry Simeone)*

On the album *Not Another Christmas Album: An Alternative Christmas* Rhino Flashback 76519 (2004)

"The Little Drummer Boy" *(Katherine Davis, Henry Onerati, and Harry Simeone)*

On the album *You Sleigh Me: Alternative Christmas Hits* Atlantic 82851 (1995)

"Losing My Religion" *(Bill Berry, Peter Buck, Mike Mills, and Michael Stipe)*

On the album *Higher Learning: Music from the Motion Picture* 550 Music/Epic Soundtrax BK 66944 (1994)

"Merman"

On the album *No Boundaries: A Benefit for the Kosovar Refugees* Sony 63653 (1999)

"Murder He Says" *(Frank Loesser and Jimmy McHugh)*

On the album *Mona Lisa Smile: Music from the Motion Picture* Epic EK 90737 (2004)

"1000 Oceans"

On the album *Here on Earth: Music from the Motion Picture* Sony 63596 (2000)

"Paradiso Perduto" *(Patrick Doyle)*

On the album *Great Expectations: The Score* Atlantic 83063 (1997)

"Professional Widow"

On the album *Escape from L.A.: Original Motion Picture Soundtrack* Atlantic 92714 (1996)

"Professional Widow" *(Armand Van Helden Remix)*

On the album *Formule Techno* Wotre 714265 (1997)

"Professional Widow" *(Armand's Star Trunk Funkin' Mix)*

On the album *Kiss in Ibiza* Polygram TV 535967 (1996)

"Professional Widow" *(Armand's Star Trunk Funkin' Mix)*

On the album *Loved Up* Prima Vera (1995)

"Professional Widow" *(Armand's Star Trunk Funkin' Mix)*

On the album *Work Out* Atlantic 82966 (1997)

"Ring My Bell" *(Frederick Knight)*

On the album *Ruby Trax—The NME's Roaring Forty* NME 40CD (1992)

"Silent All These Years"

On the album *Atlantic Records 50 Years: The Gold Anniversary* Atlantic 83088 (1998)

"Silent All These Years" *(Tales of a Librarian Mix)*

On the album *For the Next X: A Benefit CD for RAINN* RAINN (2004)

"Silent All These Years" *(live)*

On the album *Live at the World Café: Volume I* World Café WC9501 (1995)

"Silent All These Years" *(live)*

On the album *Rare on Air—Volume I* Mammoth 0074 (1994)

"Silent All These Years"

On the album *Rolling Stone: Women in Rock* Razor & Tie 89005 (1998)

"Siren" *(Tori Amos and Patrick Doyle)*

On the album *Great Expectations: The Album* Atlantic 83058 (1997)

"Stamp!" *(original mix) (with Jeremy Healy)*

On the album *Electro Breakz (Volume 2)* Streetbeat 1026 (1997)

"Stamp!" *(original mix) (with Jeremy Healy)*

On the album *Kiss in Ibiza* Polygram TV 535967 (1996)

"Talula" *(B.T.'s Tornado Mix)*

On the album *Twister: Music from the Motion Picture* Warner Bros. 46254 (1996)

"You Belong to Me" *(Pee Wee King, Chilton Price, and Redd Stewart)*

On the album *Mona Lisa Smile: Music from the Motion Picture* Epic EK 90737 (2004)

All songs written by Tori Amos unless otherwise indicated.

Guest Appearances on Other Musicians' Albums

Sandra Bernhardt

"Little Red Corvette" *(background vocals) (Prince)*

On the album *Without You I'm Nothing* Enigma 73369 (1989)

B.T.

"Blue Skies" *(vocals) (Brian Transeau)*

On the album *Ima* Perfecto/Kinetic/Reprise 46356 (1995)

Also on the album *10 Years in the Life* Reprise 78118 (2002)

Remix on the album *R & R* Nettwerk 30223 (2001)

Family Fantastic

"Doin' This Thing" *(vocals) (Val Chalmers, Vince Clarke, Jason Creasy, Phil Creswick, and Emma Whittle)*

On the album…*Nice!* Cleopatra 769 (2000)

Ferron

All songs *(backing vocals)*

On the album *Phantom Center* Chameleon 42576 (1990)

Tom Jones

"I Wanna Get Back to You" *(backing vocals) (Diane Warren)*

On the album *The Lead and How to Swing It* Interscope 92457 (1994)

Stan Ridgway

"Dogs," "Peg and Pete and Me," and "The Last Honest Man" *(background vocals)*
  (Stan Ridgway)

On the album *Mosquitos* Geffen 2–24216 1988

"Peg and Pete and Me" also on the album *The Best of Stan Ridgway: Songs That
  Made This Country Great* IRS X2-13139 1992

Al Stewart

"Last Day of the Century" and "Red Toupee" *(background vocals)*

On the album *Last Days of the Century* Enigma D2-73316 (1988)

Robert Tepper

All songs *(background vocals)*

On the album *Modern Madness* Scotti Bros. ZK-40977 (1988)

Paul Van Dyk

"Blue Skies" *(Blau Himmel Remix) (with B.T.) (vocals) (by Brian Transeau)*

On the album *Vorsprung Dyk Technik* Deviant 033 (1998)

Tori Amos's Songs as Recorded by Other Artists

"Baker Baker"
E-clypse featuring Jemima Price
On the album *The Pretty Good Years: A Tribute to Tori Amos* Dressed to Kill 176
  (1999)

"Beauty Queen"
Unto Ashes
On the various-artists CD *Songs of a Goddess: A Tribute to Tori Amos* Cleopatra
  CLP 1053 (2001)

Also on the album *Empty Into White* Projekt 147 (2003)

"Bliss"
Glampire
On the various-artists CD *Songs of a Goddess: A Tribute to Tori Amos* Cleopatra
  CLP 1053 (2001)

"Butterfly"
Casey Stratton
Performed live. Posted on the Internet at: http://www.latitudeline.com/sounds.html.

"Caught a Lite Sneeze"
E-clypse featuring Jemima Price
On the album *The Pretty Good Years: A Tribute to Tori Amos* Dressed to Kill 176 (1999)

"Caught a Lite Sneeze"
String Quartet
On the album *Precious Things: The String Quartet Tribute to Tori Amos* Vitamin 8541 (2001)

"Caught a Lite Sneeze"
Voltaire
On the various-artists CD *Songs of a Goddess: A Tribute to Tori Amos* Cleopatra CLP 1053 (2001)

Also on the album *Boo Hoo* Projekt 129 (2002)

"Charlette Corday"
Al Stewart *(Al Stewart and Tori Amos—never recorded by Amos)*
On the album *Famous Last Words* Mesa/Blue Moon 79061 (1993)

"China"
E-clypse featuring Jemima Price
On the album *The Pretty Good Years: A Tribute to Tori Amos* Dressed to Kill 176 (1999)

"Cornflake Girl"
BareNaked Ladies
Performed on radio and in concert. Never officially released.

"Cornflake Girl"
E-clypse featuring Jemima Price
On the album *The Pretty Good Years: A Tribute to Tori Amos* Dressed to Kill 176 (1999)

"Cornflake Girl"
Jawbox
On the album *Jawbox* Atlantic 92707 (1996)

"Cornflake Girl"
String Quartet
On the album *Precious Things: The String Quartet Tribute to Tori Amos* Vitamin 8541 (2001)

"Cornflake Girl"
Tapping the Vein
On the various-artists CD *Songs of a Goddess: A Tribute to Tori Amos* Cleopatra CLP 1053 (2001)

"Crucify"
E-clypse featuring Jemima Price
On the album *The Pretty Good Years: A Tribute to Tori Amos* Dressed to Kill 176
  (1999)

"Crucify"
Kiki and Herb
Performed in concert. Never officially released.

"Crucify"
Nolwenn Leroy
On the CD single *Inévitablement* Mercury France (2004)

"Crucify"
String Quartet
On the album *Precious Things: The String Quartet Tribute to Tori Amos* Vitamin
  8541 (2001)

"Crucify"
This Ascension
On the various-artists CD *Songs of a Goddess: A Tribute to Tori Amos* Cleopatra
  CLP 1053 (2001)

"Cruel"
String Quartet
On the album *Precious Things: The String Quartet Tribute to Tori Amos* Vitamin
  8541 (2001)

"Flying Dutchman"
String Quartet
On the album *Precious Things: The String Quartet Tribute to Tori Amos* Vitamin
  8541 (2001)

"Girl"
String Quartet
On the album *Precious Things: The String Quartet Tribute to Tori Amos* Vitamin
  8541 (2001)

"God"
String Quartet
On the album *Precious Things: The String Quartet Tribute to Tori Amos* Vitamin
  8541 (2001)

"God"
Temple of Rain
On the various-artists CD *Songs of a Goddess: A Tribute to Tori Amos* Cleopatra
  CLP 1053 (2001)

"Hey Jupiter"
E-clypse featuring Jemima Price
On the album *The Pretty Good Years: A Tribute to Tori Amos* Dressed to Kill 176
  (1999)

"i i e e e"
Meegs and Jessicka
On the various-artists CD *Songs of a Goddess: A Tribute to Tori Amos* Cleopatra
  CLP 1053 (2001)

"i i e e e"
The Pimps
On the album *Wouldn't It Be Great to Have All These Songs on One Album?*
  Countdown (2000)

"Leather"
Amber Asylum
On the various-artists CD *Songs of a Goddess: A Tribute to Tori Amos* Cleopatra
  CLP 1053 (2001)

"Leather"
Bimbetta
On the album *War or Love* D'Note Classics 710755102323 (1997)

"Leather"
E-clypse featuring Jemima Price
On the album *The Pretty Good Years: A Tribute to Tori Amos* Dressed to Kill 176
  (1999)

"Leather"
B. D. Wong
Performed on the TV series *Oz*. Never officially released.

"Me and a Gun"
Stabbing Westward
Performed in concert. Never officially released.

"Muhammad My Friend"
String Quartet
On the album *Precious Things: The String Quartet Tribute to Tori Amos* Vitamin
  8541 (2001)

"Party Man"
The Worldbeaters featuring Peter Gabriel (*George Acogny, Tori Amos, and Peter
  Gabriel—never recorded by Amos*)
On the motion-picture soundtrack *Virtuosity* Radioactive RARD-11295 (1995)

"Past the Mission"
String Quartet
On the album *Precious Things: The String Quartet Tribute to Tori Amos* Vitamin
8541 (2001)

"Playboy Mommy"
Allison Crowe
Never officially released. Posted on the fan site http://www.painunspoken.
allisoncrowe.com/covers.html.

"Precious Things"
Blueline Medic
On the album *New.Old.Rare* Fueled by Ramen 57 (2003)

"Precious Things" (performed as a medley with Damien Rice's "Volcano")
Corey Byrnes
Posted online at: http://www.coreybyrnes.com/html/music.html.

"Precious Things"
Finger Eleven
Recorded but never officially released (2000).

"Precious Things"
String Quartet
On the album *Precious Things: The String Quartet Tribute to Tori Amos* Vitamin
8541 (2001)

"Pretty Good Year"
Evridiki
On the album *Live…* Evridiki Greece 7243 5 40566 (2002)

"Pretty Good Year"
String Quartet
On the album *Precious Things: The String Quartet Tribute to Tori Amos* Vitamin
8541 (2001)

"Professional Widow"
E-clypse featuring Jemima Price
On the album *The Pretty Good Years: A Tribute to Tori Amos* Dressed to Kill 176
(1999)

"Professional Widow"
Night Flyte
On the album *30,000 Feet* Passion Jazz 2 (1997)

"Professional Widow"
The Pimps

On the album *Wouldn't It Be Great to Have All These Songs on One Album?* Countdown (2000)

"Raspberry Swirl"
Simple
On the various-artists CD *Songs of a Goddess: A Tribute to Tori Amos* Cleopatra CLP 1053 (2001)

"She's Your Cocaine"
St. Eve
On the various-artists CD *Songs of a Goddess: A Tribute to Tori Amos* Cleopatra CLP 1053 (2001)

"Silent All These Years"
E-clypse featuring Jemima Price
On the album *The Pretty Good Years: A Tribute to Tori Amos* Dressed to Kill 176 (1999)

"Silent All These Years"
String Quartet
On the album *Precious Things: The String Quartet Tribute to Tori Amos* Vitamin 8541 (2001)

"Silent All These Years"
Sun Yan Zi
On the album *Start* Warner Music Taiwan (2002)

"Spacedog"
Dragon Style
On the various-artists CD *Songs of a Goddess: A Tribute to Tori Amos* Cleopatra CLP 1053 (2001)

"Spacedog"
Jonathan Stiers
On the single *Masquerade* (2004). Posted on the Web at http://www.jonathanstiers.com/html/music_04.html.

"Sugar"
Rei Toei
On the various-artists CD *Songs of a Goddess: A Tribute to Tori Amos* Cleopatra CLP 1053 (2001)

"Waitress"
Sebos
On the EP *The Sage* (2004)

"Winter"
Aural Pleasure
On the album *Tell Me When* (2003)

"Winter"
Dream Theater
On the album *Subconscious* (1995)

"Winter"
E-clypse featuring Jemima Price
On the album *The Pretty Good Years: A Tribute to Tori Amos* Dressed to Kill 176
   (1999)

"Winter"
October Hill
On the various-artists CD *Songs of a Goddess: A Tribute to Tori Amos* Cleopatra
   CLP 1053 (2001)

"Winter"
R.E.M.
Performed in concert. Never officially released.

Tori Amos Covers of Other Artists' Songs

AC/DC
"You Shook Me All Night Long" *(Brian Johnson, Angus Young, and Malcolm
   Young)*
Performed in concert. Never officially released.

Aerosmith
"Dream On" *(Steven Tyler)*
Performed live on MTV (1998) and (1999).
On the limited-edition CD *B of A Pavilion: Boston, MA, 8/21/05.* (Available from
   www.toriamosbootlegs.com) (2005)

Alice Cooper
"Only Women Bleed" (original title was "Only Women") *(Alice Cooper)*
On the CD 5 maxi-single *Strange Little Girl* Atlantic Europe AT0111CD (2001)

Julie Andrews
"Do-Re-Mi" *(Oscar Hammerstein II and Richard Rodgers)*
Performed in concert. Never officially released.
"My Favorite Things" *(Oscar Hammerstein II and Richard Rodgers)*
On the limited-edition CD *Manchester Apollo: Manchester, England, 6/5/05.*
   (Available from www.toriamosbootlegs.com) (2005)
"Stay Awake" *(Richard M. Sherman and Robert S. Sherman)*
Performed on the TV show *Last Call with Carson Daly* (2002).

Bad Company
"Bad Company" *(Simon Kirke and Paul Rodgers)*
Performed in concert. Never officially released.

The Beatles
"Happiness Is a Warm Gun" *(John Lennon and Paul McCartney)*
On the album *Strange Little Girls* Atlantic 7567-83486 (2001)
"Here, There and Everywhere" *(John Lennon and Paul McCartney)*
Performed in concert. Never officially released.
"Let It Be" *(John Lennon and Paul McCartney)*
Performed in concert. Never officially released.
"The Long and Winding Road" *(John Lennon and Paul McCartney)*
Performed in concert. Never officially released.
"Penny Lane" *(John Lennon and Paul McCartney)*
Performed in concert. Never officially released.
"She's Leaving Home" *(John Lennon and Paul McCartney)*
Performed in concert. Never officially released.
"Something" *(George Harrison)*
Performed in concert. Never officially released.
"With a Little Help from My Friends" *(John Lennon and Paul McCartney)*
Performed in concert. Never officially released.

The Bee Gees
"More Than a Woman" *(Barry Gibb, Maurice Gibb, and Robin Gibb)*
Performed in concert. Never officially released.

Pat Benatar
"Love Is a Battlefield" *(Mike Chapman and Holly Knight)*
Performed in concert. Never officially released.
"We Belong" *(David Eric Lowen and Dan Navarro)*
Performed in concert. Never officially released.

Björk
"Hyper-Ballad" *(Björk)*
Performed in concert. Never officially released.

Bon Jovi
"Livin' on a Prayer" *(Jon Bon Jovi, Desmond Child, and Richie Sambora)*
On the limited-edition CD *Royce Hall Auditorium: Los Angeles, CA, 4/25/05*
   (Available from www.toriamosbootlegs.com)

The Boomtown Rats
"I Don't Like Mondays" *(Robert Geldof)*
On the album *Strange Little Girls* Atlantic 7567-83486 (2001)

Debby Boone
"You Light Up My Life" *(Joseph Brooks)*
Performed in concert. Never officially released.

David Bowie
"After All" *(David Bowie)*
On the CD 5 maxi-single Strange Little Girl Atlantic Europe AT0111CD (2001)

Bread
"If" *(David Gates)*
Performed in concert. Never officially released.

Kate Bush
"And Dream of Sheep" *(Kate Bush)*
Performed in concert. Never officially released.
"Running Up That Hill (A Deal with God)" *(Kate Bush)*
Performed in concert. Never officially released.

Hoagy Carmichael
"Georgia on My Mind" *(Hoagy Carmichael and Stuart Gorrell)*
Performed in concert. Never officially released.
"Heart and Soul" *(Hoagy Carmichael and Frank Loesser)*
Performed on E! Entertainment Television.

The Carpenters
"Superstar (Don't You Remember?)" *(Bonnie Bramlett and Leon Russell)*
Performed in concert. Never officially released.
"We've Only Just Begun" *(Roger Nichols and Paul Williams)*
Performed in concert. Never officially released.

Johnny Cash
"Ring of Fire" *(June Carter Cash and Merle Kilgore)*
Performed in concert. Never officially released.

Ray Charles
"Georgia on My Mind" *(Hoagy Carmichael and Stuart Gorrell)*
Performed in concert. Never officially released.

Maurice Chevalier
"Thank Heaven for Little Boys" *(original title was "Thank Heaven for Little Girls")*
    (Allan Jay Lerner and Frederick Loewe)
Performed in concert. Never officially released.

Leonard Cohen
"Famous Blue Raincoat" *(Leonard Cohen)*
On the album *Tower of Song: The Songs of Leonard Cohen* A&M 31454 0259
    (1995)
"Suzanne" *(Leonard Cohen)*
On the limited-edition CD *Paramount Theater: Denver, CO, 4/15/05.* (Available
    from www.toriamosbootlegs.com) (2005)

Lloyd Cole and the Commotions
"Rattlesnakes" *(Neil Clark and Lloyd Cole)*
On the album *Strange Little Girls* Atlantic 7567-83486 (2001)
Live version on the limited-edition CD *Hammersmith Apollo: London, England,*
    6/4/05. (Available from www.toriamosbootlegs.com) (2005)

Nat "King" Cole
"When Sunny Gets Blue" *(Marvin Fisher and Jack Segal)*
Performed in concert. Never officially released.

Elvis Costello
"Hoover Factory" *(Elvis Costello)*
Recorded for *Strange Little Girls* (2001) but never released.

The Coven
"One Tin Soldier (The Legend of Billy Jack)" *(Dennis Lambert and Brian Potter)*
Performed in concert. Never officially released.

Jim Croce
"Operator" *(original title was "Operator [That's Not the Way It Feels]") (Jim Croce)*
On the limited-edition CD *Auditorium Theater: Chicago, IL, 4/15/2005* (Available
   from www.toriamosbootlegs.com)

Crowded House
"Don't Dream It's Over" *(Neil Finn)*
Performed in concert. Never officially released.

The Cure
"Lovesong" *(Simon Gallup, Roger O'Donnell, Robert Smith, Perl Thompson,*
   Laurence Tolhurst, and Boris Williams)
Performed in concert. Never officially released.

Doris Day
"Sentimental Journey" *(Les Brown, Bud Green, and Ben Homer)*
Performed in concert. Never officially released.

Del Amitri
"Nothing Ever Happens" *(Justin Currie)*
Performed in concert. Never officially released.

Depeche Mode
"Enjoy the Silence" *(Martin Gore)*
On the album *Strange Little Girls* Atlantic 7567-83486 (2001)
"Personal Jesus" *(Martin Gore)*
Performed in concert. Never officially released.

Dion DiMucci
"Abraham, Martin and John" *(Dick Holler)*
Performed in concert. Never officially released.

The Doors
"Riders on the Storm" *(John Densmore, Robby Krieger, Ray Manzarek, and James*
   Douglas Morrison)
Performed in concert. Never officially released.

The Eagles
"Desperado" *(Glenn Frey and Don Henley)*
Performed in concert. Never officially released.
"Tequila Sunrise" *(Glenn Frey and Don Henley)*
Performed in concert. Never officially released.

Eminem
"'97 Bonnie & Clyde" *(Jeff Bass, Mark Randy Bass, and Marshall Mathers III)*
On the album *Strange Little Girls* Atlantic 7567-83486 (2001)

David Essex
"Rock On" *(David Essex)*
Performed in concert. Never officially released.

The Eurythmics
"Sweet Dreams (Are Made of This)" *(Annie Lennox and David Stewart)*
Performed in concert. Never officially released.

Betty Everett
"You're No Good" *(Clint Ballard Jr.)*
Performed in concert. Never officially released.

Roberta Flack
"Killing Me Softly with His Song" *(Charles Fox and Norman Gimbel)*
Performed in concert. Never officially released.

Flatt and Scruggs
"The Ballad of Jed Clampett (*Beverly Hillbillies* Theme)" *(Paul Henning)*
Performed in concert. Never officially released.

Fleetwood Mac
"Dreams" *(Stevie Nicks)*
Performed in concert. Never officially released.
"Landslide" *(Stevie Nicks)*
Performed in concert. Never officially released.
"Songbird" *(Christine McVie)*
Performed in concert. Never officially released.

A Flock of Seagulls
"I Ran (So Far Away)" *(Frank Maudsley, Paul Reynolds, Ali Score, and Mike Score)*
On the limited-edition CD *Paramount Theater: Denver, CO, 4/15/05*. (Available
   from www.toriamosbootlegs.com) (2005)

Dan Fogelberg
"Song from Half Mountain" *(Dan Fogelberg)*
Performed in concert. Never officially released.

Peter Gabriel
"Red Rain" (written by *Peter Gabriel*)
Performed in concert. Never officially released.

Judy Garland
"Have Yourself a Merry Little Christmas" *(Ralph Blane and Hugh Martin)*
On the U.K. 2-disc CD 5 maxi-single *Spark* (1998) East West AT0031 (1998)
"Somewhere Over the Rainbow" *(Harold Arlen and E. Y. "Yip" Harburg)*
On the EP *Hey Jupiter* Atlantic 82955 (1996)

Astrud Gilberto
"Carnival" *(original song title was "Manha de Carnaval") (written by Luiz Bonfá)*
On the album *Music from and Inspired by Mission Impossible 2* Hollywood
   910501 (2001)

Godspell
"By My Side" *(Stephen Schwartz)*
Performed in concert. Never officially released.
"Day by Day" *(Stephen Schwartz and John Michael Tebelak)*
Performed in concert. Never officially released.

Heart
"Magic Man" *(Ann Wilson and Nancy Wilson)*
Performed in concert. Never officially released.

Jimi Hendrix
"If 6 Was 9" *(Jimi Hendrix)*
On the limited-edition U.K. EP *Cornflake Girl* East West A7281 (1994)

Billie Holiday
"God Bless the Child" *(Arthur Herzog, Jr., and Billie Holiday)*
Performed in concert. Never officially released.
"Lover Man (Oh, Where Can You Be?)" *(Jimmy Davis, Roger "Ram" Ramirez, and
   Jimmy Sherman)*
Performed in concert. Never officially released.
"Strange Fruit" *(Lewis Allan)*
On the limited-edition U.K. EP *Cornflake Girl* East West A7281 (1994)
"Summertime" (from *Porgy and Bess*) *(George Gershwin)*
Performed in concert. Never officially released.

Billy Idol
"Eyes Without a Face" *(Billy Idol and Steve Stevens)*
Performed in concert. Never officially released.

INXS
"Need You Tonight" *(Andrew Farriss and Michael Hutchence)*
Performed in concert. Never officially released.

Joe Jackson
"Real Men" *(Joe Jackson)*
On the album *Strange Little Girls* Atlantic 7567-83486 (2001)

Jesus Christ Superstar
"Everything's Alright"*(Tim Rice and Andrew Lloyd Webber)*
Performed in concert. Never officially released.

Billy Joel
"Piano Man"*(Billy Joel)*
Performed in concert. Never officially released.

Elton John
"Candle in the Wind"*(Elton John and Bernie Taupin)*
Performed in concert. Never officially released.
"Daniel"*(Elton John and Bernie Taupin)*
Performed in concert. Never officially released.
"Rocket Man"*(Elton John and Bernie Taupin)*
Performed in concert. Never officially released.
"Someone Saved My Life Tonight"*(Elton John and Bernie Taupin)*
Performed in concert. Never officially released.
"Tiny Dancer"*(Elton John and Bernie Taupin)*
Performed in concert. Never officially released.

Rickie Lee Jones
"On Saturday Afternoons in 1963"*(Rickie Lee Jones)*
Performed in concert. Never officially released.

Janis Joplin
"Me and Bobby McGee"*(Fred Foster and Kris Kristofferson)*
Performed in concert. Never officially released.

Carole King
"I Feel the Earth Move"*(Carole King)*
Performed in concert. Never officially released.
"So Far Away"*(Carole King)*
Performed in concert. Never officially released.

Cyndi Lauper
"All Through the Night"*(Jules Shear)*
On the limited-edition CD *Royce Hall Auditorium: Los Angeles, CA, 4/25/05*
    (Available from www.toriamosbootlegs.com)

Led Zeppelin
"Down by the Seaside"*(duet with Robert Plant) (Jimmy Page and Robert Plant)*
On the album *Enconium: A Tribute to Led Zeppelin* Atlantic 82731 (1995)
"Thank You"*(Jimmy Page and Robert Plant)*
On the EP *Crucify* Atlantic 82399 (1992)
"When the Levee Breaks"*(Memphis Minnie—John Bonham, John Paul Jones,
    Jimmy Page, and Robert Plant)*
Performed in concert. Never officially released.

"Whole Lotta Love" *(Willie Dixon—John Bonham, John Paul Jones, Jimmy Page, and Robert Plant)*
Performed in concert. Never officially released.

The Left Banke
"Walk Away Renee" *(Michael Brown, Bob Calilli, and Tony Sansone)*
Performed in concert. Never officially released.

John Lennon
"Imagine" *(John Lennon)*
Performed in concert. Never officially released.

Gordon Lightfoot
"If You Could Read My Mind" *(Gordon Lightfoot)*
Performed in concert. Never officially released.

Lindisfarne
"Fog on the Tyne" *(Alan Hull)*
Performed in concert. Never officially released.

Dave Loggins
"Please Come to Boston" *(Dave Loggins)*
Performed in concert. Never officially released.

Madonna
"Like a Prayer" *(Madonna Ciccone and Tom Patrick Leonard)*
On the limited-edition CD *Hammersmith Apollo: London, England, 6/4/05.*
   (Available from www.toriamosbootlegs.com) (2005)
"Like a Virgin" *(Tom Kelly and Billy Steinberg)*
Demo recorded. Never released.
"Live to Tell" *(Madonna Ciccone and Patrick Leonard)*
Performed in concert. Never officially released.

Paul McCartney
"Band on the Run" *(Linda McCartney and Paul McCartney)*
Performed in concert. Never officially released.

Don McLean
"American Pie" *(Don McLean)*
Performed in concert. Never officially released.
"Vincent (Starry, Starry Nights)" *(Don McLean)*
Performed in concert. Never officially released.

George Michael
"Father Figure" *(George Michael)*
On the limited edition CD *Hammersmith Apollo: London, England, 6/4/05.*
   (Available from www.toriamosbootlegs.com) (2005)

Bette Midler
"The Rose" *(Amanda McBroom)*
Performed in concert. Never officially released.

Kylie Minogue
"Can't Get You Out of My Head" *(Rob Davis and Cathy Dennis)*
Performed in concert. Never officially released.

Joni Mitchell
"Both Sides Now" *(Joni Mitchell)*
Performed in concert. Never officially released.
"A Case of You" *(Joni Mitchell)*
On the limited-edition U.K. EP *Cornflake Girl* East West A7281 (1994)
"Circle Game" *(Joni Mitchell)*
On the limited-edition CD *Auditorium Theater: Chicago, IL, 4/15/2005* (Available
    from www.toriamosbootlegs.com)
"River" *(Joni Mitchell)*
Performed in concert. Never officially released.

The Moody Blues
"Nights in White Satin" *(Justin Hayward)*
Performed in concert. Never officially released.

Peter Murphy
"Marlene Dietrich's Favourite Poem" *(Peter Murphy)*
Recorded for *Strange Little Girls* (2001) but never released.

Anne Murray
"You Needed Me" *(Randy Goodrum)*
Performed in concert. Never officially released.

Nine Inch Nails
"Hurt" *(Trent Reznor)*
Performed in concert. Never officially released.

Nirvana
"Smells Like Teen Spirit" *(Kurt Cobain, David Grohl, and Krist Novoselic)*
On the EP *Crucify* Atlantic 82399 (1992)

Oasis
"Don't Look Back in Anger" *(Noel Gallagher)*
On the limited-edition CD *Manchester Apollo: Manchester, England, 6/5/05.*
    (Available from www.toriamosbootlegs.com) (2005)

Mike Oldfield
"Tubular Bells" *(Mike Oldfield)*
Performed in concert. Never officially released.

Dolly Parton
"I Will Always Love You" *(Dolly Parton)*
Performed in concert. Never officially released.

Peter, Paul and Mary
"Puff (the Magic Dragon)" *(Leonard Lipton and Peter Yarrow)*
Performed in concert. Never officially released.

The Police
"Wrapped Around Your Finger" *(Sting)*
Performed in concert. Never officially released.

Cole Porter
"I Love Paris" *(Cole Porter)*
Performed in concert. Never officially released.

Prince
"Little Red Corvette" *(with Sandra Bernhardt) (Prince)*
On the Sandra Bernhardt album *Without You I'm Nothing* Enigma 73369 (1989)
"Purple Rain" *(Prince)*
Performed in concert. Never officially released.

Public Enemy
"Fear of a Black Planet" *(Chuck D., Eric "Vietnam" Sadler, and Keith Shocklee)*
Recorded for *Strange Little Girls* (2001) but never released.

Pulp
"Common People" *(Nick Banks, Jarvis Crocker, Candida Doyle, Steve Mackey, and Russell Senior)*
Performed in concert. Never officially released.

Radiohead
"Karma Police" *(Colin Greenwood, Johnny Greenwood, Ed O'Brien, Phil Selway, and Thom Yorke)*
Performed in concert. Never officially released.
"Street Spirit (Fade Out)" *(Colin Greenwood, Johnny Greenwood, Ed O'Brien, Phil Selway, and Thom Yorke)*
Performed in concert. Never officially released.

R.E.M.
"Drive" *(Bill Berry, Peter Buck, Mike Mills, and Michael Stipe)*
Performed in concert. Never officially released.
"Losing My Religion" *(Bill Berry, Peter Buck, Mike Mills, and Michael Stipe)*
On the album *Higher Learning: Music from the Motion Picture* 550 Music/Epic Soundtrax BK 66944 (1994)

Damien Rice
"The Blower's Daughter" *(Damien Rice)*
Performed in concert. Never officially released.

Rodgers and Hammerstein
"Bali H'ai" (from *South Pacific*) (*Oscar Hammerstein II and Richard Rodgers*)
Performed in concert. Never officially released.
"Do-Re-Mi" (from *The Sound of Music*) (*Oscar Hammerstein II and Richard Rodgers*)
Performed in concert. Never officially released.
"My Favorite Things" (*Oscar Hammerstein II and Richard Rodgers*)
On the limited edition CD *Manchester Apollo: Manchester, England, 6/5/05*.
    (Available from www.toriamosbootlegs.com) (2005)
"Surrey with a Fringe on Top" (from *Oklahoma!*) (*Oscar Hammerstein II and Richard Rodgers*)
Performed in concert. Never officially released.

The Rolling Stones
"Angie" (*Mick Jagger and Keith Richards*)
On the EP *Crucify* (Atlantic 82399) (1992)
Live version on the limited-edition CD *B of A Pavilion: Boston, MA, 8/21/05*.
    (Available from www.toriamosbootlegs.com) (2005)

Bob Seger
"Turn the Page" (*Bob Seger*)
Performed in concert. Never officially released.

Dinah Shore
"Murder, He Says" (*Frank Loesser and Jimmy McHugh*)
On the album *Mona Lisa Smile: Music from the Motion Picture* Epic EK 90737
    (2004)

Shel Silverstein
"Sarah Sylvia Cynthia Stout Would Not Take the Garbage Out" (*spoken word*)
    (*Shel Silverstein*)
On the KZON various-artists charity cassette *Speaking of Christmas and Other Things* KZON (1992)

Carly Simon
"Boys in the Trees" (*Carly Simon*)
Performed in concert. Never officially released.

Simon and Garfunkel
"59th Street Bridge Song (Feelin' Groovy)" (*Paul Simon*)
Performed in concert. Never officially released.
"For Emily, Whenever I May Find Her" (*Paul Simon*)
Performed in concert. Never officially released.

Slayer
"Raining Blood" (*Jeff Hanneman and Kerry King*)
On the album *Strange Little Girls* Atlantic 7567-83486 (2001)

Bruce Springsteen
"Growin' Up" *(Bruce Springsteen)*
Performed in concert. Never officially released.
"I'm on Fire" *(Bruce Springsteen)*
On the various-artists album *VH–1 Crossroads* Atlantic 82895 (1996)
"Streets of Philadelphia" *(Bruce Springsteen)*
Performed in concert. Never officially released.
"Thunder Road" *(Bruce Springsteen)*
Performed during a radio interview with WDRE-FM New York, NY (1996). Never
officially released.

Jo Stafford
"You Belong to Me" *(Pee Wee King, Chilton Price, and Redd Stewart)*
On the album *Mona Lisa Smile: Music from the Motion Picture* Epic EK 90737
(2004)

Steely Dan
"Do It Again" *(Walter Becker and Donald Fagen)*
On the U.K. maxi-single *Spark* East West AT0031 (1998)

Cat Stevens
· "Moonshadow" *(Cat Stevens)*
Performed in concert. Never officially released.
"Wild World" *(Cat Stevens)*
Performed in concert. Never officially released.

The Stooges
"I'm Sick of You" *(Iggy Pop and James Williamson)*
Recorded for *Strange Little Girls* (2001) but never released.

The Stranglers
"Strange Little Girl" *(Jean Bumel, Hugh Cornwell, Brian Duffy, David Greenfield,
    and Hans Warmling)*
On the album *Strange Little Girls* Atlantic 7567-83486 (2001)

Barbra Streisand
"Evergreen" *(Paul Williams and Barbra Streisand)*
Performed in concert. Never officially released.

The Stylistics
"You Make Me Feel Brand New" *(Thom Bell and Linda Creed)*
Performed in concert. Never officially released.

James Taylor
"Carolina in My Mind" *(James Taylor)*
Performed in concert. Never officially released.
"Millworker" *(James Taylor)*
Performed in concert. Never officially released.

Tears for Fears
"Mad World" *(Roland Orzabol)*
Performed in concert. Never officially released.

10cc
"I'm Not In Love" *(Graham Gouldman)*
On the album *Strange Little Girls* (Atlantic 7567-83486) (2001)

Traditional
"Amazing Grace" *(John Newton)*
On the CD 5 maxi-single *Talula* East West 7567-88512 (1996)
"America the Beautiful" *(Katherine Lee Bates and Samuel A. Ward)*
Performed in concert. Never officially released.
"The Church's One Foundation" *(Samuel John Stone and Samuel S. Wesley)*
Performed as part of improvised medley during an interview with NPR Radio
    (1994).
"Danny Boy" *(Traditional)*
Performed in concert. Never officially released.
"Dixie" *(Daniel Decatur Emmett)*
Performed in concert. Never officially released.
"The Farmer in the Dell" *(Traditional)*
Performed in concert. Never officially released.
"Happy Birthday" *(Mildred Hill and Patty Smith Hill)*
Performed in concert. Never officially released.
"Home on the Range" *(Traditional)*
On the CD 5 maxi-single *God* Atlantic 85687 (1994)
"House of the Rising Sun" *(Traditional)*
Performed in concert. Never officially released.
"Kumbaya" *(Traditional)*
Performed in concert. Never officially released.
"The Little Drummer Boy" *(Traditional)*
On the KROQ various-artists charity cassette *Kevin and Bean: We've Got Your
    Yule Logs Hanging* KROQ CS–4 (1992)
Also on the album *You Sleigh Me: Alternative Christmas Hits* Atlantic 82851
    (1995)
Also on the album *Not Another Christmas Album: An Alternative Christmas*
    Rhino Flashback 76519 (2004)
"Oh Susanna" *(Stephen Foster)*
Performed in concert. Never officially released.
"Skyeboat Song" *(Traditional) (recorded as Y Kant Tori Read)*
On the album *Y Kant Tori Read* Atlantic 81845 (1988)
"There Is a Balm in Gilead" *(Traditional)*
Performed in concert. Never officially released.
"This Old Man" *(Traditional)*

On the CD 5 maxi-single *Caught a Lite Sneeze* Atlantic 85519 (1996)
"What Child Is This?" *(Traditional)*
Performed on the CNN TV series *The Music Room* (2002).
"The Wheels on the Bus" *(Traditional)*
Performed in concert. Never officially released.

Travis
"Turn" *(Francis Healy)*
Performed in concert. Never officially released.

Bonnie Tyler
"Total Eclipse of the Heart" *(Jim Steinman)*
On the limited-edition CD *B of A Pavilion: Boston, MA, 8/21/05.* (Available from
 www.toriamosbootlegs.com) (2005)

U2
"New Year's Day" *(Bono, Adam Clayton, The Edge, and Larry Mullen Jr.)*
Performed in concert. Never officially released.
"Running to Stand Still" *(Bono, Adam Clayton, The Edge, and Larry Mullen, Jr.)*
Performed in concert. Never officially released.

The Velvet Underground
"New Age" *(Lou Reed)*
On the album *Strange Little Girls* Atlantic 7567-83486 (2001)

The Village People
"Y.M.C.A." *(Henri Belolo, Jacques Morali, and Victor Willis)*
Performed in concert. Never officially released.

Tom Waits
"Time" *(Tom Waits)*
On the album *Strange Little Girls* Atlantic 7567-83486 (2001)

Anita Ward
"Ring My Bell" *(Frederick Knight)*
On the album *Ruby Trax—The NME's Roaring Forty* NME 40CD (1992)

Dionne Warwick
"The Windows of the World" *(Burt Bacharach and Hal David)*
Performed in concert. Never officially released.

Bill Withers
"Ain't No Sunshine" *(Bill Withers)*
Performed in concert. Never officially released.

Neil Young
"After the Gold Rush" *(Neil Young)*
Performed in concert. Never officially released.
"Heart of Gold" *(Neil Young)*

On the album *Strange Little Girls* Atlantic 7567-83486 (2001)
"The Needle and the Damage Done" *(Neil Young)*
Performed in concert. Never officially released.
"Ohio" *(Neil Young)*
Performed in concert. Never officially released.
"Old Man" *(Neil Young)*
Performed in concert. Never officially released.
"Philadelphia" *(Neil Young)*
Performed in concert. Never officially released.

Bibliography

Interviews

Amos, Tori. Telephone conversation with author. October 21, 1992.
Amos, Tori. Telephone conversation with author. April 19, 1996.
Folds, Ben. Telephone conversation with author. April 10, 1997.
Hudson, Sarah. Telephone conversation with author. August 12, 2004.
Jovovich, Milla. Personal interview with author. August 19, 1994.
Martin, Charlotte. Telephone conversation with author. September 22, 2004.
McLachlan, Sarah. Personal interview with author. March 22, 1994.
McLachlan, Sarah. Telephone conversation with author. June 11, 1997.
Nalick, Anna. Telephone conversation with author. March 29, 2005.
Ondrasik, John (Five for Fighting). E-mail to author. June 21, 2004.

Articles

Aaron, Charles. "Sex, God and Rock and Roll." *Spin*, October 1994.
Adams, Cameron. "Scarlet's Web." *The Herald Sun* (Victoria, Australia), October 31, 2002.
"Album Reviews." *Billboard*, June 11, 1988.
Amos, Tori. "Celebrity Real Life: Tori's Joy After Her Miscarriage Heartbreak." *She*, December 2003.
Amos, Tori. "The Mix Sessions." *Q*, June 2005.
Amos, Tori. "Q Diary—This Ain't L.A., Baby." *Q*, February 1994.
Amos, Tori. "The Wisdom of the Wild: Singer-Actress Sandra Bernhard." *Interview*, August 1994.
"Any Queries? Tori Amos" *Attitude*, September 2001.
Ashare, Matt. "One-Woman Choir: Tori Amos Unravels a Bit of Her Mystery." *Rollingstone.com*, August 8, 1998.
Baker, James Ireland. "Tori Amos." *Us*, October 1999.
Balfour, Brad. "What Really Gets to You?" *New Review of Records*, December 1993/January 1994.
Bennett, James. "The Big Interview: No Pain, No Gain." *The Times* (London), April 11, 1998.
Bergman, Justin. "Amos Challenges Self on Other Side of Microphone." *Gannett News Service*, November 22, 1996.
Billen, Andrew. "Tori the Librarian and Other Odd Tales." *The Times* (London), November 4, 2003.
Blandford, James. "Tea with the Waitress." *Record Collector*, November 1999.

Block, Francesca Lia. "The Volcano Lover." *Spin*, March 1996.

Bozza, Anthony. "Random Notes." *Rolling Stone*, November 12, 1998.

Brown, Glyn. "Tori Amos: In the Company of Men." *The Independent* (London), September 14, 2001.

Brown, Marc. "America at Her Gait." *Rocky Mountain News*, December 4, 2002.

Browne, Sally. "Tori's Own Land of Oz." *The Sunday Mail* (U.K.), May 15, 2005.

Bykofsky, Stu. "Concert Advice." *Philadelphia Daily News*, August 26, 2005.

Cady, Monica. "Tori Amos." *Rag*, May 2005.

Callahan, Maureen. "The Enchanted Forest." *Spin*, November 1999.

Chambers, Veronica. "Two for the Road." *Newsweek*, July 27, 1998.

Chandar, Chris. "Tori Amos: The Idiosyncratic Singer-Songwriter Reclaims Her Roots in *Scarlet's Walk*." *Pulse*, November 2002.

Christenson, Thor. "Tori Amos Dresses Up to Personify the Women Men Sing About." *The Dallas Morning News*, November 2, 2001.

Christman, Ed. "Atlantic Sets Precedents with Sale of Amos Download." *Billboard*, August 21, 1999.

"The College Daze of Tori Amos." *Student Advantage Magazine* , winter 1998.

Collis, Clark. "Tori Amos: Strange Little Girls." *Q*, October 2001.

Condran, Ed. "Her Stamp on Men's Words." *The Record* (Bergen County, NJ), October 5, 2001.

Condran, Ed. "Soundcheck: Tori Amos—Singer/Songwriter." *Cleveland Free Times*, August 13–19, 2003.

Considine, J. D. "Amos' Magic Shines Through." *The Baltimore Sun*, August 25, 1999.

Considine, J. D. "A Choirgirl with Charisma." *The Baltimore Sun*, May 24, 1998.

Considine, J. D. "Page and Plant Shake the Led Out in Their Latest Tour." *The Baltimore Sun*, March 19, 1995.

Curtis, Kim. "Five Questions with Tori Amos." The Associated Press, December 31, 2002.

Daley, David. "Magic and Loss." *Alternative Press*, July 1998.

Daly, Steven. "Tori Amos: Her Secret Garden." *Rolling Stone*, June 25, 1998.

Dawn, Randee. "Motherhood, Murder and the Missus." *Alternative Press*, October 2001.

Dawn, Randee. "The 25 Most Anticipated Albums of 1998." *Alternative Press*, January 1998.

Dawn, Randee. "Venus Envy." *Alternative Press*, October 1999.

Deevoy, Adrian. "Hips. Tits. Lips. Power." *Q*, May 1994.

DeFretos, Lydia Carole. "Tori Amos: Finding Her Own Fire." *Aquarian Weekly*, February 21, 1996.

DeMain, Bill. "Mother of Invention Tori Amos." *Performing Songwriter*, January/February 2002.

Devine, Julie. "Riot Poof on the Road." *UK.Gay.com*, January 8, 2001.

DeYoung, Bill. "Next-door Celebrities." *The Stuart News*, November 6, 2004.

Diehl, Matt. "Almost Amos: Amos Bends Genders in *Strange Little Girls.*" *Elle,* September 2001.

Doerschuk, Robert L. "Tori Amos: Dancing with the Vampire and the Nightingale." *Keyboard,* November 1994.

Doerschuk, Robert L. "Voices in the Air: Spirit Tripping with Tori Amos." *Musician,* May 1996.

"Donald Leslie; Creator of the Leslie Keyboard Speaker; 93." The Associated Press, September 9, 2004.

Doyle, Tom. "Cash for Questions: Alanis Morissette." *Q,* March 1999.

Doyle, Tom. "Ready, Steady, Kook!" *Q,* May 1998.

Doyle, Tom. "Single to Damascus Please…." *Q,* June 1995.

Dunleavy, T'cha. "Tori's Weird World." *The Montreal Gazette,* August 24, 2005.

Dunn, Bill. "A Date with Tori Amos." *Esquire,* October 1999.

Dunn, Jancee. "Tori Amos." *Rolling Stone,* October 31, 2002.

Erlewine, Stephen Thomas. "The Beekeeper." *AllMusic.com,* April 2005.

Everson, John. "Tight Socks and Feminist Freedom." *The Illinois Entertainer,* August 1994.

Everson, John. "Tori Amos: The Sacred and the Profane." *The Illinois Entertainer,* September 1998.

Farber, Jim. "Early Bird Artists Have a Jump on '98." *New York Daily News,* January 5, 1998.

Farley, Christopher John. "Tori, Tori, Tori!" *Time,* May 11, 1998.

"The Fifty Most Beautiful People in the World 1996." *People,* June 1996.

Foege, Alec. "Two New Feminist Voices, Tori Amos and Juliana Hatfield, Bring Women's Rock Beyond the Babe Factor." *Vogue,* June 1992.

Flick, Larry. "Label Tickled 'Pink' Over New Tori Amos Set." *Billboard,* December 4, 1993.

Flick, Larry. "Tori Amos Shares Life Lessons." *Billboard,* March 28, 1992.

Fowley, Kim. "So You Found a Girl Who Thinks Really Deep Thoughts." *BAM,* March 11, 1994.

Freydkin, Donna. "Tori Amos: Clearly in the Right Band." *CNN.com,* August 27, 1998.

Gallani, Michael. "Tori Amos—Metaphysics and Music." *Keyboard,* July 2005.

Garcia, Sandra A. "A Bottle of Red: Tori Amos." *B-Side,* May/June 1996.

Garcia, Sandra A. "Tori Amos: In the Name of the Mother." *B-Side,* April/May 1994.

Gardner, Elysa. "New Faces: Tori Amos—Ethereal Earthquakes." *Rolling Stone,* April 30, 1992.

Gardner, Elysa. "Tori Amos Keeps Her Head." *Musician,* January 1993.

Gatta, John Patrick. "It's a Free Will Planet: An Interview with Tori Amos." *Magical Blend,* winter 1998.

Graff, Gary. "Songstress Tori Amos Takes a Walk Through America a Year After September 11th." *Galleryofsound.com,* October 2002.

Graff, Gary. "Staying Creative." *The Cleveland Plain Dealer,* August 26, 2005.

Griffith, Brian. "Tori! Tori! Tori!" *Hits,* April 6, 1992.

Gulla, Bob. "Walk on the Wild Side." *Women Who Rock,* fall 2002.

Handal, Richard. Letter to the Tori Amos fan site TheDent.com, http://thedent.com/recordcoll99.html.

Harrington, Richard. "Finally, A Prodigy Finds Her Song." *The Washington Post,* March 22, 1992.

Harrington, Richard. "Tori Amos Flips the Perspective." *The Washington Post,* October 22, 2001, WE06.

Haynes, Esther. "Music Q & A: Tori Amos." *Jane,* October 1999.

Hermes, Will. "Don't Mess with Mother Nature." *Spin,* October 2001.

Hersey, Brook. "Listen to Tori Amos." *Glamour,* August 1992.

Hibbert, Tom. "Tori Amos: From Rock Chick to Twisted Mystic." *Details,* November 1992.

Hill, Michael. The Wire . "Tori Amos: Stars, Planets, Wine and Song." *VH1.com,* September 1999.

Hinckley, David. "A Fire in the Wheat Fields." *New York Daily News,* March 28, 1993.

Hochman, Steve. "An Anthem in the Waiting." *Los Angeles Times,* May 15, 1997.

Hochman, Steve. "Tori Amos Offers a Woman's-Eye View of Songs by Men." *Los Angeles Times,* July 1, 2001.

"If You Don't Have a Stalker, You Don't Rate." *She,* May 1998.

"Incoming . . ." *Q,* April 1998.

"In the Works." *Mojo,* September 2001.

"The It List: Tori Amos—The Siren." *Entertainment Weekly,* June 26, 1998.

Ives, Brian. "An American Journey Gooses the Singer-Songwriter's Imagination." *VH1.com,* October 28, 2002.

Jackson, Joe. "The Hurt Inside." *Hot Press,* February 23, 1994.

Jackson, Joe. "Tori's Story." *Hot Press,* March 26, 1992.

Jacobs, Jay S. "In The Flesh." *Philly Rock Guide,* December 1992.

Jacobs, Jay S. "Tori Amos." *Philly Rock Guide,* December 1992.

Jacobs, Jay S. "Tori Amos Breaks the Silence." *Rockpile,* May 1996.

Jacobs, Jay S. "Tori Amos CD Reviews." *PopEntertainment.com.,* 1994–2005.

Johnson, Troy. "People Are Strange…Tori Amos Rewrites Songs and Sex on Her New Album." *Slamm—The San Diego Music Magazine,* October 31 to November 13, 2001.

Knight, Molly. "Matt Chamberlain Talks About Tori, Summer Touring, and Datura's Chances." *Mollyknight.com,* August 11, 2003.

"Kooky Singer Songstress Tori Amos' Latest Offering, *Strange Little Girls,* Is a Collection of Songs Written by Men Through Which She Wanted to Talk About Men. Hey, Who Were We Not to Oblige Her?" *Boyz,* September 17, 2001.

Kuhlmann, Hannah. "A Glimpse Into the Mind of Neil Gaiman." *The Minnesota Daily,* November 18, 1999.

Lanham, Tom. "Going on 'Scarlet's Walk.'" *San Francisco Examiner,* October 30, 2002.

Laskas, Jeanne Marie. "Tori Adored." *Entertainment Weekly,* July 12, 1996.

Lynskey, Dorian. "33 Things You Should Know About Tori Amos." *Blender,* November 2002.

"Lyricists: The Sense Impressionist—Tori Amos." *Word,* February 2005.

Mark, Mary Ellen. "Tori Amos." *Us,* July 1998.

Marlow, Wil. "Tori Goes Back to the Future." The Press Association, November 10, 2003.

McCollum, Brian. "This Time Tori Amos Is Bringing a Band to Detroit." *Detroit Free Press,* April 28, 1998.

McCormack, Carlo. "Naked Angel." *Paper,* November 1992.

McNair, James. "Her Indoors: Tori's Lesson in Marital Harmony." *Mojo,* November 1999.

McNair, James. "Tori Amos: Fairytale Endings." *The Independent* (London) November 21, 2003.

McNulty, Bernadette. "Goddesses on Parade." *The Daily Telegraph* (London) June 23, 2005.

Morgan, Laura. "Rock." *Entertainment Weekly,* September 21, 2001.

Morgan, Laura. "Tori Amos Loved Leg Warmers!" *Seventeen.com,* November 2002.

Moriarty, Matthew. "Man Dies from Wreck Injuries." *Pilot.com,* November 24, 2004.

Morrison, Alistair. "Faces to Watch: Tori Amos." *Entertainment Weekly,* January 31, 1992: 30.

Morse, Steve. "Tori Amos Play-acts Pop's Images of Women." *The Boston Globe,* September 16, 2001.

Morse, Steve. "Venus of the Road." *The Boston Globe,* August 27, 1999, E14.

Nash, Jesse. "Sigerson Captures Amos' Emotional Tremors." *Billboard,* April 11, 1992.

Newman, Melinda. "Tori Amos: Atlantic's Golden Girl." *Billboard,* February 20, 1993.

Newman, Melinda. "The Beat." *Billboard,* November 24, 2001.

Nichols, Natalie. "For Amos, Passion Fuels 'Venus' Voyage." *Los Angeles Times,* September 23, 1999, 22.

"The 90 Greatest Albums of the 90s." *Spin,* September 1999.

O'Brien, Lucy. "Pianosexual." *Diva,* February/March 1996.

Orloff, Brian. "Gathering 'Round with Music." *St. Petersburg Times,* November 3, 2002.

Orloff, Brian. "Tori Amos Bears New Fruit." *RollingStone.com,* September 5, 2003.

Parker, Lyndsey. "Damian Rice Wins Shortlist Music Prize," *Launch.com,* October 6, 2003.

Patterson, Spencer. "Amos True." *The Las Vegas Sun,* July 27, 2003.

Piantadosi, Roger. "Ellen Amos: The Marbury Woman." *The Washington Post,* May 11, 1984, W13.

Picardie, Justine. "Kooky or What?" *The Independent* (London), January 16, 1994.

Pietrangelo, Julie Ann. "To Venus and Back." *Spin.com,* September 1999.

Planer, Lindsay. "It's Best to Catch Her Live." *Break,* August 14–20, 1996.

Powers, Ann. "For Female Expression, the Virility of Tori Amos." *The New York Times,* April 25, 1998.

Pride, Domenic and Chuck Taylor. "Amos Bares Soul on Atlantic Set." *Billboard,* January 13, 1996.

Quantick, David. "In the Piano Room with Tori Amos." *Blender,* August/ September 2001.

"The Reliable Source." *The Washington Post,* June 22, 2000.

Reynolds, Simon. "Do Angels Want to Wear Her Red Shoes?" *Pulse,* December 1993.

"Road Runners." *Rolling Stone,* July 8–22, 1999.

Robins, Wayne. "Songs of Sex and the Spirit." *New York Newsday,* April 5, 1992.

Robinson, Lisa. "Men No Longer God to Amos." *New York Post,* January 12, 1996.

Robinson, Steven. "Red Letter Day with Tori." *Hot Press,* November 20, 2002.

Robjohns, Hugh. "Checking in with the Choirgirl: Mark Hawley Recording and Touring with Tori Amos." *Sound on Sound,* July 1998.

Rogers, Jude. "Will the Real Tori Amos Ever Shut Up?" *Word,* August 2005.

Rooti, Sam. "Famous Amos." *Spin,* January 1993.

Rule, Greg. "Co-producer Eric Rosse: The Three Lives of Little Earthquakes." *Keyboard,* September 1992.

Rule, Greg. "Tori! Tori! Tori!" *Keyboard,* September 1992.

Savage, John. "Tori Amos." *Interview,* May 1992.

Schwartz, David. "Local Rock 'n' Roller Shoots for Stardom." *The Gazette* (Montgomery County, MD), June 22, 1988, 30.

Shapiro, Gregg. "Cover Girl: An Interview with Tori Amos." *Next,* September 5, 2001.

Shapiro, Gregg. "Walking and Talking with Tori Amos." *Windy City Times,* November 13, 2002.

Shapiro, Gregg. "Whatever Rufus Wants." *Outsmart.com,* November 2003.

Sharp, Ken. "When Tori Amos Talks, People Listen." *Concert News,* November 1992.

Shaw, William. "Earth Angel." *Details,* August 1988.

Simmons, Sylvie. "Nice!" *Mojo,* May 1998.

Sinclair, David. "Dear Diary: The Secret World of Kate Bush." *Rolling Stone,* February 24, 1994.

"Singer Tori Amos Sued." *AAP,* August 30, 2003.

Smallwood, Sue. "Amos Speaks Cryptically." *The Virginian-Pilot* (Norfolk, VA), July 27, 1994.

Smith, Chris. "Tori Amos." *Us,* July 1998.

Smith, Christopher. "Tori Amos: The Loudest Voice in the Choir." *Performing Songwriter,* September/October 1998.

Smith, Julia Llewellyn. "I Needed a Child in My Life More Than I Knew." *The Daily Telegraph* (London), September 5, 2001.

Snow, Mat. "Can We Talk?" *Q*, February 1992.

Solomon, Evan. "Tori Amos: Under the Volcano." *Shift*, April 1996.

Stone, Sarah. "Tori Amos." *RedDirect.com*, September 2001.

Stone, Tom. "Arena-sized Venues, a Band—What's Next for Tori Amos?" *The Dallas Morning News*, October 4, 1998.

Stoneman, Justin. "World of the Strange." *Virgin.net*, September 11, 2001.

"Stories." *Q*, November 1993.

"Stories." *Q*, January 1996.

"Strange Little Tori." *RollingStone.com*, October 4, 2001.

Streeter, Leslie Gray. "Tori Amos' Lyrical, Emotional Appeal." *The Miami Herald*, August 10, 2005.

Takiff, Jonathan. "Amos' Piano Pop More Than Music." *Philadelphia Daily News*, March 24, 1994.

"Talking About Nothing with Trent Reznor." *Axcess Magazine*, September 1994.

Talkington, Amy. "A Few of Tori Amos' Favorite Things." *Seventeen*, March 1996.

Taylor, Chuck. "Tori Amos Unveils 'Venus.'" *Billboard*, July 17, 1999.

Taylor, Nick. "Toritelling." *Attitude*, November 2003.

"This Month's Stories." *Q*, June 1995.

Tien, Ellen. "In the Eye of One Beholder, Only Beauty." *The New York Times*, May 12, 2002.

Tolbert, Katherine. "At 17, Student Sings a Song of Success." *The Washington Post*, December 18, 1980, MW2.

Tood, Matthew. "Tori's Glory." *Attitude*, November 1999.

"Top Teens in Talent Test." *Montgomery Journal*, March 31, 1977.

"Top Ten Singles of 2002." *USA Today*, December 31, 2002.

"Tori Amos." *Columbia House*, spring 1999.

"Tori Amos Covers All the Bases." *ICE*, September 2001.

"Tori Amos: Interplanetary, Most Extraordinary." *Time-Off*, November 24–30, 1999.

"Tori Amos' Musical Journey Across America." *CNN.com*, February 13, 2003.

"The Tori Party." *Deluxe*, May 1998.

Verna, Paul. "Tori Amos Isn't Alone in Her Hotel." *Billboard*, April 4, 1998.

Weitz, Matt. "Desperately Seeking Tori." *Dallas Observer*, June 13, 1996.

Wener, Ben. "She Seeks the Woman Within." *The Orange County Register*, November 13, 2001.

Whitehead, Michael. "Tori and Drugs." *TheDent.com*, December 28, 2000.

Williamson, Nigel. "Relative Values." *The Sunday Times Magazine* (London), May 24, 1998.

Willman, Chris. "Brazen. Precious. Poetic. Profane." *Los Angeles Times*, January 30, 1994.

Zaleski, Annie. "Journey Woman." *Boston Phoenix*, November 14, 2002.

202 Pretty Good Years

Tour Programs, Press Kits, and Releases

Atlantic Records. "Online 'Bliss': Atlantic to Sell New Tori Amos Single via Web" (press release), August 13, 1999.
Atlantic Records. "Tori Amos" (press kit), February 1992.
Atlantic Records. "Tori Amos" (press kit), January 1996.
Atlantic Records. "Tori Amos" (press kit), May 1998.
Atlantic Records. "Tori Amos Checks Into the *Choirgirl Hotel*" (press release), March 30, 1998.
Atlantic Records. "Tori Amos Set to Fly 'To Venus and Back'" (press kit), July 20, 1999.
Atlantic Records. "Tori Amos. Under the Pink." (press kit), January 1994.
Atlantic Records. "Y Kant Tori Read" (press kit), 1988.
The Bridge Entertainment Group. "Tori Amos Announces New Business Venture" (press release), October 9, 2003.
Epic Records. "Epic Records/Sony Music Soundtrax Announce the Release of the Soundtrack to *Mona Lisa Smile*, a Revolution Studio and Columbia Pictures Release" (press release), November, 24 2003.
Epic Records. "Howie Day Hits the Road with Tori Amos" (press release), September 26, 2002.
Epic Records. "*Scarlet's Walk*—A Prologue" (press kit), September 2002.
Epic Records. "*Scarlet's Walk* Hits the Road" (press release), September 2002.
Epic Records. "A Signing of Epic Proportions" (press release), July 22, 2002.
Epic Records. "Tori Amos to Release Live Bootleg Series" (press release), August 8, 2005.
Epic Records. "Tori Amos to Release Live DVD and Six-Song Companion CD 5/18/04" (press release), April 8, 2004.
Epic Records. "Tori Amos Readies New Album 'The Beekeeper'" (press release), November 1, 2004.
Epic Records. "Tori Amos' Summer of Sin" (press release), June 15, 2005.
"Little Earthquakes" (tour program), 1992.
Oxygen Cable Network. "The Tori Amos Custom Concert" (press release), March 2002.
Spivak Entertainment. "Amos Is Unrehearsed for First MTV/SonicNet Event" (press release), August 11, 1999.
Spivak Entertainment. "Tori Amos Announces Long-Awaited New Release: A Baby Girl!" (press release), September 6, 2000.

Books

Brite, Poppy Z. *Courtney Love: The Real Story*. New York: Simon & Schuster, 1998.
Campbell, Paul. *Tori Amos Collectibles*. New York: Omnibus Press, 1997.
Neely, Tim. *Goldmine Price Guide to Alternative Records*. Iola, WI: Krause Publications, 1996.

Robbins, Ira A. *The Trouser Press Guide to 90s Rock*. New York: Fireside/Simon & Schuster, 1997.

Whitburn, Joel. *Rock Tracks*. Menomonee Falls, WI: Record Research, Inc., 2002.

Television, Radio Shows, and Videos

ABC-TV. *Prime Time Live*, August 21, 1996.

Amos, Tori. *The Complete Videos 1991–1998*. Atlantic Music Video, 1998.

Amos, Tori. *Little Earthquakes*. A-Vision, 1992.

Amos, Tori. *A Sorta Fairytale*. Epic Music Video, 2002.

Amos, Tori. *Welcome to Sunny Florida*. Epic Music Video, 2004.

ARTE (French/German Television). *Music Planet 2Nite*, November 26, 2002.

BBC World Service. *Music Biz*, October 31, 2002.

ITV1 (U.K.). *Faith and Music*, February 29, 2004.

CFNY-FM (Toronto, Ontario, Canada), January 29, 1996.

KCRW-FM (Santa Monica, CA). *Morning Becomes Eclectic*, December 17, 2002.

KNDD (Seattle, WA). *End Sessions*, September 20, 1998.

KROQ-FM (Los Angeles, CA). *The Kevin and Bean Morning Show*, September 19, 1999.

KROQ-FM (Los Angeles, CA). *The Kevin and Bean Morning Show*, December 1, 2003.

KSCA-FM (Los Angeles, CA), August 24, 1994.

Mix 94.7 (Austin, TX), November 1, 2002.

MTV Unplugged: Tori Amos, June 26, 1996.

MTV Video Music Awards, September 10, 1992.

MTV Video Music Awards Opening Act, September 10, 1992.

National Public Radio —interview with Noah Adams, July 5, 1994.

National Public Radio. *Morning Edition*, November 27, 2002.

Oxygen Cable Network. *The Isaac Mizrahi Show*, March 10, 2003.

The Ryan Seacrest Show, April 15, 2004.

Spotlight Music Showcase. *Tori Amos: Tales of a Librarian*. Atlantic, 2003.

VH1 Behind the Music 2: Tori Amos, March 21, 2000.

VH1 Storytellers: Tori Amos, February 21, 1999.

Westwood One Radio Network, February 27, 1992.

W96.3 University Radio Warwick (Coventry, England), February 25, 1994.

WVRV-FM (St. Louis, MO). *The River Lounge*, December 3, 2002.

WXPN-FM (Philadelphia, PA). *World Café*, May 18, 1992.

WXPN-FM (Philadelphia, PA). *World Café*, March 1, 1996.

WXPN-FM (Philadelphia, PA). *World Café*, November 9, 2001.

Web Sites

The All Music Guide, http://www.allmusic.com.

The Covers Project—Tori Amos, http://www.coversproject.com/artist/Tori+Amos.

Here in My Head—A Tori Amos Web Site, http://www.hereinmyhead.com/.
Martian Engineering, Ltd., http://www.martianengineering.com/.
Nirvana: Anarchy in the U.K., http://www.nirvanaclub.com/nfa/anarchy.html.
The Peabody Institute of John Hopkins University, http://www.peabody.jhu.edu.
A Dent in the Tori Amos Universe, http://www.thedent.com.
Strange Little Covers, http://www.strangelittlecovers.tk.
Tori Amos Official Web Site, http://www.toriamos.com.
Toriphoria, http://www.yessaid.com.
The Trail of Tears—About North Georgia by Golden Ink, http://ngeorgia.com/history/nghisttt.htm.
The Ultimate Tori Amos FAQ, http://www.geocities.com/ultimatetrifaq/.

Index